The Secrets of Culture

OTHER BOOKS BY D. PAUL SCHAFER

The Age of Culture (2014)

Revolution or Renaissance: Making the Transition from an Economic Age to a Cultural Age (2008)

Culture: Beacon of the Future (1998)

THE SECRETS OF CULTURE

D. Paul Schafer

A New Road Book
Rock's Mills Press

A New Road Book
PUBLISHED BY
Rock's Mills Press

Library and Archives Canada Cataloguing in Publication

Schafer, D. Paul (David Paul), 1937-, author
The secrets of culture / D. Paul Schafer.

Includes bibliographical references.
ISBN 978-0-9881293-5-1 (pbk.)

1. Schafer, D. Paul (David Paul), 1937-. 2. Culture.
3. Social change. 4. Arts administrators--Ontario--Biography.
5. Educators--Ontario--Biography. I. Title.

HM621.S33 2015 306 C2015-900204-4

ABOUT THE COVER: In 1979, Mont Saint-Michel was named one of the first UNESCO World Heritage sites. Like culture, this tidal island in Normandy holds many secrets and has fulfilled many valuable functions over the course of its history. It is now an historic monument and one of France's most cherished tourist destinations. Photo credit: © Veni/iStock.

First Edition
ISBN-13: 978-0-9881293-5-1

THE SECRETS OF CULTURE

D. Paul Schafer

A New Road Book
Rock's Mills Press

A New Road Book
PUBLISHED BY
Rock's Mills Press

Library and Archives Canada Cataloguing in Publication

Schafer, D. Paul (David Paul), 1937-, author
The secrets of culture / D. Paul Schafer.

Includes bibliographical references.
ISBN 978-0-9881293-5-1 (pbk.)

1. Schafer, D. Paul (David Paul), 1937-. 2. Culture.
3. Social change. 4. Arts administrators--Ontario--Biography.
5. Educators--Ontario--Biography. I. Title.

HM621.S33 2015 306 C2015-900204-4

ABOUT THE COVER: In 1979, Mont Saint-Michel was named one of the first UNESCO World Heritage sites. Like culture, this tidal island in Normandy holds many secrets and has fulfilled many valuable functions over the course of its history. It is now an historic monument and one of France's most cherished tourist destinations. Photo credit: © Veni/iStock.

First Edition
ISBN-13: 978-0-9881293-5-1

Contents

PREFACE *vii*

1 The Formative Years 1
2 Studying and Teaching Economics 22
3 Soul Searching Abroad 49
4 Embarking on a New Career Path 76
5 Striking Out on My Own 100
6 Coming to Grips with Culture 129
7 Writing about Culture and Cultures 146
8 A New Beacon for the Future 169
9 Assessing the Economic Age 194
10 Entering a Cultural Age 215
11 Flourishing of a Cultural Age 234
12 Living a Cultural Life 250

ACKNOWLEDGEMENTS AND REFERENCES 266

Preface

I believe we need to pass out of the present economic age and into a future cultural age. In order to do this, it is necessary to unlock and capitalize on all the diverse and dynamic secrets of culture.

This book describes the long and fascinating journey I have had over my life attempting to achieve this objective and make the case for a cultural age. It begins with a project I did in public school on Marco Polo, and concludes with my quest to live a cultural life today. But the most important part of the journey is all the jobs, projects, problems, breaks, and turning points I have had along the way. For, as John Stuart Mill observed many years ago, the most essential part of any journey is not arriving at the destination, but rather the route that is taken to get there.

Unlocking and capitalizing on the secrets of culture and entering a cultural age were the farthest things from my mind when I was young. Despite the excellent education I had in the arts in my youth, I studied economics at university and then taught economics for a number of years in the early '60s. I marvelled at the power of the economic age to generate vast increases in material and monetary wealth. I also felt this economic age (as I came to call it) was capable of solving most if not all the world's problems. Not only had it improved living standards and the quality of life for billions of people in the years since Adam Smith wrote *The Wealth of Nations* in 1776, but it had also yielded phenomenal achievements in industry, agriculture, education, science, technology, the arts, and many other areas of life.

I was so taken with the power and potential of the economic age to make improvements in the world situation — which has always been a real passion of mine — that I thought I would stay in this field and teach economics for the rest of my life. In order to do so, it was necessary to get a Ph.D., since I only had a Master's degree at that time. So I enrolled in a doctoral program in economics at the University of Michigan with this purpose in mind.

The first inkling I had that there was something wrong with this decision came when several faculty members at the university told me that I would not be permitted to write a Ph.D. thesis on the economics of the arts — another real passion of mine — because there was no such thing as "the economics of the arts."

As my studies at the university progressed, other problems began to emerge that troubled me a great deal. One was the mathematical nature of economics. Another was the tendency of economists (and others) to see everything in the world in economic terms. But the most serious problem of all was the fact that the natural environment was treated as a "given" and ignored, largely because it was deemed to exist outside the realm of economics. This bothered me immensely. The natural environment is vital to the survival and well-being of everything and everybody. How could it be ignored?

With reservations like these weighing heavily on my mind, I decided it would not be wise to remain at the University of Michigan. But what was I to do? Most of my training had been in economics, and I was ill-equipped to do much else. Since I was still interested in many aspects of economics, I decided to pursue my interest in the economics of the arts, as well as my dream of helping to make the world a better place for all, in some other place and in some other way.

After a long and illuminating trip to Europe and Morocco to sort things out, I eventually landed a job at the Ontario Arts Council. This was the first real step in the "cultural leg" of my journey. Although I didn't know it at that time, I was destined to spend the next fifty years of my life attempting to broaden and deepen my knowledge and understanding of culture and cultures and making the case for a cultural age.

My job at the Ontario Arts Council was followed by a job as director of the Program in Arts Administration at York University, which was arguably the first academic program in the world for training arts administrators and cultural policy-makers. After this, I spent the better part of a decade working on numerous projects as a self-employed person. This included undertaking several missions for UNESCO to different parts of the world, as well as writing publications on culture, the world system, Canadian cultural policy, and Canada's international cultural relations.

But the most important job I ever had was at the Scarborough campus of the University of Toronto. I went there in the early '80s to participate in the creation of two new cooperative programs, one in arts administration and one in international development. It wasn't long before I discovered that the campus library had an incredible collection of books, articles, and other documents dealing with culture, which, by this time, had become my principal preoccupation in life.

What I discovered in the library amazed me and changed my life. I learned that cultural scholars have had an enormous amount to say about culture that is relevant to improving the world situation. This is true not only for the many different ways culture manifests itself in the world – from the arts and humanities to the organizational forms and structures of different species – but also for making improvements at every level, from the individual, institutional, and municipal level to the regional, national, and international level.

By this time, I had become much more concerned about the economic age and its consequences. As with every age, there was a tendency to focus on the strengths of the economic age but ignore its shortcomings. One shortcoming was the devastating effect this age was having on the natural environment. Another was the tendency to justify everything in terms of its "economic impact." A third was putting too much emphasis on the material and quantitative side of life, and a fourth was placing a much higher priority on the production and consumption of wealth than on distributing wealth more equitably.

As I delved more deeply into these matters, I began to realize that there was a basic flaw in the economic age that could not be corrected in my view. It stemmed from the fact that (as mentioned earlier) the natural environment was treated as a given and consequently as an "externality." This problem eventually caused me to conclude that the economic age could not be transformed from the inside, since it was impossible *after the fact* to insert the natural environment into a system of thought and practice that had evolved progressively and relentlessly over more than two centuries.

Even several decades ago, it was apparent that dire consequences were in store for humanity if it persisted in giving priority to economic concerns over everything else. The rapid rate of world population growth, growing shortages of natural resources, escalating pollution, and undue pressure on the finite carrying capacity of the earth all added up to a prescription for a catastrophe of monumental proportions if these matters were not addressed. More than once, I recalled Einstein's observation that "the significant problems we face cannot be solved by the same level of thinking that created them."

As my investigations into culture intensified, I began to realize that everything was there to make a compelling case for a cultural age as the next great age in human history.

For one thing, culture is rooted in nature, not materialism. This is because the term culture derives from the Latin verb *colo,* meaning "to plant, till, and cultivate." For another thing, many cultural activities — such as the arts, humanities, education, life-long learning, social interaction, spiritual renewal, and the quest for the sublime — are capable of bringing a great deal of happiness and fulfillment in life, as well as reducing our huge ecological footprint, because they are largely labour-intensive rather than material-intensive. Moreover, culture is capable of coming to grips with the enormous amount of complexity and diversity in the world, primarily because it is perceived, defined, and manifests itself in the world in many different ways and not just one way.

But the most compelling argument of all for the importance of culture — when we take it in the all-encompassing sense as "the complex whole" or a people's "total way of life" — is that culture is, by definition, holistic. This is undoubtedly one of culture's best-kept secrets and most valuable assets. It makes it possible to see the big picture, come to grips with key components and strategic relationships within that all-inclusive perspective, and achieve more balance, stability, and sustainability in the world.

It is important to emphasize that the strengths of the economic age would not disappear or be rejected in a cultural age. On the contrary — a cultural age would incorporate these strengths, along with many other strengths, into a broader, deeper, and more fundamental way of looking at and dealing with life, living, reality, history, the human condition, and the world system. Clearly we will need strong economies in the future, but we will need them properly positioned in a comprehensive cultural context, as well as informed by environmental, historical, and cultural values and not just industrial, commercial, technological, and financial values.

But the most important point of all is this. When all the different thoughts, ideas, and insights of generations of cultural scholars are brought together and considered collectively, they produce a powerful portrait of what a cultural age would be like — what our future could be like — if we choose to move in that direction.

From the moment when I realized the full potential of culture several decades ago, virtually all of my research and writing has been concerned with fleshing out what is required to create a cultural age and to enable it to flourish.

These matters have been addressed in several books, including *Cul-*

ture: Beacon of the Future, *Revolution or Renaissance: Making the Transition from an Economic Age to a Cultural Age*, *The Age of Culture*, and now *The Secrets of Culture*. This is also the principal objective of the World Culture Project, which was created in 1989 to commemorate the World Decade for Cultural Development. The Project is designed to show in theoretical and practical terms how it is possible for culture and cultures to play a mainstream rather than marginal role in the world.

That culture should be at the centre of human life is as it should be. Not only is this consistent with reality; it is also the key to the future. While preoccupation with the economic age has produced countless benefits and opportunities, it is not capable of carrying humanity forward into the next great epoch in human history. For this, a cultural age is required. Such an age possesses the potential to capitalize fully on all of culture's profuse and profound secrets, as well as to create the conditions for a more equitable, sustainable, and harmonious world.

D. Paul Schafer
2015

Do not go where the path may lead. Go instead where there is no path and leave a trail.

RALPH WALDO EMERSON

CHAPTER ONE

The Formative Years

It all started when I was very young. My teacher in grade five asked me to do a project at home that I could present to the class at school. So I decided to do a project on Marco Polo.

I am not sure why I picked this topic. Perhaps it was because one day when I was seven or eight, I asked my mother what lay directly beneath where we were standing in our house. Her answer was "China." And when I asked her how far away China was, she said, "Why don't you dig a hole to China in the backyard and find out?" So this is what I did. I got a shovel from the garage and started digging a hole to China.

After that, whenever I bothered my mother — which was often — she would send me to the backyard to work on that hole. I only got wise to this when the hole was well over my head and the earth was getting heavier and heavier and the digging harder and harder. It slowly but surely dawned on me that I would never reach China regardless of how long I spent digging. I would have to find out about China some other way.

The Marco Polo project provided this opportunity. No sooner was I started than my interest in China — indeed my interest in all things Chinese — grew by leaps and bounds. The project taught me a great deal about a person and part of the world I knew nothing about, as well as introducing me to one of the most fascinating countries in the world.

What I didn't know at the time was that this project would have a profound effect on my entire life because it was concerned with culture and a specific culture in the world. Broadening and deepening understanding of culture in general and the world's many diverse cultures in particular eventually became my principal passion and life's work. What I also didn't know at the time was that I would become actively involved in many aspects of Chinese culture later in life — from brush painting and Chinese opera to tai chi, qi gong, and involvement in a number of Chinese organizations — as well as writing a number of books on culture that would be translated into Chinese and published in China.

But I'm getting ahead of myself here. In my project, I traced Marco Polo from the time he left Italy with several family members and friends and made his way through present-day Turkey, Iran, Iraq, Afghanistan, and Pakistan until he arrived in China. I was particularly interested in the time he spent in China (the "Middle Kingdom" as it was sometimes called, because many Chinese felt it was situated at the centre of the world) and especially the time he spent in Peiping, which, of course, we know as Beijing today. He had many captivating experiences there, including meeting many different kinds of people, eating diverse types of foods, and enjoying banquets and festivities in the courts of Kublai Khan and other rulers. I found myself growing more and more immersed in the project as it evolved.

This was not the only encounter I had with culture when I was young that would have an important impact on my life. A couple of years after presenting the Marco Polo project to my class, my mother enrolled my brother Murray and me in Saturday morning art classes at the Art Gallery of Toronto (now the Art Gallery of Ontario). One day on our way to the gallery, we were confronted by a little old lady who asked us if we would light her stove for her because she was Jewish and not allowed to light her stove on the Sabbath. It was the first time that I can recall being exposed to a person whose culture and cultural customs were different than mine. Like the Marco Polo project, this experience kindled in me a keen desire to learn more about culture and all the various cultures and religions of the world.

Nor were these the only experiences I had when I was young that had a profound effect on my life. My mother read stories to Murray and me about other cultures, customs, peoples, and ways of life. We would lie spellbound in the bunk beds my father had created for us, listening breathlessly to such stories as *Ali Baba and the Forty Thieves*, *The Seven Voyages of Sinbad the Sailor*, *Peter Pan*, and *Tom Sawyer*, as well as fairy tales by Hans Christian Andersen, the Brothers Grimm, and many other authors.

I think the red-covered books that included these stories were called *Journeys through Bookland*. They were compiled by Charles H. Sylvester, and were part of a universal anthology of some of the greatest literary masterpieces created especially for children. These masterpieces ran the gamut of possibilities. There were short stories, long stories, epic tales, everyday adventures, poems, and virtually everything else. They were drawn from every conceivable part of the world — east, west, north, and south — and, like the experiences with the little old Jewish lady and the Marco Polo project, filled me with a keen desire to learn about all the different cultures of the world.

It wasn't long before I was observing the cultural habits, customs, traditions, and beliefs of others. This was especially true of my friends and classmates at school. Most had habits and customs that were similar to mine, perhaps because their parents, grandparents, or more distant relatives came from the same part of Europe as my ancestors. However, some had beliefs that were very different, especially those whose parents, grandparents, or more distant relatives came from Asia, Africa, Latin America, or the Middle East. They were the really interesting ones — the ones who held out the greatest attraction for me — because they did things, believed in things, celebrated things, and valued things that were very different than the things most familiar to me.

These early encounters with cultures and people different from myself were accompanied by many different artistic experiences, most of which were provided by my parents. Not only did I enjoy the classes I took at the Art Gallery of Toronto, but also I enjoyed all the paintings on display there, as well as the many stately rooms in which they were displayed.

Since authorities at the Gallery were anxious to celebrate European masters, tastes, techniques, and styles, most of the paintings were by artists such as Gainsborough, Constable, Turner, Goya, Vermeer, Van Dyck, and others. I also seem to recall a painting by Rembrandt, and one or two by the French Impressionists. These paintings had a lasting effect on me because they exposed me at a very early age to some of the greatest painters and paintings in the world. There were, however, few if any paintings by Canadian artists that I can remember. But I do seem to remember someone at the Gallery named A. Y. Jackson and someone else named Arthur Lismer. What I didn't know was that these two individuals were not just art teachers, but members of Canada's Group of Seven, without doubt the finest group of artists Canada has ever produced.

Shortly after being enrolled in the art classes, my mother enrolled me in the choir at Grace Church on-the-Hill in the central part of Toronto. This proved to be one of the most important, if not *the* most important, experiences in my life. I loved singing the hymns — especially hymns like "A Mighty Fortress Is Our God," "O Perfect Love," "Abide with Me" and especially "Jerusalem"— as well as many beautiful anthems. There was a great deal of exquisite music of other kinds, too, most notably George Fredrick Handel's *Messiah*, Felix Mendelssohn's *Elijah*, and many cantatas and masses by Johann Sebastian Bach, Franz Schubert, and many other European composers.

My experience in the choir filled me with an appreciation for music in general, and religious music in particular, that has brought me an enormous amount of happiness in life. Whenever I am depressed, I usually realize it is because I am not listening to enough music to keep my spirits high. Whenever this happens, I turn on my radio or CD player. Almost immediately, I feel revitalized. Today, I enjoy music of all types, styles, eras, and from all parts of the world: popular and classical; sacred and secular; ancient, medieval, and modern; and African, Asian, Latin American, Middle Eastern, European, and North American. However, it was my early exposure to religious music that made all this possible.

I reaped many other benefits from singing in the choir at Grace Church on-the-Hill. One was singing *The Messiah* every Christmas at Massey Hall in downtown Toronto, although we were so far up in the second balcony that it was virtually impossible to see the conductor, Sir Ernest Macmillan, who was one of Canada's most distinguished conductors and musicians at the time. Another benefit was singing at weddings at Bishop Strachan School across from the church. This involved singing a great deal of beautiful music and also being paid handsomely for the privilege of doing so.

Yet another benefit was going to choir camp every summer. The best thing about this — quite apart from getting away from the heat of the city for two weeks every summer in the days before air conditioning was common — was enjoying everything nature had to offer. Since the camp was located in a different place each year, this provided an opportunity to become familiar with a great deal of exquisite scenery in Muskoka and other areas north of Toronto. It also provided an opportunity to enjoy many pristine lakes, rivers, and streams, take long walks in the country and the forest, and eat freshly grilled fish for breakfast most mornings.

This was not the only encounter I had with nature when I was young that was destined to have a profound effect on my life. We were fortunate to have a huge ravine — Cedarvale Ravine — located a few blocks from where we lived. I spent an incredible amount of time there, something which, in addition to my experiences at choir camp, accounts for the fact that I have had a keen interest in nature and the natural environment ever since. I should also mention that I have always had a keen interest in horticulture, which springs largely from the fact that I worked in a florist shop for several years when I was in high school. At one time, I even entertained the idea of becoming a florist.

But back to the ravine. There was always a great deal to see and do there in every season of the year. This included enjoying all the beautiful trees, plants, and wildflowers, exploring two or three large caves in the sides of hills surrounding the ravine, and wading in the ravine's small brooks and streams and a couple of decent-sized pools. My friends and I spent countless hours there enjoying everything the ravine had to offer. We particularly enjoyed skating on its ponds, tobogganing on its hills (and especially going over the "camel's hump"), and playing hide-and-seek and Cowboys-and-Indians in many different locations in the ravine, despite the fact that it was not the ideal landscape for the latter purpose. We discovered this when we started watching Roy Rogers, Tom Mix, and Lone Ranger movies at the movie theatre on Saturday afternoons. Most of these movies were shot in Arizona, New Mexico, Death Valley, and the Badlands of South Dakota, places that looked very different than our ravine in Toronto!

While singing in the choir and enjoying nature were among the most memorable and important experiences I had when I was young, listening to classical music with my father was another. We would lie on a couch in the living room together listening to the old "78's" for what seemed like hours on end. Each record played for only three or four minutes before it had to be changed. (This was before automatic record changers, which let you stack many records on the record player and listen to them sequentially, rather than having to change them by hand.)

My father loved the music of Brahms, Beethoven, Schubert, Rachmaninoff, Chopin, and many other composers, and instilled this love in me. He was particularly fond of Schumann, who (he said) had a remarkable capacity for creating musical problems for himself and then extricating himself from these problems with great beauty, imagination, and ingenuity.

There were piano lessons, too, paid for in monthly installments by my parents. Unfortunately, I couldn't play the piano very well. My teacher said it was because my fingers were too short and I had a "lazy left hand." This irked me immensely because I was — and still am — left-handed, and one of the most talented pianists in the world at the time was Arthur Rubinstein, who had the shortest fingers I have ever seen. Nevertheless, I did manage to pass both the grade eight piano examination and the grade two music theory exam at the Royal Conservatory of Music in Toronto.

My parents also exposed me to a number of theatrical productions when I was young. One of the most memorable was a production by a group of aboriginal actors and actresses on the Six Nations Indian Reserve near Brantford, Ontario, one crisp fall evening in late September. I cannot remember the name or content of this production, but it had a powerful effect on me nonetheless. Perhaps it was about Hiawatha, the legendary chief of the Onondaga tribe who founded the Iroquois Confederacy and was immortalized in a poem by Henry Longfellow. But more likely it was about Joseph Brant, the brilliant Mohawk leader who was friendly with the British and led the colonial Loyalists and Indian troops against the Americans during the American Revolutionary War. He eventually settled in what is now Ontario on a plot of land given to him by John Graves Simcoe, the Governor of Upper Canada at the time.

One of the most fascinating things about the education I received in the arts when I was young was that my parents did not have an education in the arts themselves. This was because they came from farming stock — my mother Belle from Manitoba and my father Harold from Saskatchewan — and were forced to leave school rather early to earn a living and help support their parents. However, my mother did manage to go to normal school and then teach school for a number of years before getting married, although my father was forced to leave school in grade ten despite the fact he had done very well in school up to that point.

Despite this, my parents understood the value of an education in the arts, much as many parents do. It is not coincidental that many parents want piano, singing, dance, or art lessons for their children, even if they have been deprived of such opportunities themselves. They understand the value of an education in the arts for happiness, fulfillment, and well-being at all stages in life.

My parents certainly did. I don't know where this conviction came from, but it was certainly there. Perhaps it was because they had ancestral roots stretching back to Europe and were able to profit from the high value Europeans generally place on the arts. Perhaps it was because they saw people around them whose children were benefitting from an education in the arts and wanted this type of education for their children. Or perhaps it was because they had taught themselves to play musical instruments or paint pictures and thought this would be good for their children as well.

Interestingly, my mother taught herself to play both the piano and the violin when she was young and played in a dance band and community orchestra for a number of years, although she never took lessons on either instrument. My father also taught himself to play the piano, although not as well as my mother, and would often sit down at the piano after dinner and play the first movement of Beethoven's *Moonlight Sonata,* Debussy's *Clair de Lune*, or the first page or two of Chopin's *Étude in E Flat* before it got too difficult. He also taught himself to paint pictures without the benefit of any lessons, and produced many beautiful water colour and pastel paintings, several of which are hanging in our home today.

Given their own interests, it is not surprising, then, that my parents wanted their children to have an excellent education in the arts — the kind of education that was deeper, richer, and broader than the one provided by elementary and secondary schools in those days and perhaps even today.

There is one other matter related to the education my parents gave me in the arts that should be mentioned. It was the nature of the home my parents created for us. While this was not something as concrete and specific as piano or art lessons, singing in a choir, being exposed to great literature, or attending a theatrical performance, it nevertheless embodied everything my parents knew and valued about the arts.

We have all been in enough family residences to know that there is a huge difference between a *house* and a *home*. A house has all the trappings and accoutrements that are necessary for life and living — tables, chairs, beds, lamps, sofas, pots, kettles, a stove, a refrigerator, a furnace, carpets, wall hangings, paintings, and the like. However, this doesn't make it a home. It only becomes a home when these things are attractively displayed, cleverly presented, and a great deal of artistic mastery and ingenuity goes into ensuring that they serve aesthetic functions and not just commonplace and practical functions.

This is seldom a matter of money. More often than not, it is a matter of taste. Many people who have a great deal of money to spend on family residences and furnishings are incapable of making a house a home. Conversely, many people who do not have a lot of money to spend are more than capable of doing this. We have all been in family abodes where people with a great deal of money to spend on household items end up producing something that is cold, impersonal, and unattractive, rather than warm, inviting, and enjoyable. And usually the more money they spend the worse things get! Unfortunately, their artistic sensibilities and sensitivities have not been developed to the point where they are capable of making a house a home.

Not so with my parents. They knew exactly how to make a house a home and had an incredible knack for this, which I believe was intimately tied up with their awareness of and appreciation for the arts. They seemed to know where everything fit, what went with what and what did not, and how to achieve the maximum effect. This was especially true for my mother. Although she had to be careful with every penny, she knew how to use pictures, wall hangings, craft objects, carpets, and the like to warm a room, create intimacy and effect, make every room unique, and blend all the various parts of the home together to form a harmonious whole. As a result, we enjoyed living in our home immensely. Although it was not situated in the best of neighbourhoods and was semi-detached, this didn't matter to us. It had an artistic ambiance and aesthetic appeal that was as cherished as it was rare. It made life and living for me, Murray, and my parents much more memorable and enjoyable than it would have been otherwise.

Looking back on all this makes me realize how fortunate I was to be exposed to the arts when I was young. I am sure most people feel this way, even if they lacked the good fortune to have had as rich, varied, and intensive exposure to the arts as I did. There is only one thing I would change if it were possible to do so. I would see to it that every person was educated in the architectural, cinematographic, culinary, horticultural, and material arts. For although I had an intensive education in the musical, visual, and literary arts — and was exposed to a fair amount of drama — I was not educated in these other areas. I had to wait until I was well into my forties and had travelled a great deal before realizing how important knowledge of these other arts is for a fulfilling life.

What is especially interesting about all this is the fact that I didn't make any distinction between *the arts* and *culture* when I was young. Probably that was because these terms were used interchangeably by virtually everyone I knew. However, I do recall feeling even then that there could be some basic differences between the two concepts. Culture seemed to imply something broader and deeper than the arts, because it included things like habits, customs, traditions, and beliefs, and even a whole way of life.

In retrospect, I can see that I could not have had a better introduction to culture than through the arts. This is because the arts epitomize culture and provide a gateway to the cultural world and understanding culture. However, more about this later — much more! Here I simply want to mention that the arts and culture were seen as one and the same when I was young, even if I had an intuitive feeling that they could well be very different.

While the education I had in the arts was provided primarily by my parents, it was augmented at the high school I attended. There were the usual art and music classes, which were concerned largely with playing musical instruments and painting pictures, as well as opportunities to engage in other artistic activities, such as going to community theatrical productions, joining the photography club, or participating in the school play or annual music night.

It was at high school that my musical horizons were broadened quite considerably. Although I had already listened to a great deal of classical music and had sung an enormous amount of sacred music in the choir, I had not been exposed to much music of other kinds. This changed — and changed dramatically — when I was in high school. I have been grateful for this ever since.

It was in high school that I was exposed to musicals for the first time, since they were very popular when I was growing up in the 1950s. Most of these musicals were written by American composers and lyricists, such as Jerome Kern, Alan Jay Lerner, Frederick Loewe, and especially Richard Rodgers and Oscar Hammerstein II. Three of my favourite musicals were *Brigadoon*, *Carousel*, and *Oklahoma*, which were all performed at the high school I attended although I was not involved in any of the productions. But they filled me with a love for musicals in general, and American musicals in particular, that has grown steadily over the years and endured to this day. Among the other musicals I love are *Showboat*, *South Pacific*, *The King and I*, *Porgy and Bess*, and, more recently *The Sound of Music* and *Les Misérables*.

These musicals, and countless others, have many beautiful songs in them — songs such as "If I Loved You" and "You'll Never Walk Alone" from *Carousel*, "Some Enchanted Evening" from *South Pacific*, "Old Man River" from *Showboat*, "Oh What a Beautiful Morning" from *Oklahoma*, "Climb Every Mountain" and "Edelweiss" from *The Sound of Music*, and "I Dreamed a Dream" from *Les Misérables*. I wish these and other musicals were performed more often, since they are filled with many songs and melodies that linger in the mind and memory for decades. They also provide a "vision of the future" that is far more compelling than most visions in vogue today. This is particularly true of the work of Oscar Hammerstein II, who had a remarkable knack with words and an incredible capacity to combine those words with exquisite music by Richard Rodgers and other composers in musicals such as *Carousel* and *The Sound of Music*.

I was also exposed to a great deal of popular music when I was in high school and developed a keen appreciation for it. As a result, I enjoy popular music today as well as classical music and musicals, and don't make much distinction between them. If I like a piece of music and find it beautiful, I will listen to it regardless of what people think or whether it is popular, semi-classical, or classical in nature.

Many popular songs were all the rage when I was in high school, such as "Love is a Many Splendored Thing," "Unchained Melody," "Shangri-La," "My Prayer," "I Believe," "I'm a Stranger in Paradise," "When We Come of Age," "Moon River," and my all-time favourite, "Tammy," especially when it is sung by Debbie Reynolds. Singers and groups popular at the time included Rosemary Clooney, Patti Page, Perry Como, Frank Sinatra, Frankie Lane, the McGuire Sisters, The Four Lads, the Platters, and many others. I enjoy listening to these singers and groups immensely whenever I hear them, which is regrettably far too seldom, as well as the songs and music of many other fine singers and composers popular at the time. They never fail to move me and make me nostalgic, which I know is also true for many other people who enjoy the commitment made by PBS and other broadcasters to "bringing back the oldies."

Although there were other opportunities to enjoy the arts when I was in high school, I was aware that most students lacked the kind of intensive education in the arts that my parents gave me. And I was aware of something else. There was a great deal of friction between the arts and sports when I was in high school.

This was made abundantly clear by an experience I had with the French horn in grade eleven. I decided to take music as an option that year, and was told by the music teacher that I would have to learn to play a musical instrument. So I decided on the French horn, because it had a mellow tone and sounded nice. I was also involved in a number of sports at the time, especially football and basketball.

Whenever I had to take the French horn home to practice — which was often — I would leave school early for fear of being ridiculed, because I didn't want my teammates on the football or basketball team to see me carrying the awkward-looking French horn case. So I would slink along side streets and over backyard fences, much like the cats in Dylan Thomas's *Child's Christmas in Wales,* hoping that no one would see me and being exceedingly grateful it was not something far larger, such as a tuba or a double bass. You can imagine how embarrassing it would have been for me if my teammates had seen me carrying a musical instrument home from school when I was the quarterback and captain of the football team and we were well on our way to winning a district football championship.

The friction between the arts and sports was palpable when I was in high school. And it was not confined to students playing sports. It affected every boy and girl in the school, since sports were generally deemed to be "male activities" and the arts "female activities." But the consequences were the same. This distinction kept boys out of the arts, and girls out of sports. I have often wondered if things have changed in this respect, now that girls are so much more involved in sports than when I was in school. My impression is that things haven't actually changed all that much, but I have no empirical evidence to back this up.

I was obsessed with sports when I was in high school, so much so that in addition to all the sports I played and watched during school hours, I would often skip class to watch or play sports outside of school as well. Not only did we have football and basketball practices before and after school every day — it was impossible to win championships without this — but I was constantly playing football and ball hockey on the street, ice hockey at the local rink, and basketball in every church basement and community centre in our neighbourhood. Talk about being "hooked on sports"! I was so obsessed with sports that I couldn't think about much else, with the exception of snooker, which also commanded a great deal of my time and attention and caused me to skip school on numerous occasions.

While most high school teachers did not take kindly to sports because they thought they had an unfavourable effect on too many students' academic work — that was certainly true of me as I will explain momentarily — I must say that I learned a great deal from playing and watching sports in high school. For one thing, I learned how important sports are for physical conditioning, exercise, and good health later in life. For another, I learned the value of teamwork and developing cooperative skills and abilities, getting along with others, meeting challenges, capitalizing on opportunities, and learning to win and to lose gracefully. It is amazing what can be accomplished when people set aside their egos and differences and participate collectively in something that can't be achieved working as individuals. While sports are not the only activities that are capable of teaching such lessons, they are certainly one of the best.

But there was another side to my involvement in sports at high school that should be mentioned. By the time I was in grade twelve (or should I say grades ten, eleven, and twelve because I had passed some subjects and not others in each of these years!) I was so deeply immersed in sports, and in snooker, that I was doing dreadfully at school in the academic sense. Not only was I getting very poor grades in the subjects I somehow managed to pass, but I was failing others and failing them miserably. This was because I had little interest in academic matters when I was in high school, and spent little time and energy on them.

This was not only because of my obsession with sports and snooker. It was also because I didn't take to the high school curriculum at all well. I know things have changed a great deal in this area since I was in high school, so my comments on this may be less relevant today. However, when I was in high school, all students were required to take many compulsory subjects, such as English, French, Latin, physics, chemistry, trigonometry, algebra, and geometry. This was not exactly an inspiring slate of courses for someone who had been well schooled in the arts, was obsessed with sports and snooker, and was wrestling with all the problems young people wrestle with at this particular stage in their lives.

I always thought I should be taking some elementary courses in psychology, sociology, and perhaps even philosophy, since they were far more relevant to the problems I was experiencing at the time. Subjects like these were of considerable interest to me because I was struggling with a whole series of questions like: *What is the meaning of life? Why do I behave the way I do? Why do I get along with some people and not others?* And, most importantly, *what is most essential in life, where should I be going, and how can I get there?*

Unfortunately, my teachers had other ideas. They expected me to master a whole set of courses that had little or nothing to do with the problems I was experiencing at that stage in my life, perhaps because of pedagogical beliefs and convictions that were carried over from classical times and were deemed to constitute the "ideal education." I can only say that it delights me no end to see that in recent years this traditional way of thinking about the high school curriculum has changed in many educational institutions and jurisdictions throughout the world. It is now possible for students to choose from a much broader array of courses — courses that are far more interesting than the ones I was compelled to take, and pass, when I was at high school.

There was, however, one course I took at high school that I enjoyed immensely and which had a profound effect on me. It was ancient and medieval history. I took this course in grade eleven, and it was totally different from the history courses I took in grades nine and ten and again in grade twelve. These latter courses, which were concerned primarily with Canadian, American, and world history, were filled with dates, places, names, wars, politicians, political events, and treaties of one type or another. They were predicated on the memorization and regurgitation of a great deal of information and data, most of which was political in nature and forgotten quickly.

Ancient and medieval history — at least the way my teacher taught this course — was very different. It was filled with great achievements and terrible tragedies. Over the course of the year, we studied the rises and falls and strengths and weaknesses of numerous cultures and civilizations in the ancient and medieval worlds. We travelled to Egypt, Greece, Persia, and Rome. We saw the Pyramids, the Parthenon, Persepolis, and the Coliseum. We fought with Agamemnon, Ulysses, Hector, and Achilles in the Trojan wars, engaged in hand-to-hand combat with Xerxes, King Darius, and Cyrus, and conversed with Homer, Socrates, Plato, and Aristotle about crucial philosophical issues and worldly matters. We also met Marcus Aurelius and Julius Caesar, and saw the horrors of the Christians being fed to the lions. Later, we travelled through medieval Europe to enjoy the wonders of Venice, Florence, Avignon, Toledo, and many other cities, as well as to witness catastrophes like the Black Death and the Crusades.

The year was filled with triumphs and tragedies, saints and sinners, surges and setbacks. It opened my eyes to a very different world. If I could enter a time capsule and travel either backward or forward in time, I would definitely travel backward in order to see all the cultures, peoples, and civilizations that provide so many valuable insights into what life, living, and the world are all about. By doing so — and my high school course was, in fact, something like a time machine — I would learn how different civilizations coped with countless calamities and adversities but still managed to survive and move forward. Without doubt, the course I took in ancient and medieval history was the highlight of my high school years in an academic sense — despite the fact that it still paled by comparison with sports and snooker! — as well as the shining star in a lackluster slate of courses.

Apart from this one course, I floundered badly in the academic sense in high school and had virtually no hope of going further in school. Fortunately, however, I started hanging around with many Jewish students at this time, largely because they seemed to be interested in the same things I was interested in, especially sports, billiards, and the arts. But there was one significant difference. Virtually all of these students were doing extremely well in school and planning to go to university. This was due to the high value Jewish people and Jewish culture generally place on education and learning.

Had it not been for this, as well as one other remarkable development I will tell you about in a moment, I probably never would have thought of going to university. I was doing so poorly in high school it was simply out of the question. But listening to my Jewish friends constantly talking about what they were planning to take at university made me wonder if I might be able to go to university as well, especially when several of these students offered to help me with the courses that I was doing badly in and that were holding me back.

This was the first time in my life that I began to understand that other cultures are not just fascinating because they are based on different customs, tradition, beliefs, and way of life. *There is an incredible amount to learn from other cultures that is relevant to how we can solve the problems we are confronted with, and in doing so, enrich our own lives*. Nor would this be the last time I would realize this fact and find it extremely helpful in overcoming problems I myself faced, therefore enhancing my life in ways I never dreamt possible.

These were not the only rewards I reaped from my association with Jewish students when I was in high school. There were many others. One was going to play basketball at the YMHA (the Young Men's Hebrew Association) on the corner of Spadina Avenue and Bloor Street in the central part of Toronto. Not only were there many Jewish students who were outstanding basketball players attending high schools in that part of Toronto, especially at Harbord Collegiate and Central Commerce, but also the YMHA had a much better basketball court than any of those I played on at my high school or in the local community.

It was also through my Jewish friends at the "Y" that I got my first taste of Chinese food. While my father had taken us for many years to Studleigh's Restaurant in downtown Toronto — a Victorian restaurant on King Street that was famous for its buffets, roast beef, and mile-high mince meat pie — this was the extent of my exposure to food from other cultures and parts of the world until my friends at the Y took me to what was known as "12A," a small Chinese restaurant over a grocery store on Elizabeth Street in that area of Toronto known as Chinatown.

I will never forget my first Chinese meal. It consisted of won ton soup, egg rolls, barbecued pork spare ribs, shrimp fried rice, beef chow mien, sweet and sour chicken balls, and fortune cookies. I remember thinking: "What have I been missing all these years!" Anyone who has grown up on food from the British Isles will know exactly what I mean, since our meals at home usually consisted of tough meat, under-cooked potatoes, and an overcooked "veg."

My mouth still waters whenever I think of my first Chinese meal. I can taste it today like it was yesterday. Chinese food has been a favourite of mine, and an integral part of my life, ever since. Years later, I went often to the Sai Woo Restaurant on Dundas Street near Bay Street. It was extremely popular with many Torontonians because its founder, Bill Wen, really knew how to throw a banquet, and was renowned throughout Toronto for creating fabulous food, helping Chinese immigrants to get settled in the city, and participating in the creation and development of a seniors' home for elderly Chinese people in the downtown core. Like many long-time Toronto residents, I can still remember his superb banquets with their many sumptuous courses, delicious dishes, impeccable service, unbelievable organization, and colourful decorations. It is probably the closest I will ever get to knowing what it was like for Marco Polo and his entourage to eat at the court of Kublai Khan.

However, I am getting ahead of myself once again! By the time I was in high school in the early to mid-1950s, Canada was on the move after a long, painful period that included the Great Depression and the Second World War. The years of thrift and penny-pinching were finally over. People were starting to earn real money again and spend it more freely. New washers, dryers, refrigerators, radios, and possibly even a new car, television set, or house were on most people's minds. A new era had opened up in Canada, one that was driven by a dynamic economy, a dramatic expansion in the country's educational system, and major advances in science, industry, commerce, and technology. Canadians were once again excited for the future.

These were busy years for my parents. While they did not have a lot of money to spend and were not involved in many community activities, they were caring, sharing, and compassionate people who channelled most of their time, energy, and attention into working hard and helping others. This was particularly true with respect to immigrants and refugees who suffered badly during the Second World War and came to Canada (and especially Toronto) hoping for a better, safer, and more secure life. Many of these immigrants came from countries like Italy, Greece, France, and Germany that had suffered horrendously during the war, although some came from elsewhere in Europe, as well as from other parts of the world. They made their way to Canada on their own, or they were brought to Canada by relatives, friends, church groups, or other organizations.

My parents were always anxious to help people like this. They often invited them to our place for a home-cooked meal, to experience the Canadian way of life, or to get to know a typical Canadian family. I have fond memories of this. Immigrants and refugees were always turning up at our door for Christmas dinner, Easter celebrations, or some other festive occasion. It was fascinating to hear their stories about customs, traditions, and cultures back home. Occasionally they might even say something about their experiences during the War, although most of them were reluctant to talk about this. Several of them remain close friends today, including Attila and Elfriede Bimbo, who came from Hungary and Germany respectively and are godparents to our two daughters, Charlene and Susan. They lived upstairs on the other side of our semi-detached house. I have known them for more than sixty years and they are integral parts of our family today.

My parents also took in a refugee from Hungary after the 1956 Hungarian Revolution, in order to help him learn English and prepare for life in his new country. I distinctly recall travelling by streetcar to a social welfare agency in downtown Toronto with my mother — my father must have been away at the time on a business trip for Imperial Oil, his employer — to pick up Laszlo, or Leslie as he came to be called, shortly after he arrived in Canada. He couldn't speak any English and we couldn't speak any Hungarian, so all we could do on our way home on the streetcar was smile at each other and then look the other way.

What stands out most vividly in my memory is how quickly Leslie learned English. When I got to know him better, I learned that he was fluent in four or five languages, which he had learned at school or in the ethnically and linguistically diverse area of Hungary where he had lived close to the Yugoslavian border. He taught me a great deal about this particular part of the world and its many diverse cultures, languages, and peoples, things I was to learn about in far more detail when I travelled there years later. He also taught me a great deal about opera, especially the operas of Puccini, Verdi, Mozart, Wagner, and other European composers, all of which he knew like the back of his hand. He also introduced me to Beethoven's *Ninth Symphony* when he gave me a recording of this remarkable symphony for Christmas one year. Am I ever glad he did! It has been a favourite of mine ever since, much as it is for millions of people around the world.

There is one final experience I had when I was young that was destined to have a profound effect on my life. It has to do with the battle I was waging to get out of high school and go to university.

By this time, I had been in high school for more years than I care to remember but was very keen to go to university. I even gave up sports and snooker — incredibly hard for me to do at the time! — in order to concentrate on my studies. The problem was that my academic record was so abysmal and my study habits were so poor that I had little chance of being accepted to university, regardless of how badly I wanted to go.

While it normally took students five years to finish high school, I was still in high school in my seventh year, which says a great deal about all the time I spent playing sports and snooker and the problems I had with the high school curriculum. Although I had acquired five of the nine grade thirteen credits that were required in order to graduate from high school, I still needed four credits — English literature, English composition, French literature, and French composition — to graduate from high school and have any chance of getting into university. I had done reasonably well in three of the grade thirteen courses where I seemed to have a natural aptitude, namely algebra, geometry, and trigonometry, and had squeaked through history and geography. However, my Achilles heel was — and always had been — languages. I did very poorly in languages, regardless of whether it was English, French, or Latin. This is ironic in view of the fact that I have been a writer most of my life, but it was a major stumbling block for me at the time.

I was most concerned about the final exam I had to write in English composition because this course always gave me the most trouble. So I made a pact with myself at Easter time in my seventh year to work as hard as I possibly could on the remaining four grade thirteen courses I had to pass — and especially hard on the English composition course — in order to fulfill my dream of going to university.

I put my whole heart and soul into studying in the months leading up to the four final exams in June. I even went to a series of special classes given by my English teacher, Miss Helen Waugh, to get the help I needed to prepare properly for the exams. I distinctly recall Miss Waugh saying, "Paul, whatever you do, make sure you write a wonderful first sentence for the essay you are required to write on your English composition exam, because this will make the marker want to read your entire essay." Since the essay counted for 80 percent of the total mark, writing a good essay and a captivating first sentence was imperative.

For weeks prior to the English composition exam, I prayed I would get a terrific topic to write about — they were usually as dull as dishwater — as well as hoping I would be able to write a fantastic first sentence that would really grip the marker's attention.

When I received the questions for the final exam in the exam room in June — it was the first of the four examinations I had to write and pass in order to be admitted to university — I was thrilled to discover that my prayers had been answered. There, staring me in the face, was the topic "music as a hobby." I couldn't believe my eyes. Since I had taken piano lessons and sung in a choir, I remember thinking, "This is the perfect topic for me." There simply couldn't have been a better one.

What happened next progressed steadily from a fervent dream to an incredible nightmare. I wrote the first sentence of my essay, stared at it for a minute or two, and then, remembering what Miss Waugh had told me, said to myself: "Paul, you can write a better first sentence than this." So I crossed this sentence out and wrote another one on the top of the next page. Once again, I stared at this sentence for a minute or two, and said to myself: "Paul, you can write an even better first sentence to start your essay." So I crossed out this sentence and wrote yet another one on the top of the next page.

You won't believe this, but after an hour and a half — grade thirteen exams were two-and-a-half hours in those days — I was still on my first sentence. I had gone through fourteen or fifteen examination books by this time with a sentence at the top of each page, but always with the sentence crossed out and replaced by another sentence on the following page, and then with this one crossed out as well.

By this time, I was in a real panic, and was getting more frantic and frustrated by the moment. I called the supervisor over and told him how distraught I was. I said I wanted to leave the examination immediately because I couldn't cope with the stress and tension any longer. More than half the time allotted for the exam was over and I had nothing to show for it. The supervisor said that there were a couple of other questions on the exam, and that I should answer these questions "to the best of my ability" and then turn in everything I had written.

Since the essay accounted for four-fifths of the final mark and the remaining questions only one-fifth, I didn't see any point in continuing. I couldn't possibly pass the exam, and pleaded with the supervisor to let me leave the exam room because I was getting more despondent and depressed by the moment. However, he insisted that I finish as much as I could and turn in everything I had written, including the fourteen or fifteen exam books with a sentence on the top of each page that had been crossed out and replaced by another on the next page. So this is what I did. I completed the remaining questions as best I could, turned in all my exam books, and left the exam room and the school as quickly as possible.

I cried all the way home. I had let myself down, my parents down, and my teachers down. Since this was the first of the four final grade thirteen examinations I had to write and pass in order to have any hope of getting into university, there seemed to be no point in writing the three remaining exams. After all, I knew for sure that I failed the English composition exam. It was one of the most excruciating experiences I have ever had in life. With tears rolling down my cheeks, I hoped none of my friends or classmates would see me.

When I got home, I instantly called my father to tell him what had happened, sobbing profusely all the time. He told me not to worry and said he would leave work immediately and be home in an hour. And this is what he did. After listening to my tale of woe and calming me down, he suggested we go for a drive in the country. He said he would even let me drive the car a little on a back road, although I didn't have a license at the time. He knew from experience that it was useless to rehash my disastrous experience and far better to get my mind on something else such as driving the car, which I had wanted to do for some time.

By supper time, I had calmed down considerably, but had decided not to write the remaining three exams. Universities were very strict in those days in requiring nine grade thirteen credits in order to quality for admission, and since I had failed English composition, that was now out of the question. However, my parents eventually persuaded me to study as hard as I could under these adverse circumstances and do as well as I could on the three remaining exams. "You never know what might happen," they told me. Besides, if I passed the three remaining exams, at least I would not have to repeat those three courses the following year if I decided to go back to high school, an option that I absolutely dreaded. This made a great deal of sense, so I studied as hard as I could and wrote the three remaining exams.

When the marks came in July, they were very much as I had expected. I managed to squeak through the three exams in English literature, French literature, and French composition — I think my marks were all in the low fifties, but this was enough to pass in those days — but I received a resounding 13 on my English composition exam. It was the worst mark I ever received in school. I was totally heartbroken and distraught. Failing English composition meant that I would likely never go to university. Since I didn't want to go back to high school for yet another year, I probably would have had to leave school and get a job in a department or grocery store.

But this is when my mother stepped in. Since she had been a teacher when she was young, she was not without experience in such matters. She suggested that we go to see our family doctor and tell him exactly what happened on the exam. I resisted this suggestion like the plague because I felt it was utterly useless; there was no way I would be admitted to university when I was short one subject, especially a subject like English composition and a university like the University of Toronto. But my mother persisted . . . and persisted . . . until finally I gave in.

The doctor listened patiently while I recounted my horrific experience. Then he sat there for a couple of minutes in silence. Finally, he said, "I am going to write a letter to the Registrar of the University of Toronto and explain exactly what happened to you during your final exam." He went on to say that he would point out that I was in a state of severe distress shortly after the exam commenced until I was unable to remain in the exam room any longer.

I was certain this wouldn't work, but my mother, who was very determined, said, "Let's go ahead and submit an application to the University of Toronto, attach the letter from Dr. Evelyn, and see what happens. At least you will know that you have tried everything in your power to get into university and explored every option available." So this is what I did.

Several weeks passed, and then a month. Finally, toward the end of August, a letter addressed to me arrived from the Registrar at the University of Toronto. I opened it breathlessly, and couldn't believe its contents. It said: "You have been admitted to the University of Toronto subject to the provision that you complete grade thirteen English composition by the end of your first year at university." It went on to say that even if I passed my first-year courses at the university, I would not be admitted into the second year until this stipulation had been met. This I was able to do, but only by the skin of my teeth. I think I got 51 on the final grade thirteen English composition exam when I wrote it for the second time the following June.

The day I was admitted to the University of Toronto was undoubtedly one of the happiest days of my life. After struggling for so many years, I had finally put my disastrous academic experience at high school behind me and was going on to university, and the University of Toronto to boot.

It was the beginning of a whole new phase in my life, one that has had a profound effect on virtually everything that has occurred in my life ever since. I am not sure how my life would have turned out if I had not been able to go to university. However, I do know that I would not have been able to spend the bulk of my life attempting to come to grips with the secrets of culture. Many doors were opened to me as a result of this timely stroke of good luck. We all need breaks at crucial times in our lives, and this was certainly one of the greatest breaks — if not *the* greatest break — I have ever received in life.

When I look back now, I realize how fortunate I was to have had the parents I had, and how grateful I am to them for everything they did for me and gave to me in life. They were always there for me, and made it possible for me to embark on many things that would not have been possible otherwise. In so doing, they provided me with a superb "foundation for life."

It is a foundation that has enabled me to come to grips with the many challenges and opportunities I have been presented with over the years, achieve my basic goals and objectives, and live a happy, fruitful, and fulfilling life. It is a life that has been devoted largely to probing culture in breadth and in depth, learning as much as I could about all the diverse cultures and civilizations in the world, and wanting the best for all people and countries and for humanity as a whole. What is especially fascinating is how all these areas of interest have broadened, deepened, intensified, and manifested themselves over the course of my life. It is to the next stage in this remarkable journey that I now turn.

CHAPTER TWO

Studying and Teaching Economics

I am not sure why I enrolled in commerce and finance when I went to the University of Toronto in 1957. Perhaps it was because the Canadian economy was booming at the time and this choice of subjects seemed to make a great deal of sense. Perhaps it was because my brother Murray was a composer and I thought it might help him later in life. I was aware that Vincent van Gogh's brother Theo had given Vincent a great deal of help when he was struggling as an artist and thought I might be able to help Murray in much the same way.

But much more likely it was because my father was an accountant and I thought it would be wise to follow in his footsteps. Not only would a degree in commerce and finance give me something concrete to fall back on if other possibilities did not materialize, but also it had a practical ring to it and was an obvious asset for anyone interested in having a family, a nice home, a decent standard of living, and the ability to help others.

University was a real eye-opener for me. I enjoyed it from beginning to end. For the first time in my life, I felt I was involved in something relevant to my life, even if I didn't take a course in the arts, psychology, or sociology. I did, however, take a course in philosophy, although I had to fight like mad with authorities at the university to take this course rather than another accounting course.

What immediately struck me about the University of Toronto was the atmosphere and environment there. They were much more conducive to studying and learning than the environment and atmosphere at high school. Since one of my favourite movies was *Goodbye, Mr. Chips* — it still is — I had no difficulty adjusting to the hallowed halls of the University of Toronto and its many fine Gothic buildings.

Fortunately, a strong humanistic tradition existed at the University of

Toronto when I was there. I am not sure why this was so. Perhaps it was because the university had been strongly influenced by the great humanistic tradition of English universities. All I know is that this tradition had somehow found its way into the University of Toronto in general and the commerce and finance faculty in particular. As a result, I received a broad, humanistic education there, despite the fact that I took only one liberal arts course. It certainly wasn't the kind of specialized and technical training I would have received at most American universities, and perhaps at some other Canadian universities.

There were many outstanding professors in the commerce and finance faculty when I was at the University of Toronto. Included among them were William Ashley, who taught the introductory course in commerce and finance and looked very much like Mr. Chips in his long, flowing gown; Ian Macdonald, who had just returned from Oxford and taught Principles of Economics; William Hood and Edward Neufeld, who taught Money and Banking and went on to play major roles in the federal government and Bank of Canada; and Mel Watkins, who taught Canadian Economic History and was deeply involved in the New Democratic Party and the development of the left-leaning Waffle Group in the late 1960s and early 1970s.

But the professors who had the greatest influence on me and affected me to the most were undoubtedly Karl Helleiner and Vincent Bladen. They were both distinguished scholars from Europe and were steeped in the European tradition. They arrived at the University of Toronto later in life, and took a broad approach to the courses they taught which I found especially attractive.

Karl Helleiner taught European Economic History (his specialty was the medieval period). He exposed us to all the great European economic historians over the course of the year, including Henri Pirenne, Marc Bloch, Eli Heckscher, and many others. We also learned about some of Europe's greatest commercial and financial centres in medieval and early modern times, including Ghent, Bruges, Antwerp, Amsterdam, Hamburg, Lübeck, and Venice. I can still remember how impressed I was with these cities when I visited them several years later. I was amazed to find that they were not just great financial and commercial centres, but also great artistic and cultural centres. I wondered why this was so, and what the reasons were for it.

But the professor who affected me the most and had the greatest impact on my life was Vincent Bladen. He was a graduate of Oxford and very much in the tradition of a long line of distinguished British economists, most notably Alfred Marshall, Joan Robinson, A. C. Pigou, and John Maynard Keynes. Like Keynes, who was a chairman of the Arts Council of Great Britain and a member of the Bloomsbury group, Professor Bladen was very involved in the arts in Canada and was chairman of the National Ballet School in Toronto for several years.

Bladen's specialty was the history of economic thought. He was a well-known international authority on Adam Smith and *The Wealth of Nations*, which he knew like the back of his hand. As a result, the bulk of his course on the History of Economic Thought was taken up with information and insights into this remarkable individual and his famous book, despite the fact that the course was advertised as a course on the history of economic thought from Adam Smith to John Maynard Keynes. The course gave me a keen insight into the person who is largely responsible for the type of world we are living in today, as will be discussed momentarily. I have often wondered what the world would be like if Adam Smith had not been born and *The Wealth of Nations* had never been written.

The word soon got out among the student body that Vincent Bladen thought that "in the beginning God created Adam Smith." I once confronted him with this and he merely laughed, shrugged his shoulders, and said, "No, you have it wrong. In the beginning, Adam Smith created God." I thought about this years later when I read a fascinating book by Arthur Herman called *How the Scots Invented the Modern World*. Adam Smith was featured in it, along with many other famous Scottish scholars and statesmen, as an individual who literally created the world we are living in today.

It wasn't long before I realized that the commerce and finance faculty at the University of Toronto was much more concerned with economics than commerce and finance. Most of the faculty members were economists rather than experts in commerce and finance, and, as a result, many of the courses I took in the program were economics courses. This caused me to become much more interested in economics than commerce and finance.

As my studies progressed, I began to realize why economics was such a powerful force in the world, as well as why the world was dominated far more by economics, economies, and economic growth than anything else. Not only was economics seen as the key to producing material and monetary wealth, improving standards of living, and creating a better quality of life — much as Adam Smith had envisaged this two centuries earlier — but also it was also deemed to be the key to virtually everything in life. This was because economics was concerned with jobs, income, and sources of livelihood, as well as making improvements in virtually every aspect and dimension of the human condition, from food, clothing, shelter, transportation, and communications to education, politics, recreation, the sciences, and the arts.

I also began to realize something else as my studies in economics progressed. I began to realize that economics did not suddenly vault into a position of prominence on the world scene as a result of the success of the Marshall Plan, post-war European recovery, or the fascination with economies and economic growth after the Second World War. On the contrary, the pre-eminence of economics was based on a long and distinguished tradition of economic thought and practice over several centuries. It was a tradition that was deeply rooted in the works of the classical, Marxian, neoclassical, Keynesian, and post-Keynesian economists, as epitomized by such influential books as Adam Smith's *The Wealth of Nations*, David Ricardo's *Principles of Economics*, Karl Marx's *Capital* (*Das Kapital*), Alfred Marshall's *The Principles of Economics*, and John Maynard Keynes's *General Theory of Employment, Interest, and Money*. It was a tradition that was every bit as powerful and pervasive as the tradition underlying most of the great religions of the world, and therefore such books as *The Bible*, *Quran*, *The Upanishads*, *The Analects of Confucius,* and others. Since I was anxious to learn as much as possible about economics and why economics, economies, and economic growth were so powerful and pervasive in the world, I began to think seriously about doing some graduate work in economics after my undergraduate studies were completed. I also began to think about focusing my attention on the history of economic thought, since that was such an integral part of my interest in economics at the time.

During the time I spent at the University of Toronto, my education in the arts was curtailed to a great extent, although I continued to listen to good music and visit art galleries and museums as often as possible. I was not able to take any courses in the arts because the commerce and finance program was very demanding and time consuming. As a result, I had to settle for enjoying the arts in my spare time and leisure moments, although they were never far from my mind.

There was one experience in the arts I did have in my undergraduate years, however, that had a profound effect on me. Like many other such experiences over the years, it was in the field of music. It did a great deal to expand my musical horizons, largely by exposing me to an area of music that was not too familiar to me at the time but has been a favourite of mine ever since.

The experience occurred one spring afternoon as I was walking past Hart House in the central part of the campus. Suddenly, I heard the most exquisite music lofting out of one of the windows at Hart House. I stood there for the longest time listening to this music because it was so beautiful and I had never heard it before. When it was over, I went to the music room at Hart House to find out what it was and who composed it. It turned out to be *The Four Seasons* by Antonio Vivaldi, one of the greatest composers of baroque music. While I had been exposed to a great deal of baroque music by Johann Sebastian Bach and George Fredrick Handel as a result of singing in the choir at Grace Church-on-the-Hill, I had not been exposed to much music by other baroque composers and certainly nothing by Vivaldi that I can remember.

Hearing *The Four Seasons* opened up a whole new musical world for me. It instilled in me a strong desire to learn more about the music of Vivaldi — the so-called "Red Priest" — as well as many other baroque composers, such as Arcangelo Corelli, Giovanni Gabrieli, and Tomaso Albinoni from Italy, François Couperin, Jean-Baptiste Lully, and Jean-Philippe Rameau from France, Henry Purcell, William Byrd, and John Stanley from England, Georg Philipp Telemann from Germany, and Dietrich Buxtehude from Denmark.

This turned out to be a real find for me. Put simply, I love the music of baroque composers. It is so uplifting, majestic, and accessible that it never fails to move me and fill me with a great deal of joy and inspiration whenever I hear it. This is confirmed by the experiences of many other people. In fact, contemporary research is revealing that baroque music has a favourable effect on people because it is very regal and evocative in nature, and affects that part of the brain that produces positive feelings and emotions.

But more about this later. Here, it is important to point out that after my undergraduate studies were concluded and I received my Bachelor of Commerce degree in 1961, I decided to enroll in the Master's program in economics at the University of Toronto. Not knowing what to do before starting my graduate work, but remembering that one of my professors had recommended taking a trip abroad after our undergraduate studies, I decided to go to Europe for the summer.

I immediately set my sights on England, Ireland, and Wales, as many

Canadians do. I went to England first, and visited many museums and art galleries in cities such as London, Oxford, Cambridge, and York, as well as cathedral towns like Ely, Wells, Canterbury, Peterborough, Norwich, and others. I then set off for southern Wales, which evoked strong memories of another favourite movie of mine – *How Green Was My Valley*. I visited many important mining towns there, and even rode in a coracle, a small, light, wooden boat dating back to Roman times. But the thing I remember most about southern Wales was the people, many of whom invited me to stay with them and had interesting stories to tell. I was amazed to discover that virtually everyone in southern Wales knew Dylan Thomas personally or was related to him in some way – especially after he became famous! – and had fascinating tales to tell about him.

Following my stay in southern Wales, I headed off to Ireland where I hitch-hiked around the entire coast of this emerald-green isle. I got a ride on everything imaginable: donkeys, lorries, vans, horses, bicycles, motorcycles, cars, and indeed anything and everything that moved and was capable of carrying people. I visited as many pubs, churches, town halls, and community centres as possible, from Cork and Limerick in the south to Galway and Dublin in the centre and Donegal and Belfast in the north. I also kissed the Blarney stone, as every good traveller to Ireland must do. It was about as intensive a tour of the perimeter of a country as anyone could have in a short period of time. I learned a tremendous amount about Irish culture and Irish people from it.

Following this, I returned to London for a few days and then set off to Germany for a two-week stay in Bad Gotesberg in the Rhineland with a group of students from the University of London.

We visited many famous castles and historic sites on the Rhine river, as well as many wonderful medieval towns such as Rüdesheim, Dinkelsbühl, and Rothenberg ob der Tauber. My stay in Germany was captivating, perhaps because it wasn't long after the Second World War and my grandparents were born in Germany, although they came to the United States at the end of the nineteenth century and settled in Erie, Illinois where my father was born and lived for several years before his family emigrated to Canada.

Like most North Americans with European roots, I was curious to see the land of my grandparents. My grandfather on my father's side was born in a town called Hildesheim in central Germany, which is famous for a rose bush that has grown on the side of a cathedral there for more than a thousand years. I was anxious to explore my ancestral roots, and hoped that I might be related to some famous European family and have royal blood flowing in my veins.

These hopes were dashed one day when I was in a small town on the Rhine River. I was in a phone booth and happened to see the name Schäfer printed on a sign above a store window across the street. Thinking that it might be a relative, I immediately opened the telephone book to get the phone number of the store. You can imagine my surprise when I discovered that many people in the town were named Schäfer. When I returned to the hostel where I was staying, I asked people what Schäfer meant in English. They told me it meant "Sheppard." Suddenly, it was all clear to me. The reason why so many people in the town were called Schäfer – as was the case in many other German towns I visited in the years to follow – was because half the inhabitants of the town were probably shepherds going back several centuries. My illusions of grandeur were shattered that day and have never returned since, especially as I know my relatives on my mother's side came from peasant stock in Scotland and were part of the Rose clan.

Following my trip to Germany, I decided to go to Greece with another group of students from the University of London. We had to choose between a classical tour around the Peloponnesus, which included a lengthy stay in Athens and visits to Delphi, Tiryns, Mycenae, Sparta, Argos, and other famous sites, or a boat cruise in the Cyclade Islands off the coast of Greece. Remembering how much I had enjoyed the course on ancient and medieval history when I was in high school, I opted for the tour around the Peloponnesus in the hope that I might be able to visit the Cyclade Islands, and other famous Greek islands, later in life.

One evening on the way to Delphi to visit the famous oracle, we happened to come across a wine-tasting festival in a small town that I believe was called Daphne. For three or four drachma, the equivalent of roughly 50 cents Canadian, we were entitled to admission to the festival, a great deal of food and drink, and lots of entertainment. We spent the entire evening devouring freshly grilled lamb and souvlaki, eating Kalamata olives, sampling too many glasses of freshly harvested retsina wine, and talking to local residents. The experience was enriched by a great deal of bazooka music and many traditional Greek folk dances. I will never forget that magical evening in southern Greece.

After Daphne, it was on to the Delphi, world famous for the oracle and the sanctuary of Apollo. I found the setting breathtaking, situated as it is high on the slopes of Mount Parnassus with a phenomenal view of the surrounding countryside and its many beautiful valleys and mountains. It was not difficult to imagine countless people being attracted to this site in classical times to receive predictions about the future and information about the issues of the day. Following this, it was on to the Tiryns of the Cyclopean walls, made famous in Greek mythology for its one-eyed monsters and walls made of colossal stones.

Next was a trip to Mycenae, surely one of the highlights of the trip because it is said to be the home of Agamemnon, one of the greatest leaders of the Greeks during the Trojan wars. Mycenae became internationally famous in the nineteenth century when Herman Schliemann, an amateur archeologist from Germany who believed that much of Greek mythology and especially Homer's *Iliad* and *Odyssey* were true rather than make-believe, unearthed a funeral mask made of gold in a burial shaft. Schliemann believed this was the funeral mask of Agamemnon. Though this was later disputed because many archeologists felt the mask was found farther down the shaft than would have been the case had it dated from Agamemnon's time, the discovery nevertheless excited Schliemann so much that he sent a telegram to the Government of Greece saying that he had "gazed on the face of Agamemnon." After this, we visited many other ancient sites in the Peloponnesus, including Argos and especially Sparta, a rival to Athens that was well-known for its disciplined people and skilled warriors.

These experiences sparked my interest in Greece as a country. I began to wonder why Greece was so much poorer than England and Germany, and what could be done about this.

When my trip to Greece was over, I returned to London for several days and then boarded a plane back to Canada. It was late August of 1961 by this time, and I was anxious to commence my graduate studies in economics at the University of Toronto. I took The History of Economic Thought from Douglas Hartle, who was carrying out a number of major studies for the federal government at the time; Economic Theory from Burton Kiersted, who was one of Canada's and the world's most respected economic theorists; and Underdeveloped Countries from Stephan Triantis, a well-known authority on what is today called development economics or international development. These studies immersed me much more thoroughly in the discipline of economics than was possible during my undergraduate studies.

Since I had become fascinated with Greece and was getting more and more interested in how economics could help people and countries in other parts of the world and the world as a whole, I decided to write my Master's thesis on "Greece as an Underdeveloped Country." Professor Triantis, who was an expert in this area and also happened to be Greek, was the logical person to supervise this thesis. There was only one problem. I didn't read Greek and was totally dependent on English sources of information. This proved to be a real difficulty because most literature in English about Greece and the Greek economy was produced by the Government of Greece, which was actively promoting foreign investment and tourism in Greece and was very biased in its presentation of the situation there.

Nevertheless, I derived numerous advantages from writing my thesis on this remarkable country. I learned a great deal about Greece as a country as well as the Greek economy and Greek culture, particularly in classical times. This provided me with indispensable insights into what is generally regarded as "the cradle of western civilization," and, as such, the forerunner of many different cultures in the world today, especially in the west. I also learned of the high value the Greeks placed on the visual, architectural, literary, and theatrical arts, as well as on scholarship, philosophy, democracy, and so forth. In addition, I learned a great deal about the long period of Turkish rule in Greece, which ended with the Greek War of Independence in 1821. I began to understand what it is like for a country and a people to be occupied and oppressed by another country and people for an incredibly long period of time.

What also fascinated me was the fact that Greece was apparently very alluvial in classical times, with a great deal of greenery and vegetation. However, by the time I visited Greece, and presumably for many centuries prior to this, it was anything but fertile and green! Some people told me that the Greeks have a saying that God created all the other countries in the world, and threw what was left over his shoulder and that became Greece. In any case, it was easy to see why life in Greece was so difficult, since most of the fertile land and vegetation were gone and there was not much left but arid land, stones, and spindly trees.

By the time my thesis on Greece was completed and my Master's program at the University of Toronto came to an end, I had added underdeveloped countries to the history of economics and economic theory as the three areas in the discipline that were of greatest interest to me. The history of economic thought was of interest because it provided an opportunity to understand how economics had evolved as a discipline over the centuries, as well as why economics was such a dominant force in the world. Economic theory was of interest because it gave me an excellent insight into the foundations of the world system and the functioning of individuals, institutions, economies, and countries in that system. And the subject of underdeveloped countries was of interest because it provided an opportunity to understand why it was so difficult to improve living standards and the quality of life in Africa, Asia, Latin America, the Caribbean, and the Middle East, where conditions were very different than those in North America and Europe.

What I didn't realize at the time – and what turned out to be a total surprise to me – was that I would be *studying* economics at the University of Toronto in the spring of 1962 but by the fall of that same year I would be standing in front of a group of eager undergraduate students at Dalhousie University *teaching* economics. Here is how this unexpected turn of events came about.

Shortly after completing my Master's degree in May 1962, I received a call from a Cannon Puxley, who was then the president of King's College in Halifax, Nova Scotia. He was in Toronto looking for someone to teach three courses in economics as part of a general agreement King's had with Dalhousie to provide a specified number of instructors to teach courses in three or four different disciplines each year. I had been recommended to teach the courses by Professor Kiersted, who I mentioned earlier.

You can imagine how thrilled I was when Cannon Puxley called me a few days after our interview to offer me the job at King's, which I immediately accepted. I felt very honoured: King's is the oldest university in Canada; I wanted to pursue a teaching career in economics; and King's seemed an ideal place to get started.

I was even more thrilled when I learned that I would be teaching courses in the three areas that were of greatest interest to me and that I knew the best, namely two third-year courses, The History of Economic Thought and Underdeveloped Countries, and a first-year course on The Principles of Economics. I knew teaching these courses would provide a marvellous opportunity to broaden and deepen my understanding of economics and why it was playing such a powerful and pervasive role in the world.

The entire world was preoccupied with economics at this time, and with it, the production of goods and services and creation of material and monetary wealth. This preoccupation was accompanied by many concomitant developments. Corporations were growing rapidly in size and being accorded a central position in society; citizens were becoming more focused on consumption and maximizing their consumer satisfaction in the marketplace; economic growth was dominating public and private policy and decision-making; governments were becoming increasingly involved in the economic affairs of nations; and people and countries in more and more parts of the world were looking to economics to solve both their economic *and non-economic* problems.

I worked all summer preparing lecture notes for the three courses I was required to teach. A professor at the University of Toronto advised me to take far more material than I thought I would use into my first lecture, because I would likely get very nervous standing in front of a class of thirty or forty students for the first time in my life and go through far more material than I expected. This turned out to be sage advice. I got so nervous, in fact, that I used virtually all of the material I had prepared over the entire summer for the course on The History of Economic Thought in my very first lecture!

What was I to do? I returned to my suite at King's College where I was a don in residence wringing my hands in grief and wondering what I would do for the next lecture in the course which was only two days away.

After spending an agonizing day and night, I finally decided what to do. I would go into the second class and say as casually as I could: "Look, what I was really doing in the first class was giving you an overview of the entire course. Now I want to go back to the beginning and start the course in earnest."

It worked! Fortunately, the course began with Adam Smith and *The Wealth of Nations,* which, as you will recall, I knew like the back of my hand because I had studied it with Vincent Bladen, the acknowledged master in the field. Nevertheless, I thanked my lucky stars that day for "necessity being the mother of invention." It literally saved my life. It also made me aware that starting a course with a general overview makes a great deal of sense. I don't know how many times students have come up to me over the years to thank me for starting a course that way. They say it makes it possible for them to situate everything in context and understand what the course is designed to accomplish. They often added that they wish all professors would start their courses this way.

I enjoyed teaching at Dalhousie immensely. Although I didn't look much older than most of my students — something which presented its fair share of problems — I enjoyed exchanging thoughts and ideas with the students ever so much. Since my mother had been a school teacher prior to getting married, I thought I was following in her footsteps — and also in my father's footsteps in a curious kind of way — although I was attracted to Dalhousie University far more by wanting to teach economics than by wanting to teach in general.

As my preparations for the class in The History of Economic Thought intensified, I began to realize why Vincent Bladen was so enamored of Adam Smith and *The Wealth of Nations*. I also began to understand why Adam Smith was deemed to be the "founder of economics." Little wonder Max Lerner called him "a gentle sage with dynamite flowing from his pen."

There is no doubt that Adam Smith changed the course of history. He did so by focusing on the one thing that most countries have been concerned with over the past few centuries and particularly over the last fifty years, namely the production, distribution, and consumption of goods and services and creation of material and monetary wealth. Of course, people and countries were concerned with this issue long before Smith arrived on the scene. However, Smith was the first person to examine this matter in a systematic, sustained, and sophisticated manner. He did so by equating goods and services and material and monetary wealth with "the necessaries and conveniences of life," as he liked to call them, rather than with "gold, silver, and precious metals," as was popular at the time.

When the necessaries and conveniences of life are increasing, people are better off, according to Smith. When they are decreasing, people are worse off. The only exception to this general rule is when the necessaries and conveniences of life are increasing, but at a slower rate than population growth. In this case, people are becoming worse off rather than better, and this is why Smith was so adamant that the necessaries and conveniences of life must increase faster than the population.

What sets Smith apart from most other economists is the fact that Smith created a comprehensive and elaborate theoretical and practical *system* to show how the necessaries and conveniences of life (or net domestic product as we would say today) can be increased most effectively. Among the main components in Smith's system were:

- making economics the centrepiece of society and principal preoccupation of a country's development;
- recognizing labour as the principal source of all value and wealth;
- promoting the "division of labour" or "labour specialization" as the main prerequisite for increasing wealth;
- expanding the size of the market to facilitate labour specialization;
- asserting the importance of "productive" as opposed to "unproductive" labour;

- utilizing the market as the main vehicle for discharging economic functions;
- facilitating as much capital accumulation, trade, and colonial development as possible; and
- relying on an "invisible hand" and "enlightened self-interest" to guide the economy, the marketplace, and society generally.

In Smith's view, if countries wanted to enhance the standard of living of their citizens and play a forceful role in the world, they should commit themselves to these requirements and build an economic system worthy of the task.

While many people may quibble over the details, this is more or less what has happened in the world over the last two centuries. The creation and expansion of goods and services and material and monetary wealth has been the central objective of the world system, as well as the principal preoccupation of municipal, regional, national, and international development. The centrality of economics has been justified on the grounds that it is deemed to provide the wherewithal that is required to satisfy people's needs and wants *in all areas of life*.

In consequence, building strong, dynamic economies is now seen as the principal goal of public and private policy and decision-making in most if not all parts of the world. People are encouraged to specialize in one or two production functions rather than generalize on many production functions, the market is seen as the main vehicle for discharging economic transactions and generating economic growth, and a strong commitment is made to capital accumulation, trade, and "enlightened self-interest." Above all, people are encouraged to believe that the "invisible hand" of market forces guides the economy and society generally, ensuring that everything will turn out for the best. And while these days a great deal of wealth is created through the use of technology, many economists would still argue that labour is, ultimately, the primary source of wealth: after all, it is labour that *creates* the technology that in turn "adds value."

What made *The Wealth of Nations* so influential in Smith's day, and even today, is the fact that it set out a comprehensive system for generating wealth efficiently and effectively. This prospect held out a ray of hope for the masses that they themselves, and not just the rich and privileged classes, could improve their lot in society.

This crucial fact is what distinguishes Smith from other economists during the century that followed the publication of *The Wealth of Nations* in 1776, most notably David Ricardo, Thomas Robert Malthus, and Karl Marx. Whereas these individuals were pessimistic about the ability of all classes to benefit from wealth creation, Smith was optimistic. Smith believed that, while it would take time, all classes in society (and possibly all countries in the world, although I am less certain about this) would in the end benefit from wealth creation. Even John Stuart Mill, who was more optimistic than Ricardo, Malthus, and Marx about future prospects, remained pessimistic about the ability of *all* classes to benefit from the creation of wealth. However, Mill did set out a number of public policy prescriptions designed to assist the poorer classes and not just the rich, largely by making a distinction between the production of wealth and the distribution of wealth.

Mind you, Smith did not lay the foundations for modern economics all on his own. While he did develop the first truly comprehensive theoretical and practical system of economics, it was Ricardo who turned economics into the highly specialized, rigorous, and autonomous discipline it became. He did so by casting economics in far more abstract and conceptual terms than Smith, as well as by according economics the highest priority in society. According to Ricardo, economic issues must always be considered first, before any other activities are considered. Economics leads and everything else lags. This was especially true in relation to politics. Only after economic issues had been considered and dealt with in totality and in depth should attention be given to politics and other activities in society in Ricardo's opinion. This point of view is still held by many individuals and institutions throughout the world today.

Karl Marx played an even stronger and more fundamental role than David Ricardo in the evolution of economics as a discipline and the powerful impact it has had on the world. He did so by contending that economics constitutes the basis of *everything* in life.

Many contend that it was Marx's indictment of capitalism and evocative theories of communism and socialism that had the greatest impact on the world. After all, Marx had such strong convictions about these matters that they ended up dividing the entire world into capitalist and communist components and producing a cold war between the two that raged for more than half a century. *Nevertheless, it is Marx's economic interpretation of history that has had by far the greatest impact.* The reason for this is not difficult to detect. While Adam Smith laid the theoretical and practical foundations of economics as the centrepiece of the world system, Marx provided the historical and philosophical underpinnings and justification for it. Marx achieved this by claiming that economics is the "cause" and "basis" of everything in human society.

He did this by dividing all human societies into an "economic base" and a "non-economic superstructure." The base is economic, according to Marx, because it is concerned with the modes of production and the material conditions of life, and therefore with the wherewithal that is required to support developments in all other areas of society. The superstructure is non-economic because it depends on the economic base for its existence. This quickly gave rise to the conviction that there is a one-way relationship between the base and the superstructure: changes that occur in the economic base can cause changes in the non-economic superstructure, *but not the other way around*. Although Marx was less assertive about this one-way relationship than many of his colleagues and followers, nonetheless in the Marxian view of the world economics soon came to be regarded as the "cause," and everything else as the "effect."

If Marx had been content to limit his views to the society in which he was living, it is quite possible that his impact on future developments throughout the world would not be as powerful as they have been. But Marx went much farther than this. He contended that the economic base — non-economic superstructure theory is not just true at a particular point in time. *It is always true: it has always been true; and it always will be true*. Moreover, it is true in space as well as in time, said Marx, because it applies to all parts of the world, not just some parts.

This claim of universality eventually turned Marx's economic base and non-economic superstructure theory, and more fundamentally his economic interpretation of history, into the most powerful ideology in the world. The entire world is now locked in the economic interpretation of history and has been ever since Marx propounded these theories. Everywhere it is assumed, either implicitly or explicitly, that everything in the world has to do with economics to begin with, or can be traced back to economics in the end. While this view is starting to change, as we will see later, it is still the dominant force in the world.

It is clear in retrospect why Marx interpreted history in economic terms. He was living at a time when the Industrial Revolution was in full swing and society was assuming a highly materialistic and physical orientation. Nowhere was this more evident than in England, the very place where Marx was living and working when he created his economic interpretation of history and theory of economic determinism. It was one thing, however, to interpret what was going on in England at the time in exclusively economic terms; it was quite another to interpret the whole of human history in these terms.

This is not to say that economics and materialism do not play an extremely powerful role in the world; it would be foolhardy to deny it. But it is to say that everything in the world cannot be reduced to economics and materialism because economics and materialism are only part – albeit an extremely important part – of a much deeper, broader, and more fundamental reality. This matter will also be discussed in detail later in the book when attention is shifted from the economic interpretation of history to a cultural interpretation of history. However, suffice it to say at this point that Marx's economic interpretation of history continues to have a dominant effect on the world, as is epitomized in the popular belief that "as the economy goes, so goes the world," as well as popular catchphrases like "it's the economy, stupid."

Before leaving Marx, a word should be said about his place in history. There is a great deal of irony here, given Marx's economic interpretation of history on the one hand and his strong convictions about capitalism, communism, socialism, labour, value, and wealth on the other. There is no doubt that Marx's vigorous attack on capitalism and capitalists, as well as his wholehearted embrace of communism and socialism, contributed greatly to his posthumous popularity. This popularity was due largely to the impact his attack had on the distribution of income, the arguments he made for more equitable allocations of income and wealth, and the influence of Marxism on the creation of labour unions and better labour-management practices in many if not most parts of the world. However, and this is where the irony comes in, Marx's economic interpretation of history also opened the doors for capitalists and capitalism to play a much larger and more assertive role in the world, largely because of the high priority that was placed on economics and economic growth.

Once Marx had established and justified the centrality of economics, economists began to study economies, and especially how people and institutions function within economies. Such study was viewed as a basic prerequisite for understanding how material and monetary wealth could be increased most effectively, and how people, countries, and the world as a whole could benefit from this. In the decades to follow, elaborate theories began to emerge with respect to the effective functioning of economies. Created largely through the work of neoclassical economists such as William Stanley Jevons, Carl Menger, Léon Walrus, Alfred Marshall, and others, they focused on consumers, consumer satisfaction and behaviour, corporations, supply and demand, prices, markets, and the marketplace.

Since consumers and corporations — buyers and sellers — were the principal players in economies, a great deal of attention was focused on these two groups, as well as on the way prices were determined in specific market situations through the interaction of supply and demand. What slowly but surely began to emerge was the belief that consumers, corporations, and the marketplace play the principal roles in economic development. Corporations produce the material and monetary wealth that is required to "drive" economies and countries; consumers buy the goods and services produced by corporations; and the marketplace facilitates exchanges between the two groups.

With the acceptance of this theory came the belief that economies grow as rapidly and function as effectively as possible when corporations maximize their profits and compete as vigorously as possible, consumers act rationally and maximize their consumer satisfaction in the marketplace, and markets are as free as possible from governmental intervention and political constraints. While very different approaches to wealth creation, economic growth, and consumer behaviour were emerging in Russia, Eastern Europe, China, and other parts of the world where communism was starting to take hold — approaches that were based on planned economies, fixed rather than fluctuating prices, and a highly centralized approach to the production, distribution, and consumption of wealth — in the capitalist parts of the world this "neoclassical model" was deemed to produce the best possible conditions for producers and consumers, the greatest corporate and consumer satisfaction, the most efficient allocation of resources, and optimum rates of economic growth.

The neo-classical model had a profound effect on political and governmental thinking, policies, practices, and decision-making in the capitalist parts of the world. This is especially true in respect to corporations and corporate development. In Western Europe, the United States, and elsewhere in the capitalist world, corporations moved into a position of preeminence in society because of the indispensable role they were deemed to play in wealth creation and economic growth. Not only did they grow rapidly and without a great deal of political intervention or governmental interference, but also they enjoyed economic privileges and commercial advantages that were difficult to restrain or prevent.

This led to the creation of powerful corporations with numerous monopolistic and oligopolistic privileges, the concentration of wealth and power in fewer hands, and greater inequalities in income and wealth between rich and poor people as well as rich and poor countries. In the western world, most people believed the neoclassical ideal set out in the works of Jevons, Menger, Walras, Marshall, and others would be realized most effectively when there was little or no political involvement in the economy, the marketplace, and society generally. It was felt that there was a "self-regulating" and "self-correcting" mechanism at work in the economy and marketplace that tended to restore equilibrium whenever there was a real deviation from it. All governments had to do was sit back and let this mechanism solve the problem.

Everyone knows what happened next. When the Great Depression struck in the late 1920s and early 1930s, governments and politicians waited for the self-regulating, self-correcting mechanism to kick in and restore equilibrium at or near full employment. Meanwhile the bread lines were getting longer, unemployment was skyrocketing, consumption was sagging, investment was plummeting, and economies were stagnating. Clearly something had to be done — anything — to address this problem. As time marched on, it became clear that the economic elevator could just as easily get stuck in the basement as on the roof. In other words, a return to prosperity was impossible without a great deal of political and governmental intervention in the economy, the marketplace, and society generally. Most governments did intervene. In the United States, President Franklin Delano Roosevelt introduced the New Deal and many governments in the world followed suit.

The person who was largely responsible for this shift in policies and practices was the British economist John Maynard Keynes. Unlike Smith, Ricardo, and most of the classical and neo-classical economists, Keynes believed governments have a powerful role to play in the economy and the marketplace, especially when the economy is stalled or stuck in a recession or depression. This "Keynesian economics" eventually brought with it a great deal more governmental involvement in the political and especially economic affairs of nations. In the years to follow, economists intensified their efforts to flesh out the system of economics set out in Keynes's popular book, *The General Theory of Employment, Interest and Money*. They did this by examining national income, national expenditure, consumption, investment, saving, monetary policy, interest rates, and government intervention in the economy in a systematic and sustained manner.

Their efforts made it possible to produce a much more detailed portrait of economies and the way they function than was possible in classical,

Marxian, or neo-classical economics. It was a portrait that focused on *aggregate demand for goods and services* as "the real engine of economic growth." While consumption formed the principal component of demand in this sense, strategic roles were reserved for saving, investment, and government expenditure. Saving was important because it constituted a withdrawal from the income stream that had to be replaced in some way if economic growth was to be maintained. Investment was important because it was highly volatile in nature and provided the impetus for capital formation, corporate development, and economic growth. Saving and investment taken together were important because they were carried out by different groups of people and there was no logical reason why they had to be in balance. Indeed, the fact that an imbalance could occur shed a great deal of light on the causes and consequences of business cycles. And government expenditure was important because it could be adjusted upwards or downwards depending on actual and anticipated conditions in the economy and the marketplace.

All these ideas provided the justification needed for governments to play a powerful *economic role* in society. Prior to Keynes, the role of governments had been seen largely as political and circumscribed in nature. Governments focused primarily on such matters as legislation, regulation, law enforcement, and public policy. Governmental intervention in the economy and the marketplace was called for only in cases of monopoly, oligopoly, imperfect competition, and to provide various (usually modest) welfare programs.

Keynes and the Keynesians changed that. They did so by contending that governments can — indeed *must* — play a powerful economic role in society by controlling monetary and fiscal policy, regulating business and industry, managing debts, deficits, and surpluses, stimulating economic growth, dealing with business cycles, and spending public funds to boost the level of aggregate demand. According to Keynes, governments should produce budgetary surpluses in times of prosperity in order to have the funds necessary to spend on economic stimulation and recovery in times of recession and depression.

This particular notion made a great deal of sense to me in personal terms because it was consistent with what my parents had taught me in my youth about how to manage my money and set something aside for a rainy day. However, many governments did not heed Keynes's sage advice on this particular point, due largely to their desire to grow economies as rapidly as possible. As a result, many governments are now saddled with huge debts and deficits and find themselves unable to respond to unfavourable economic conditions. Because they did not generate the budgetary surpluses in good times required to address economic problems in bad times, in recent years many governments have been forced to introduce stringent austerity measures. These austerity measures have proven unpopular with many citizens and may even have delayed economic recovery.

As the popularity of Keynesian economics grew, governments expanded accordingly. Combined with the demands that were manifesting themselves at the same time for more government services and involvement in the economy and the marketplace, greater control over business and industry, and the desire for more social service programs and welfare benefits, the stage was set for a dramatic expansion in the size, scope, growth, and power of governments in virtually all parts of the world.

This opened the doors for economic concerns to become not just private matters but issues of great public interest, deemed of vital importance to governments, politicians, civil servants, and ordinary citizens, and not just to corporations, corporate executives, commercial and financial institutions, and businesspeople. Without this shift, it is unlikely that economic concerns would attract the media attention, political involvement, and citizen awareness and engagement they do today.

With the Keynesian revolution, all the prerequisites were in place to move economics and economies into a central position in society and the world system. Just as Adam Smith and Karl Marx created the theoretical, practical, historical, and philosophical underpinnings for this system and the neo-classical economists opened up a commanding place for corporations and consumers at the very core of it, so the Keynesian economists drew governments fully and forcefully into the economic affairs of nations. The result was that economics began to occupy a position far more prominent than had once been the case. Indeed, governments became so completely immersed in the economic affairs of nations that their principal function became economic rather than political, regardless of whether they were democratic, communist, socialist, conservative, or republican. All that was left to do was to extend this ideology from the western world to the rest of the world, so that governments and institutions in all parts of the world would be committed to the centrality of economics, economies, and economic growth in the overall scheme of things.

This extension started to occur with the notion of *development*. It commenced when President Harry Truman made his inaugural speech to Congress and the American people in 1949. In his address, Truman talked about the importance of development in order to increase production and productivity, achieve prosperity and peace, and bring about basic improvements in the diverse economies of the world in general and the economies of the "underdeveloped countries" in particular.

It wasn't long before economists began to wonder how the "miracle of development" could be spread from the "more developed" countries of North America and Western Europe to the "less developed" countries of Eastern Europe, Africa, Asia, Latin America, the Caribbean, and the Middle East. In the decades to follow, countless "development economists" travelled to different parts of the world, initially economists like Paul Rosenstein-Rodan and Ragnar Nurkse, and eventually economists such as Albert Hirschman, Gunnar Myrdal, Arthur Lewis, Harvey Liebenstein, Raul Prebisch, and many others. They brought with them a variety of views and theories about how development could be achieved.

The United Nations reinforced this process when it committed itself to "decades of development" in the 1960s. In 1962, the UN published *The Development Decade: Proposals for Action,* which set out the rationale for the first development decade. The intention was to promote development throughout the world in general and in the "less developed" parts of the world in particular. And how was development — and with it developmental goals, objectives, and priorities — perceived? Almost entirely in terms of economics, economies, and economic growth.

By this time, the whole world had been divided into two parts: a "developed" part that had already achieved high levels of development and a great deal of sophistication; and an "underdeveloped" or "developing" part that had (in this view) a long way still to go. The Cold War had heated up considerably by this time, with the capacity to economically assist underdeveloped nations being one of the main areas of competition between the United States and the USSR.

This was the situation that existed when I taught the course on underdeveloped countries at Dalhousie University. The course provided me with an opportunity to examine in great detail how all the various theories about capitalism, communism, and development could be applied to parts of the world that had been unable to benefit from wealth creation and economic growth to any great extent. I was deeply concerned about the huge inequalities in income and wealth that existed throughout the world, as well as by the urgent need to help countries in Africa, Asia, Latin

America, the Caribbean, and Eastern Europe to improve their standards of living and quality of life.

Issues and concerns like this were constantly buzzing around in my head when I was teaching economics at Dalhousie between 1962 and 1964. Each of the courses I taught broadened my knowledge of the powerful role played by economics and economies in the overall scheme of things. My teaching also deepened my understanding of the pivotal role that consumers, corporations, governments, and citizens play in this process, as well as why everyone seemed to be caught up in the "miracle of development" and believed that economics was the key to solving most if not all the world's problems.

By this time, it was generally assumed that economic growth and development would make it possible for countries in the west to achieve ever higher levels of material prosperity and monetary wealth, creating for their citizens more and more leisure time and possibly even freedom from work entirely. It was assumed that this utopian state of affairs, once achieved, could be extended, *albeit with far greater difficulty*, to the rest of the world. While I had many reservations about this, I was so caught up in teaching economics and struggling to learn as much as I could about this discipline that I tended to downplay these reservations. I had the sense that any reservations I harboured would disappear in the fullness of time as I learned more about economics and its central role in the world.

If I had been able to stay at Dalhousie teaching economics for many more years, that might very well have occurred. I was enjoying teaching very much, and the interaction I was having with students and other faculty members was fulfilling and rewarding. Moreover, I enjoyed living in Halifax very much. It was wonderful to be living in another part of Canada, especially one as scenic and historic as Nova Scotia.

During my time in Nova Scotia, I was able to take many trips along the southern and eastern shores to visit fishing villages like Chester, Lunenburg, Mahone Bay, Clam Harbour, Ship Harbour, Sheet Harbour, and others. I also took several trips to Cape Breton and Prince Edward Island to enjoy the magnificent scenery there. This was augmented by long walks with friends and colleagues in Point Pleasant Park and the Public Gardens in Halifax, as well as spending many a Saturday afternoon sailing on the Arm. What impressed me most about Halifax and Nova Scotia, however, were the people, culture, and way of life there, which were very different from what I had known in Ontario. The people were more friendly and down-to-earth, the culture was older and more established, and the pace of life was slower and more relaxed. So it is easy to see why I would have stayed at Dalhousie for many more years if this had been possible.

Unfortunately, however, it wasn't possible. The chairman of the economics department came into my office one day and said I would have to get a Ph.D. if I wanted to secure a long-term teaching position at Dalhousie or probably any other university in North America or the western world. As a result, he advised me to enroll in a doctoral program at a university in Canada, the United States, or possibly England. When I discussed this matter with other faculty members and some close friends, they confirmed what the chairman had told me. So after a great deal of thought and reflection, I decided to pursue a Ph.D. in economics after completing my second full year of teaching at Dalhousie.

I was strongly advised to go to the United States because American universities were leading the field at that time, having long since surpassed most English universities in this particular area. So this is what I did. I applied to a number of universities in United States with strong reputations and faculties in economics and, in the end, it came down to choosing between the University of Chicago and the University of Michigan. It proved to be a difficult choice.

The University of Chicago was attractive because it had an excellent reputation in economics and a well-known economist named Bert Hoselitz was there. I was strongly attracted to the approach Hoselitz took to economics, largely because he situated economics in a broad social, cultural, and historical context. Moreover, he was the founder and editor of a new journal called *Economic Development and Cultural Change*, which seemed to dovetail very nicely with my interest in economic development and underdeveloped countries on the one hand and the arts and culture on the other. In retrospect, I probably should have gone to the University of Chicago because I have spent a great deal of time in my life trying to understand economics and culture and the complex connection between them. However, I discovered before I made a final decision that Bert Hoselitz was an outcast in the economics department at Chicago because his views on economics conflicted with those of most other faculty members.

So I decided to go to the University of Michigan. I did so for three reasons. In the first place, it also had an excellent reputation in economics and the choice seemed compatible with my interest in development economics and the history of economic thought. Secondly, Michigan offered me an attractive teaching fellowship, which meant that I could earn some income while completing my Ph.D. Finally, and most importantly, Kenneth Boulding was there. He was generally regarded as one of world's greatest economists at the time and a real pioneer in economic theory and practice. He was well-known for the expansive approach he took to economics – an approach that I also found attractive – as well as for the innovative work he was doing on ecological and evolutionary economics, interdisciplinary studies, systems theory, peace studies, ethics, and other areas.

Unfortunately, when I arrived at the University of Michigan in late August 1964 to commence my doctorate, I was shocked to learn that Professor Boulding was not at the University. When I enquired about this, I was told that he was in Latin America on long-term leave and would likely not be returning for at least two years. I also learned that Boulding, like Bert Hoselitz, was an outcast in the department because of the expansive approach he took to economics and the fact that he was pursuing interests that most faculty members felt lay outside the realm of economics and had little relevance to it. This did not auger well for me, as I was attracted to the University of Michigan primarily because Boulding was there.

To make matters worse, I learned that the economics department at the University of Michigan was controlled by a small group of economists who were strongly committed to mathematical economics and building elaborate "econometric models" to explain economic behaviour and the operations of different types of economic systems. While these approaches were all the rage in many American universities at the time – especially as Keynesian economics took hold and became more refined, sophisticated, and systematized – they held little interest for me in view of my concern with broader and more humane approaches to economics, even though I had done well in mathematics in high school and the one calculus course I took at the University of Toronto.

Another matter was of even greater concern. By the time I went to the University of Michigan, I was keenly interested in the economics of the arts and wanted to write my Ph.D. thesis on this subject. My interest in this area emanated from the education I had received in the arts when I was young, the intimate connection I discovered between economics and the arts when I took the course on European Economic History at the University of Toronto, and especially the trip I had taken to Europe between my undergraduate and graduate years. I had hoped to write a thesis on this subject under the supervision of Professor Boulding in view of his strong interest in interdisciplinary studies and his innovative approaches to economics and other disciplines. Now this was obviously impossible.

When I discussed my interest in writing a thesis on the economics of the arts with faculty members in the department, I was told *in no uncertain terms* that there was no such thing as "the economics of the arts." When I persisted with this by saying that, like all other individuals and institutions in society, artists and arts organizations have economic problems and the arts have played an important role in the development of countless cities, countries, and economies throughout the world, I was told that this really had very little if anything to do with economics. Consequently I was advised to select another thesis topic because it would not be possible to find a faculty member in the economics department — or indeed in any department at the University of Michigan — who would be willing to supervise a thesis on this subject. It was just too far removed from economics to be of any real benefit, concern, or consequence.

As the fall term progressed, I began to feel more and more uneasy about my situation at the University, especially as I would have to spend a year completing all the necessary course work, and then another two or three years writing a thesis on a subject that was unknown to me and might be of little interest. Nevertheless, this was not the only problem I was having trouble with at the time. I was starting to have some doubts about economics as a discipline and the direction it was headed in the future.

In addition to becoming highly mathematical in nature, economics was growing more and more isolated from other disciplines and areas of activity in my view, despite the fact that it was responsible for creating enormous increases in material and monetary wealth and improving living standards and the quality of life for countless people and numerous countries, especially in the west. While I was not blind to these accomplishments, or the myriad benefits that were derived from making economics, economies, economic growth, and development the centrepiece of the world system, I felt insufficient consideration was given to the *context* within which economics, economies, and economic growth were situated. While these feelings were rather vague, ill-defined, and intuitive at the time, they were unsettling nonetheless.

These feelings were compounded by the fact that virtually no consideration was given to the natural environment in economics at that time. This was because most economists and the economics profession as a whole believed that the natural environment was given to humanity by

God or by nature and was therefore best treated as a "given" and an "externality" because it existed outside the realm of economics.

I was also concerned about the tendency in economics to view development almost exclusively in economic and material terms. This seemed to me to put too much emphasis on the material and quantitative side of development and life compared to the non-material and qualitative side. What was required in my view was a much better balance between these two major components of development and of life, much as my parents had taught me about this many years earlier.

When I added all these concerns up and considered them in totality, I began to wonder if it was advisable to stay at the University of Michigan. Not only was I having some very real difficulties with economics as a discipline, but also I was having some real reservations about whether or not I would be able to find a suitable thesis topic. This was complicated by the fact that a great deal of "bad blood" had been spilt over whether there was — or was not — such a thing as the economics of the arts. After a great deal of anguish, self-scrutiny, and reflection, I decided to leave the University of Michigan at the end of the fall term in 1964.

Do you know what happened next! Shortly after I left the University of Michigan, a book was published in the United States called *Performing Arts: The Economic Dilemma*. It was written by two prominent American economists, William Baumol and William Bowen, and examined the economic problems confronting artists and arts organizations in the performing arts in the United States in great detail. They concluded that artists and arts organizations have economic problems not because they are financially irresponsible or can't manage their money properly, but rather because their work is primarily labour-intensive and therefore they can't take advantage of technological gains and opportunities the way most industries and businesses can. As a result, they experience an "income gap" between their total expenses and earned income from sales of their works, ticket sales, and the sale of ancillary services. This gap must be filled in some way through government grants, corporate gifts and sponsorships, private donations, or some combination of the three. Arts organizations do not differ substantially from hospitals, educational institutions, and governments in this respect, since these organizations are also compelled to rely on funds from other sources to cover the shortfall between their expenses and income.

Not long after the Baumol and Bowen book was published, I received a call from a faculty member in the economics department at the University of Michigan saying yes, there *was* such a thing as the economics of the arts and he would like me to return to the University to write a thesis on the economics of the arts in the state of Michigan. However, so much bad blood had been spilt over this matter and I was having so many difficulties with economics as a discipline that I decided not to return to the University as he proposed. I would just have to pursue my interest in the economics of the arts in some other place or in some other way. So this is what I did.

CHAPTER THREE

Soul Searching Abroad

The decision to leave the University of Michigan was very painful. My vision of the future was based on getting a Ph.D. in economics and then spending the rest of my life teaching in this field. Now, several months later, this vision was shattered and I was being put to the test.

My immediate thought was to find another university where I could earn a Ph.D. in economics and write a thesis on the economics of the arts. However, my experience indicated there was little room in universities for people who were interested in working at the intersections of academic disciplines, which in those days were highly specialized in nature and very separate. Nor was there much interest in interdisciplinary studies. While with a great deal of hard work and some really good luck I might have been able to find a university where I could research the economics of the arts and write a thesis on this subject, chances were my quest to do so would result in frustration and failure rather than fulfillment and success.

If this had been the only problem I was wrestling with at the time, I probably would have persisted in this matter. However, as indicated earlier, I was wrestling with a number of other problems as well. It wasn't that I didn't understand why economics was so essential and why it was such a powerful force in the world. After all, economics is concerned with the production, distribution, and consumption of goods and services and creation of material and monetary wealth. Since these things affect people's jobs, income, and sources of livelihood, they were, are, and will likely always be of fundamental importance.

Nevertheless, economics was moving far beyond this in my view. In the quest to make economics the centrepiece of the world system and the foundation of development, it was being given precedence over everything else. It was as if Marx's theory about economics being the "cause" and "basis" of everything in life and his economic interpretation of history were becoming self-fulfilling prophecies. This bothered me immensely, since I didn't think it was justified in philosophical, theoretical, or practical terms.

It also didn't jibe with reality. There are many things in life – such as living a full and upright life, finding one's place, role, responsibilities, and identity in the world, creating artistic and humanistic works, experiencing happiness, fulfillment, and love in life, and evolving a way of life that respects the needs and rights of other people and other species – that have little or nothing to do with economics. However, they are also of fundamental importance. To reduce everything to economics was inconsistent with the true nature of reality, the world situation, and the human condition in my view.

With concerns like this constantly buzzing around in my mind, I decided it would be unwise to look for another university where I could complete a Ph.D. and write a thesis on the economics of the arts. What I really needed was some time to get away from everything and work things out.

But where? And how? Remembering how much I had enjoyed my trip to Europe between my undergraduate and graduate years and had benefited from this, I decided to return to Europe for a much longer and closer look. Fortunately, I had saved up enough money when I was teaching at Dalhousie University to cover the cost of such a trip.

I focused first on Germany, land of my ancestors on my father's side. I recalled how much I had appreciated the time I spent in the Rhineland and decided I wanted to learn more about this country, its people, and its culture.

After spending a couple of weeks in Cologne soaking up everything this beautiful city and its exquisite cathedral have to offer, I travelled extensively in Germany over the next few weeks. I was particularly interested in southern Germany, and visited many famous sites there, including Heidelberg, Bayreuth, Nuremberg, Stuttgart, Munich, Rothenberg ob der Tauber (once again), the three castles of Ludwig II of Bavaria (Neuschwanstein, Linderhof, and Herrenchiemsee), and the *romantische strasse* from Würzburg to Füssen. Then it was off to northern Germany to visit Hamburg, Lübeck, Travemünde, and especially Eckernförde, a small town close to the Danish border that was formerly part of Schleswig-Holstein and was the birthplace of my grandmother on my father's side.

While I was in Eckernförde, I had a remarkable experience. I was walking on a back street one day when I happened to see a very old man. Since he must have been in his eighties or early nineties, I wondered if he might have known my grandmother. In my very broken German, which I had learned at the Goethe Institute in Toronto prior to my departure, I asked him if he knew the family Duuck, my grandmother's surname before she got married. He hesitated for a minute and then mumbled, "The family Duuck, the family Duuck, they went to America a few years ago." Although he was totally confused about the date due to his advanced years — they had actually gone to America in the final years of the nineteenth century — it turned out that he had played with my grandmother on that very same street some eighty years earlier. It was one of those rare experiences we all have in life that we remember for a lifetime.

The time I spent in Germany was rewarding. Not only did it provide an opportunity to learn more about my ancestral roots, largely through information I acquired about my grandmother and her family in the town hall in Eckernförde, but also I was exposed to a country, people, and culture very different from my own.

My travels in Germany were filled largely with tramping around large cities and small towns, devouring a great deal of bratwurst, sauerkraut, and roast potatoes, drinking lots of good German beer and wine, making merry in the most delightful gasthofs and taverns imaginable, visiting myriad art galleries, museums, cathedrals, and historical sites, and going to numerous plays and concerts. It was good to be getting an in-depth exposure to Germany and German culture, even if it was confined largely to the things tourists do.

When my travels in Germany were over, I headed north to the Scandinavian countries. This seemed a logical thing to do as I was in northern Germany at the time. I had originally planned to spend a month or so travelling around Scandinavia, but the weather did not permit this. It was incredibly cold, damp, and wet when I was there. As a result, I started to wonder what I was doing in this part of Europe when climatic conditions were so uncooperative! So I cut my stay there short after seeing Denmark and a bit of Sweden and headed directly south to Spain. Was I ever glad I did. The weather was delightful. It was wonderful to wake up every morning to clear blue skies and the warmth of the sun.

The moment I hit Spain, I felt like I was in a different world. I had read a great deal about Spain for the course I took on European Economic History and was well acquainted with its "golden era," which had been characterized by a great deal of domestic development, the establishment of a highly evolved colonial system, and the flow of an unbelievable amount of gold, silver, and other precious metals into Spain from Central and South America. It was also an era characterized by a great deal of bloodshed, brutality, violence, and oppression, not only in Spain because of the actions of the Spanish Inquisition and other atrocities, but also in the colonies as a result of the intense conflict there between Spaniards and the indigenous peoples.

While I was fascinated by the way all countries in Europe maintained their cultural heritages and incorporated them into everyday life, Spain seemed a country apart. There was evidence of their golden era and rich cultural heritage everywhere— in shops, markets, restaurants, cathedrals, city streets, and so forth. Wherever I went in Spain, I encountered shields, swords, and other pieces of armour, life-size pictures of conquistadors marching into battle on powerful steeds, images of Don Quixote and Sancho Panza tilting at windmills, and portraits of Cervantes, Ferdinand and Isabella, El Cid, and many other Spanish heroes.

I don't want to leave the impression that Spain and Spaniards were living in the past because this was not the case. But there was a definite sense that the country and its citizenry wanted numerous reminders of their past around them in their everyday life. I have never seen a country where this stands out more clearly or more powerfully. I had the impression that Spaniards had come to grips with their past, both in the positive and negative sense, were extremely proud of it, and wanted it around them every minute of every day.

I travelled in Spain for the better part of a month. During this time, I came to appreciate the uniqueness of Spain, the Spanish people, Spanish culture, and the Spanish way of life, which was very different from what I encountered in most other European countries. It was not just the climate, geography, and topography that were different, since Spain shared certain similarities with Portugal and Greece in this regard. More fundamentally, it was the sights, sounds, smells, textures, and tastes of Spain. There were few parallels in other parts of Europe to match Spanish architecture, music, crafts, paintings, and food, not to mention the bullfights, siestas, parades, and so forth.

My travels in Spain took me initially to Barcelona. I had my first real encounter with *tapas* there, the famous Spanish delicacies that are eaten any time of the day or night, as well as *paella*, the country's national dish made of chicken, rice, clams, vegetables, and saffron. I also ate incredible amounts of seafood. Then it was on to Madrid. While most of my time was spent in the Prado Museum marveling at paintings by Diego Velázquez, Francisco de Goya, El Greco, and Pablo Picasso, I quickly discovered, as I did later in Paris and Vienna, that virtually every major capital in Europe has a ring around it of fascinating towns and places to see — a ring that includes palaces, cathedrals, castles, and much more. Madrid was no exception. Within a short drive of Madrid were such fascinating places as El Escorial, Ávila, Aranjuez (made famous by Joaquín Rodrigo and his *Concierto de Aranjuez*), Segovia, Toledo, and others.

Segovia turned out to be one of the most beautiful places I have ever seen and a highlight of my trip. It has a magnificent setting, perched high on a hill overlooking fertile valleys. It also has a famous aqueduct dating back to Roman times, as well as a wonderful medieval castle at one end of the town and a superb Gothic cathedral at the other. I fell in love with Segovia the moment I saw it, and have thought about it many times since.

The same holds true for Toledo, which I discovered on my way to southern Spain. Like Venice and Florence, Toledo is one of those rare places in the world that defies description. One could spend days gazing at it from the adjacent hills. It stands majestically on the top of a huge hill — much as Segovia and many other medieval towns in Europe do — and is a tribute to the finest things human beings are able to create. As attractive as its cobblestone streets, enchanting squares, and outstanding landmarks are, what is particularly fascinating about Toledo is the fact it was home during earlier times and especially the tenth century to countless Christians, Jews, and Muslims who worked together in peace and harmony rather than conflict and confrontation. It was one of those rare times and places where people from many different races and religions got along very well and worked hard to ensure that everything turned out for the best.

After Toledo, it was out to the coast to visit Valencia, and then down the Costa del Sol to spend some time in Alicante and Málaga. After that, I went inland to visit Granada, Cordoba, and Seville. Here, as well, a new world opened up for me. I knew the Moors had come across from North Africa and invaded Spain in 711, dominating much of the country for more than eight centuries after that. What I didn't know was how powerful and pervasive their impact on Spain really was.

I remember "Moorish Spain" as though it was yesterday. The Moors were incredibly refined and sophisticated, something which is evident in the remarkable centres they created in southern Spain, most notably Granada, Cordoba, and Seville, but also in many other places. I was bowled over by the architecture of the many palaces, mosques, and forts I visited there, as well as the profound understanding the Moors had of nature, landscape, sound, and water. Everything was perfectly situated in the natural environment, and the gardens were magnificent. One could sit in these gardens for hours enjoying the sights and sounds of water cascading down cleverly constructed troughs and flowing into exquisite pools and fountains. Designed for beauty, elegance, grace, and serenity, they were oases of tranquility — oases capable of transporting people into a very different time and space. These highly creative people knew exactly what they were doing when they created these remarkable places.

While many things in Spain left a lasting impression on me, I was particularly taken by the music. I was instantly drawn to Flamenco music, which I heard a great deal in the caves and taverns of Andalusia in southern Spain, as well as guitar music played by such masters as Andrés Segovia and Celedonio Romero and his three sons Celin, Pepe, and Angel. However, I was most intrigued by the music of Joaquín Rodrigo, Enrique Granados, Isaac Albéniz, Manuel de Falla, and many others since it was so characteristic of Spain and its culture. I know there are many musicologists who frown at the idea that music captures the heart and soul of a people, country, or culture, but I felt this was especially true of Spanish music. It seems to say more about Spain and Spanish culture than anything else.

If Spain transported me to a different world, Morocco transported me into what seemed like a *fantasy* world. I didn't originally plan to go to Morocco. However, after my stay in Seville, Cordoba, and Granada, I travelled to Cadiz and Gibraltar. While I was there, someone suggested I would really enjoy Tétouan, a small town situated across the Straits of Gibraltar in North Africa. It turned out to be an excellent suggestion. I was so enthralled with my experience there that I decided to see much more of Morocco.

Like many places in northern Morocco, there was evidence of both Spanish and Moorish influences in Tétouan. However, it was the Moorish influence that intrigued me and captured my attention. No sooner was I walking in the medina in Tétouan than I was reminded of the stories my mother had read to Murray and myself when we were young, most notably *Aladdin and the Magic Lamp*, *Ali Baba and the Forty Thieves*, *Sinbad the Sailor*, and *Scherazade*.

The medina and souks of Tétouan were mysterious and exciting. There were rows upon rows of shops selling exotic spices, wonderfully embroidered caftans and shawls, exquisite carpets and rugs, outstanding leather work ranging from handbags and purses to sandals and slippers, and many gold, silver, and copper masterpieces fashioned by skilled craftsmen. The architecture was equally superb, and certainly on a par with what I saw in southern Spain. And the food! It was out of this world.

I remember one night in Tétouan eating a multi-course meal in a conical, five-floor restaurant with the most enchanting honeycombed arches and architecture I have ever seen. At the outset of the meal, our hands were washed as we luxuriated on pillows, carpets, and blankets. Following this, we were served a marvelous *bstila*, the famous Moroccan dish made from filo pastry, stuffed with ground pigeon, and seasoned with ginger, sugar, saffron, cinnamon, and other spices. This was followed by a chicken *tagine* accompanied by lemons and prunes and cooked to perfection for hours in a special pot, as well as a slowly roasted lamb *méchoui* and, needless to say, the ubiquitous *couscous*. For dessert, we had the most succulent oranges I have ever tasted — even better than the ones I had in Valencia — floating in syrup and cinnamon. And this was all washed down with the most pungent and sweet mint tea I have ever tasted. What I didn't know at the time was that Morocco has one of the greatest cuisines in the world. Unfortunately, like Turkish and several other cuisines, it is one of the world's best kept secrets.

With experiences like this constantly percolating in my mind, I was anxious to see other cities in Morocco. So this is what I did. I went to three of the four imperial cities of Morocco: Fez, Meknes, and Rabat. There were also trips to many other well-known places, including Moulay Idriss, Volubilis, Casablanca — of Humphrey Bogart and Ingrid Bergman fame — and Tangier.

Fez and Meknes were undoubtedly the highlights. This is especially true for Fez, which occupies a location of unparalleled beauty surrounded by rolling hills. It was the intellectual, cultural, and religious centre of Morocco at one time, and possesses the oldest university in the world. It has many fine mosques, palaces, and sites of historical interest, including the Great Mosque, the Karaouyine Mosque, the Royal Palace, the Dar-El Beïda Palace, and the Batha Palace.

Meknes rivals Fez in many ways. Like Fez, it profits from a superb location surrounded by hills and a great deal of dessert. It is situated some forty miles west of Fez, and also possesses many fine mosques, such as the Great Mosque and the Er Rouha Mosque. But the most impressive place in Meknes is the Imperial "city within a city" of Dar Kebira and other palaces, sultan's gardens, and the tomb of Mulay Isma'il. It is entered by way of the Bab Mansour gate, a gigantic horseshoe arch cut into the walls of the city and flanked by two ornamental bastions decorated with green ceramic tile. Although Meknes's colossal walls were badly in need of repair when I was there, the city was completely fortified with gateways cut through the gigantic walls. The city owes its origins to an ancient Berber tribe, the Meknassa.

Unfortunately, I was not able to go to Marrakech, the fourth imperial city of Morocco, although I did get to Rabat in addition to Fez and Meknes. I have been kicking myself ever since, since Marrakech is situated in the very centre of the country and is described as the "jewel of Morocco" and "the most Moroccan city of all." Positioned close to the Atlas Mountains, it is dominated by a huge square — the famous Djemaa el Fna square. I am told it is possible to see the whole of humanity and Moroccan culture spread out before your eyes in this square. There are snake charmers, storytellers, money lenders, water sellers, musicians, actors, teachers, merchants, spiritual leaders, cooks, doctors, and many other kinds of people, all plying their trades, hawking their wares, and living their lives. It is apparently the closest one can get to experiencing the Moroccan way of life and culture in all their diversity, originality, vitality, and richness.

Morocco had a profound effect on me. Put simply, I fell in love with the place and will never forget it. Morocco was different than anything I had ever seen or experienced up to that point in my life. It made me realize how many diverse cultures there are in the world and how little we know about them. It wasn't until my travels in Morocco that this fact became fully apparent to me.

Following my trip to Morocco, I found myself getting anxious to see France. I travelled back through Spain, stopped to spend some time in Valladolid, Burgos, Bilbao, and San Sebastián, and then crossed over the border to visit Biarritz and Bayonne in southern France. From there, it was eastward to see more of southwestern France. After visiting two of the best-preserved medieval towns in the world — Carcassonne and Les Baux-de-Provence — I spent some time in Albi, a walled-city, and then travelled southward to visit Marseille, Cannes, Nice, and Aix-en-Provence.

I then doubled back a bit and worked my way northward to spent some time in Nîmes, Arles, Orange, and Avignon, where I danced *Sur le Pont d'Avignon* as all good tourists do. My interest in this area of France was piqued by some of the best preserved Roman ruins in the world and a chance to see some paintings by Vincent van Gogh and other Impressionist artists. Also noteworthy was the fact that Avignon was one of the world's greatest religious, administrative, and cultural centres in medieval and early modern times. Small wonder, since some of the Popes lived there for a time and it was the centre of the Roman Catholic Church. Its setting is magnificent, the landscape superb, and the weather splendid. It thrived for centuries as a major hub linking the north and south of France together.

After Avignon, I went by way of Lyon and Dijon to see Paris, "the city of light" and one of greatest urban centres in the world. I did everything tourists do there. I visited virtually every famous site: Notre Dame cathedral, the Eiffel Tower, Le Sacré-Coeur, Sainte-Chapelle, Saint-Sulpice, the Louvre, Les Invalides, L'Opéra, the Left Bank, the Champs-Elysées, the Tuilerie Gardens, the Place de la Bastille, Les Halles (unfortunately now situated in another location), L'Arc de Triomphe, and many others. I marveled at how the great nineteenth-century architect and urban planner, Baron Georges-Eugène Haussmann, was able to create the most expansive boulevards and exquisite squares and parks in Paris, especially the Boulevard Haussmann that bears his name. More than once I was totally exhausted after walking these boulevards from one end to the other. Things that seemed close at hand to the eye usually required an eternity to reach on foot.

While the attractions of Paris impressed me greatly, I must say I tired of them rather quickly and longed to experience the many different districts and neighbourhoods of Paris. There was nothing I liked better than to focus on some particular district or neighbourhood and explore it in depth — walking its streets, exploring its shops, sampling its food, eating in its restaurants, and talking to local people. While I didn't stay in Paris very long, I explored many such areas and have returned to them (and many others) often. I distinctly recall discovering a marvelous Turkish restaurant in a district near the Sacré-Coeur on one of my trips to Paris to attend a UNESCO conference. For a few francs I was able to get a fantastic three-course meal — a meal probably rivalling those served in some of the best three-star Michelin restaurants in France. The same holds true for many other inexpensive meals I had in the diverse regions of France. I often experienced terrific meals in the most humble and down-to-earth restaurants imaginable.

Once my explorations in Paris were over, I decided to explore the area around the city. As with the area around Madrid, I was glad I did. I visited most of the famous cathedrals in close proximity to Paris, including

Amiens, Reims, and Rouen — where Claude Monet painted the cathedral many times at different times of the day and Joan d'Arc was burned alive at the stake — as well as Chartres with its exquisite stained-glass windows. These cathedrals rivaled, if not surpassed, many of the cathedrals I visited in England, including the ones in Salisbury, Wells, Peterborough, York, and Canterbury. Whenever the opportunity presented itself, I was only too happy to tramp around another cathedral to enjoy the wonderful architecture and music I discovered there.

When my cathedral tour was over, I visited many famous chateaux in the Loire Valley, most notably Chambord, Blois, Amboise, Chenonceau, Azay-le-Rideau, Chaumont, Cheverny, and Ussé. I marvelled at these places, as well as the amount of time it took to build them and the many intriguing activities that took place in them. I wonder if colossal edifices like these could be built today, since they would probably take far too long to build and be much too expensive.

I had been travelling in France long enough to get a feel for the country's regional character. Perhaps more than any other country in the world, France is made up of very distinct regions — Normandie, Brittany, the Loire Valley, Champagne, Burgundy, the Savoy, the French Alps, Alsace-Lorraine, the Bordelaise, the Pyrénées, the Côte d'Azur, and so forth. Each is a region — *or a culture* — in its own right, with numerous things that make it different and unique. It may be chateaux, as is the case in the Loire Valley; it may be cheese, as is the case in Normandie; or it may be wine, as is the case in Burgundy and Bordelaise. I discovered years later that the French Ministry of Culture had mapped all the various regions of France in great detail, documenting every town, city, theatre company, symphony orchestra, art gallery, museum, community centre, artifact, and historic site with scientific precision and artistic flair.

As I reflect back on this now, I must say that what struck me the most about France was the incredible attachment people had to "the land." The French know their country and its regions exceedingly well. This deep knowledge is reflected in the work of the Impressionist painters, many of whom went to extraordinary lengths to paint the landscapes with a great deal of imagination and care.

It is not coincidental in this respect that the French are deeply committed to agriculture. This commitment goes back centuries. I remember discovering this fact when I studied European economic history at the University of Toronto. Unlike the English, who embraced commerce and industry — probably because Britain is an island and its people have always been heavily dependent on the sea and resources from abroad – the French embraced agriculture, the land, and agrarian activities. This contrast shows up most clearly in the differences between the two countries in terms of food, cuisine, and cooking. Whereas it is often said that the English "eat to live" – which was reflected for many years in their relative disinterest in cuisine although this has changed greatly recently – it is also often said that the French "live to eat," as reflected in their keen interest in food and everything related to it. There is nothing the French like better than fresh food from the land – be it meat, game, or vegetables – prepared to perfection.

This love of food and the land was not the only thing that impressed me about France and the French. I was also impressed with the overall way of life I discovered there, limited though my exposure was to it. It was a way of life that was very different than what I experienced in Germany, Spain, and Morocco. The French have evolved a very sophisticated way of life because they have keen insights into what life and living are really all about and what matters most. *Joie de vivre* is the phrase that captures this best.

While in France (as everywhere) economic considerations are important, they are not so important that they override the importance of the arts, literature, language, conversation, food and drink, and so forth. For the first time in my life, I was exposed to a people and a country that seemed to put culture – and particularly their love, appreciation, and practice of it – ahead of economics. As a result, I learned a great deal about life, living, and culture when I was in France. While earning a living is an essential part of French life, my impression is that culture is an even greater part. I found this very exhilarating – and reassuring – because it was consistent with what I had been taught by my parents was most worthwhile in life, what I experienced growing up, and what I felt within myself.

Everything seemed to be done with consummate care and sophistication in France: the use of language; the preparation and consumption of food; the selection of wines and cheeses; and the baking of bread. This showed up in French music as well. I was amazed to find that France has a musical tradition that is every bit as developed, sophisticated, and cultivated as the musical tradition of Germany, even if it is not as well known in most parts of the world. Interestingly, it rivals the German musical tradition step by step and century by century, but is very different. When the Germans had Scheidt, J. S. Bach, and Telemann, the French had

François and Louis Couperin, Rameau, and Lully. When the Germans had Brahms, Beethoven and Schumann, the French had Debussy, Ravel, and Saint-Saëns. Whereas German music tended to be deeper and heavier — much like their food — French music was lighter and more delicate. I found this fascinating because it confirmed my conviction that the arts in general and music in particular often reflect people's and countries' temperaments, cultures, and ways of life.

While I was in this part of Europe, I decided to visit Belgium and the Netherlands. I had read a great deal about these countries in the course I took on European Economic History, largely because in earlier periods of history they were not only dynamic centers of trade, industry, and commerce, but also great centres of art and culture.

Neither country disappointed me. I was most intrigued with Belgium, as it had several cities I wanted to see very badly, especially Brussels, Ghent, Liege, and Antwerp, which had been major ports and key textile centers in medieval and early modern times. But the city I liked the most and had the greatest impact on me was Bruges. While it is not very well known outside of Europe, it was a real gem to discover. I would definitely count it among the most enjoyable cities I have even seen, and on a par with Carcassonne, Rothenburg ob der Tauber, Segovia, Toledo, Granada, Florence, and Siena as one the most charming and enchanting medieval cities in Europe. I never tired of strolling its cobblestone streets, enjoying its numerous canals, and spending time gazing into the water from its many beautiful bridges. I would return there at the drop of a hat if the opportunity presented itself.

Belgium fascinated me for another reason as well. Like Canada, it has a long history of interaction between two major linguistic and ethnic groups. In the case of Belgium, it is the Flemish and the Walloons; in the case of Canada, of course, it is the French and English. Whereas the Flemish speak Dutch, the Walloons speak French. Much as in Canada, there have been numerous conflicts between these two peoples and their languages. For centuries, Belgium's professional, managerial, and administrative ranks were filled and controlled largely by Walloons, thereby leading to a great deal of friction and countless complaints by the Flemish that they were living under the thumb of the Walloons, just as the French in Canada complained that they were living under the thumb of the English. There were — and still are — strong feelings on both sides, with numerous tensions percolating just below the surface. These pressures never seem to get resolved, thereby leaving open the possibility that Belgium, like Canada, could split apart, even if history and common sense suggest otherwise.

After visiting Belgium, I headed north to the Netherlands. Although there were several cities in the Netherlands I was anxious to see, such as Amsterdam, Groningen, Leiden, Rotterdam, Delft, and Edam, I was interested in this country for a very different reason. I wanted to see how the Dutch had wrestled with nature and the sea, and had won this battle despite numerous setbacks.

Subduing nature in the Netherlands was an amazing feat that required the construction of myriad dikes and the reclaiming of a great deal of "unclaimable land." I marvelled at the industriousness and creativity of the Dutch in the face of great adversities and virtually insurmountable odds. Not only were they able to win the battle with the sea, but, like the Spaniards, they had a "golden era" in their history that was punctuated by countless economic, social, artistic, and cultural achievements, as discussed at length in Simon Schama's book *The Embarrassment of Riches: An Interpretation of Dutch Culture in the Golden Age*. For instance, the Dutch produced great painters like Hieronymus Bosch, Frans Hals, Jan Vermeer, Rembrandt, and Vincent van Gogh. As was the case with the Louvre in Paris and the Prado in Madrid, I spent countless hours in the Rijksmuseum and other major galleries in Amsterdam enjoying the incredible paintings housed there.

After exploring the museums and art galleries of this veritable "Venice of the north," I was anxious to see the real thing. I decided that the best way to do this was to travel through France, Germany, and Switzerland and then to Italy.

After spending some time in Strasbourg and Alsace-Lorraine (of which Napoleon once said, "It is fine if the people in this region speak German as long as they think in French") I cut through the Black Forest at Freiberg in Germany and found myself in northern Switzerland.

I marveled at this beautiful country and the ingenuity of the Swiss people. I knew the Swiss profited greatly from their location at the crossroads of Europe. However, the ingenuity of the Swiss seemed to go far beyond this. Whether it was their capacity to produce outstanding products for everyday use like butter, eggs, milk, cheese, and chocolate, their ability to engineer superb watches and clocks, their expertise in banking and financial matters, their capacity for maintaining elaborate defense systems, their aptitude in bringing together four very distinct linguistic groups to live in peace and harmony rather than conflict and confrontation, or their penchant for law, order, and solving complex political problems through referendums, the Swiss seemed to be able to make a great deal out of little. The fact Switzerland is one of the most exquisite and scenic countries in the world no doubt helped considerably. But there seemed to be a degree of creativity, imagination, and innovation in Switzerland that went far beyond this.

I enjoyed the German, French, and Italian parts of Switzerland very much, and especially cities like Bern, Basel, Zurich, Lucerne, Lausanne, Geneva, Lucarno, and Lugano. However, I was far more taken with Switzerland's smaller towns and cities, most notably Interlaken, Wengen, Grindelwald, Saint Moritz, Andermatt, Thun, Montreux, Appenzell, Stein am Rhein, Zermatt, and others. There was something about the manageable size and scale of these places that I found especially appealing. They seemed to be much more in keeping with the real nature of Switzerland, as they were closer to (and farther up) the mountains, and spoke more directly to the challenges of the incredibly difficult natural terrain that the Swiss confronted and overcame.

The Italian part of Switzerland proved to be an excellent introduction to Italy itself. No sooner did I leave Lugano and Lucarno than I was in the exquisite lake district of northern Italy. Is there a more beautiful part of the world than this? Lake Maggiore, Lake Como, Lake Orta, Lake Lugano, and Lake Garda all proved to be incredible, as did the Borromean Islands, Isola Bella, Isola Madre, and Stresa. But the place that left the greatest impression on me was Bellagio. I stayed there for five days in a villa, never tiring of walking the city's narrow streets and refreshing myself in its lush and lovely gardens.

There was more to come. No sooner had I left the Italian lake district than I was in Milan enjoying its incredible cathedral, one of the largest and most beautiful in Europe, as well as its many busy streets and fine boutiques. The cathedral was begun in 1386, and bristles with belfries, gables, pinnacles, and statues. It occupies a magnificent setting at the end of a long esplanade, and is best seen in the late afternoon or early evening when it is bathed in golden light from the setting sun. Following this, it was on to Genoa, Italy's largest port city, then to Portofino, one of the most alluring cities on the Italian Riviera, and finally to Lucca and Pisa, the latter made famous by the Leaning Tower. I discovered that there was much more to Pisa than the Leaning Tower, as the city was a well-known intellectual and artistic centre in the Middle Ages. I also learned that the Leaning Tower was much more than an architectural wonder and great engineering feat. It was the place where Galileo, quite possibly the world's greatest astronomer and physicist and a native son of Pisa, studied the movement of pendulums, worked out the laws governing the acceleration of falling bodies, and fought with numerous colleagues over different astronomical theories.

After Pisa, it was inland to Florence. For a person interested in the arts and culture, Florence proved to be a real eye-opener. From my studies, I knew this city was famous for its economic as well as its cultural accomplishments. It was home not only to the Medici family — noted for their financial clout in addition to being major patrons of the arts — but also to many other wealthy families and patrons, including the Pittis, the Strozzis, and the Pazzis.

But it was Florence's fame in the arts that captured my attention. I was fascinated by everything there, from the architecture of Brunelleschi and sculpture of Ghiberti, Donatello, Luca della Robbia, and Benvenuto Cellini, to the paintings of Giotto, Masaccio, Fra Angelico, and Botticelli. I marvelled at all the splendid architecture, museums, and art galleries, especially the Cathedral of Santa Maria del Fiore and its famous doors to the Campanile, as well as the Uffizi Museum and the Bargello and Pitti palaces and galleries, which contained some of the greatest paintings and sculptures in the world. The magnificent views of the city from the adjacent hills reminded me of how Toledo had looked, viewed from a distance in the hills of central Spain.

From Florence it was on to Siena via the medieval town of San Gimignano, famous for the fourteen colossal towers that dominate its skyline. They are not unlike the huge skyscrapers constructed by modern banks and insurance companies today, each one built higher than the one before it in an effort to outdo all the others.

While it was fascinating wandering through the narrow streets of Siena and visiting the cathedral in the Piazza del Duomo — construction commenced in 1065 but was not completed until the fourteenth century — it was the Palio delle Contrade that had the greatest effect on me. The Palio is a famous celebration that is held on the second day of July and sixteenth day of August in the Piazza del Campo, a huge square in the central part of the city. It has been celebrated every year since 1653! It begins with a procession of seventeen *contrade* in fifteenth-century costumes carrying their emblems, continues with the *alfieri* brandishing their banners, and concludes with the municipal guard, armed with halberds and arquebuses. This is followed by the famous horse race around the square. The *palio*, a standard inscribed with the coat of arms of the city, is awarded to the winner. It is not to be missed if one finds oneself in Siena at the right time of year.

After Siena and Florence, Rome was a bit of a disappointment. It is not that it is a disappointing city to visit; far from it, since there are many well-known things to see there including the Roman Forum, the Palatine Hill, the Coliseum, the Caracalla Baths, the Catacombs, Castel Sant'Angelo, Saint Peter's Cathedral, the Sistine Chapel, the Vatican, and so forth. Moreover, there are countless museums and arts galleries to visit, not to mention the chance to stroll down well-known boulevards and visit many famous shops and districts. However, I soon found myself tiring of these things and in a state of exhaustion. I was glad to have seen Rome and spent several days there. However, I was also glad to leave and work my way north and east to towns and cities that were substantially smaller in size, had far fewer residents, tourists, and attractions, and were much more manageable, including such places as Assisi, Perugia, Gubbio, and Urbino.

While all these towns and cities left an indelible impression on me, the jewel was undoubtedly Assisi. I had long known of Saint Francis and his love of animals and nature, but I had no idea "this city of birds and silence" was so exquisite. Built of pink stone, it is spread out in the shape of a huge fan on the slopes of Monte Subasio. The town, which has not changed a great deal since medieval times, is enclosed by ramparts and includes such attractions as Saint Francis Bascilica, the Church of Saint Clara, and many others.

Assisi proved to be an excellent introduction to Perugia, Gubbio, and Urbino, since these are also famous medieval towns surrounded by walls and ramparts, with colours, glows, and characteristics all their own. Perugia was originally one of twelve Etruscan strongholds and is famous for its artists, many of whom were trained by Florentine masters; Gubbio is known for its yellow ochre buildings, the toast-like tint of its Romanesque roofs, and its outstanding ceramics; and Urbino is built on two hills and is bathed in golden light most of the time. Its narrow, steep streets are lined with many palaces, and provide evocative glimpses of the town and its various courtyards, not to mention the local countryside. So you can understand why I was so glad to be out of Rome and into the Italian countryside, where I could explore medieval towns and cities and the wonderful Umbrian countryside and life to my heart's content. I stayed there much longer than anticipated, but it was worth it.

Following my stay in the Umbrian region of Italy, I traveled through

San Marino – one of the smallest and most ancient states in the world – to Rimini on the Adriatic. Then it was on to Ravenna. While it is not well known, Ravenna was the capital of the Roman Empire at one time, and was called "the Byzantium of the West." It is famous for its mosaics, which are considered to be the finest in Europe and surpass even those in Constantinople, now Istanbul, as well as the ones in Palermo and Venice. The mosaics are found in many of the basilicas, baptisteries, tombs, and churches of Ravenna, and are made of small cubes irregularly shaped and deliberately inlaid in order to catch and reflect the rays of the sun. Containing doves, peacocks, stags, and human figures ringed in black, they are so eye-catching that Dante called them "symphonies of colour."

After Ravenna, it was north to Verona and Vicenza on my way to Venice. What delightful places these two cities are! At one time or another both were major centers of art and culture, as well as trade and commerce. Verona is known as "the city of Romeo and Juliet," made famous by Shakespeare, Tchaikovsky, and Prokofiev. The two lovers belonged to rival families: Romeo to the Montecchi or Montagues, who were Guelphs and supported the Pope; and Juliet to the Capuleti or Capulets, who were Ghibellines and supported Emperor Frederick I. The scenes of the ball, the balcony, the secret marriage, the farewells, and the suicides of Romeo and Juliet were all set in Verona, and took place in 1302 or thereabouts. Like Assisi, the town contains many fine buildings in red, ochre, and pink marble. It is one of the most delightful towns in Italy in which to stroll day or night with an Italian ice cream cone – gelato – in hand, especially around the Centro della Città, Piazza delle Erbe, and Piazza dei Signori.

And Vicenza! It doesn't have to take a back seat to Verona. It is well-known for its Piazza dei Signori with its famous clock tower, basilica, and twelfth-century belfry, its hundred or more palaces, its exquisite buildings along the Corso Andrea Palladio, and especially its Greek Theatre. The theatre was completed in 1583 and has one of the finest stages in the world, with superimposed niches, columns, and streets in false relief created by Scamozzi.

But the highlight of my travels in Italy – and indeed my entire trip – was undoubtedly Venice. I fell in love with the place, as do tourists from all over the world. Built on more than a hundred islands with 150 canals and some 400 bridges, Venice invites strolling and idling like no other city. One could spend days (but preferably weeks and even months) exploring its incredible architectural, artistic, and cultural treasures, from Saint Mark's Square, Saint Mark's Basilica, and the Doge's Palace to the

Grand Canal, the Rialto Bridge, the Bridge of Sighs, and countless others. The Grand Canal is two miles long and is lined with more than two hundred marble palaces from the twelfth to eighteenth centuries. It was in Venice that I listened to some of the finest baroque music I have ever heard in my life, including the music of such great masters as Gabrieli, Corelli, and Vivaldi.

Unlike Paris and Rome, which I found exhausting, I never seemed to tire of Venice. There was always something to see or do, regardless of whether it was enjoying the sites, soaking up the sun, sitting in the myriad squares watching the world go by, or exploring galleries, museums, palaces, churches, and "golden houses" like the Ca' d'Oro. Each time you think you will never see anything more beautiful, another treasure of even greater beauty presents itself. I marvelled at this historic city – without doubt one of the greatest human achievements in the world – and its sundials inscribed with the immortal words, *Horas non numero nisi serenas* ("I count only happy hours"). I know Venice has been the scene of innumerable tragedies, intrigues, and a great deal of violence and corruption over the centuries. In recent years it has also been threatened by severe floods and will slowly sink into the sea if contemporary reclamation efforts are not successful. But Venice certainly served as a great source of inspiration for me. It represented the best humanity has to offer, and did a great deal to strengthen my resolve to broaden and deepen my understanding of the world's greatest artistic and cultural accomplishments.

I could have stayed in Venice forever. But the time had come to move on, though not without an enormous amount of regret, as well as the hope that I would be able to return one day. However, it was time to make my way to Yugoslavia, another country I was anxious to see. I did so by driving through Trieste, and then down the upper part of the Dalmatian coast and into what is now Croatia.

I had been anxious to see Yugoslavia for many years. While I didn't know a great deal about this country, I knew it was made up of six "people's republics" – Croatia, Bosnia-Herzegovina, Macedonia, Serbia, Slovenia, and Montenegro – that traced their individual histories back for centuries. While the effort to unify these republics and the assassination of Archduke Franz Ferdinand in Sarajevo were among the causes of the First World War, it was not until the late 1940s that Yugoslavia was unified under the Communist leader Marshall Tito, who defeated the leader of the royalists, General Draza Mihailović, with the help of the USSR and the British government. Tito immediately developed strong ties with the

Soviet Union and turned Yugoslavia into a communist state. However, he broke with the Cominform and the USSR in 1948 and pursued an independent course of action, largely by establishing "national communism" and pursuing his own foreign policy.

What made Yugoslavia interesting to me was the fact that it was a multicultural country much like Canada, although Canada was not declared an *official* multicultural country in the political sense until the 1970s. I was anxious to see how it was possible to keep so many diverse ethnic and linguistic groups together, when relations between the French and the English in Canada were so difficult. I soon realized Yugoslavia's unity would not have been possible without an iron-willed dictator like Tito, but even this fascinated me. While Yugoslavia was united and communist when I was there — although there seemed to be little evidence of the latter, as I was free to roam the country without a visa or other restrictions — there was a general feeling that it was only a matter of time before the country would break up. And this is exactly what happened after Tito died. Almost immediately, the country was split up into separate republics, with Slovenia and Croatia taking the lead.

While I didn't have the good fortune to travel extensively throughout Yugoslavia during my first trip there, I did get as far down the Dalmatian coast as Dubrovnik and Split. Fortunately, it was at a time when the Dalmatian coast was not well-known as a major tourist destination, which suited me fine. I was able to see these exquisite places before the tourist onslaught, and at a fraction of the price of a comparable trip today. Dubrovnik proved to be especially fascinating. Like Rothenburg ob der Tauber, Carcassonne, Segovia, Toledo, Assisi, and other famous medieval cities, it was in an excellent state of preservation, with strong protective walls encircling the entire city. And like the others, it invited endless hours of idling, strolling, and soaking up the sun.

Once I had my fill of Dubrovnik, Split, and the Dalmatian coast, I went overland to see Mostar and Sarajevo, and then on to Belgrade and Zagreb. Mostar and Sarajevo were real eye-openers, particularly given the incredible mix of peoples and languages I encountered there. They reminded me a great deal of places I had visited in southern Spain and Morocco, complete with many fine mosques and minarets and large Muslim populations. Mostar was, and continues to be, an ethnically divided city. It is joined together by an historic stone bridge that was destroyed during the turmoil in Bosnia-Herzegovina in the 1990s but rebuilt more recently. Sarajevo is also a very ethnically diverse city, filled with many enticing sights as well as a number of outdoor markets that have few equals in the world. It is hard to believe that these two cities were in great turmoil only a few decades after I visited them, as they seemed so tranquil when I was there. Belgrade and Zagreb were bustling metropolises, even when I visited them in the sixties. Although they are not as large as many cities in western Europe, they possess cultural and commercial traditions dating back many centuries. I have returned to these cities many times, especially Zagreb which holds out a particular attraction for me due to its countless artistic treasures.

Although Yugoslavia shared certain geographical similarities with Spain, Italy, and Greece, it was very different in other ways. The people were more diverse, the languages more distinct, the colours of the landscape clearer and stronger, the crafts more varied, and the costumes and clothing more colourful. But the thing I liked most about Yugoslavia was the food. I discovered that I had a great love of Balkan food, especially *čevapčići, ražnići,* Serbian bean soup, stuffed peppers, and so forth. In fact, I loved the food of Yugoslavia so much that when I returned to Toronto I immediately began scouring the city for restaurants that served food from this part of the world. After a long search, I finally found a restaurant on Elm Street in downtown Toronto called The Balkans, which quickly became my favourite. It was decorated in typical Balkan style, which made you feel like you were sitting in a large tent, living the life of a pasha, and enjoying food that was simply "out of this world." I went there many times over the years with family and friends and it never failed to remind me of all the wonderful times I spent in Yugoslavia.

While I would have liked to stay in Yugoslavia much longer, I knew I would return there some day. Besides, Austria and Vienna were beckoning, and I felt I simply could not put off a trip there any longer. So I travelled north from Zagreb, stopping briefly in Graz to enjoy its famous tower and outdoor clock, and then went on to Vienna. It was early August by this time, and I was anxious to soak up everything Vienna had to offer. I did just that, visiting all the sights for which the city is famous. This included the Hofburg, the favourite residence of the Hapsburgs who ruled the Austro-Hungarian Empire for so long; Saint Stephen's Cathedral; the Church of Saint Charles, close to where Johannes Brahms lived; the Belvedere; the Ring; the Opera; Schönbrunn Palace; the Prater — made famous for its Ferris wheel in the movie *The Third Man;* and especially the Art History Museum with its famous paintings by Jan Van Eyck, Rubens, Frans Hals, Rembrant, Brueghel the Younger, Brueghel the Elder,

Albrecht Dürer, Titian, Tintoretto, Caravaggio, Veronese, and many others. Given my interest in music, painting, opera, and theatre, Vienna proved to be a real treasure-trove, and I took full advantage of it.

But what made the most lasting impression on me was Grinzing. It is a small, bohemian area where Beethoven, Brahms, and Schubert spent a great deal of time – it is now officially part of Vienna – that is known for its *heuriger*, or wine taverns. It had a wonderful "laid-back quality" that invited idling, strolling, sampling excellent Austrian wines and beers, and devouring a great deal of wonderful food. This, and the restaurants and coffee houses of Vienna, were of great interest to me, since they seemed to speak directly to the slow, easy pace of life in Vienna compared to most other western European cities I visited.

Once I had my fill of Vienna, it was on to other parts of Austria. I traveled from Vienna to Salzburg – Mozart's city – via Melk, Linz, and the Salzkammergut. I was anxious to see the Benedictine Abbey at Melk, since I was very interested in the music of Anton Bruchner and he lived at this Abbey for many years. Most musicologists think Bruchner's symphonies are too long, which probably explains why they are rarely heard today. For me, however, his symphonies have an ethereal quality about them that might well have something to do with his long stay at the Abbey. While there was nothing particularly distinctive about Linz, especially after Melk, this was made up for in the Salzkammergut. As the name suggests, it was a great centre of salt mining in early periods of history, but today serves primarily as a centre for spas and thermal baths. These proved to be the ideal way to wind down and relax after Vienna and Melk, particularly in charming towns like St. Wolfgang and Bad Ischl in the heart of the Salzkammergut.

After the Salzkammergut, it was on to Salzburg. Many consider Salzburg to be the jewel in Austria's crown. Like Segovia, Toledo, Carcassonne, and many other medieval cities, it profits greatly from a superb location. It is best seen from the Mönchsberg hill, whose rocky mass hems in the old town from the banks of the Salzach river to the Hohensalzburg castle. The modern town spreads out widely along the right bank of the Salzach river, while the old town, which bristles with domes and church steeples, extends along the left bank and nestles at the foot of the Hohensalzburg castle. Lurking in the background are famous mountain peaks in the Berchtesgaden Alps, the Kapuzinerberg, and the Gaisberg.

Like many cities with ancient origins, Salzburg invites strolling, gazing, and sightseeing. There is a great deal to see there, such as the "old town," the cathedral, the treasury, St. Peter's Church, and the Getreidegasse, one of the most picturesque streets in Salzburg. It was on this street that Leopold Mozart, father of Wolfgang Amadeus and a superb musician in his own right, lived from 1747 to 1773. Wolfgang Amadeus Mozart was born on this street at number 9. A visit to this house, with its many fine reminders of Wolfgang's youth, is a must for anyone visiting Salzburg. After this, it was on to see many other famous sights in Austria, including Krimml, Innsbruck, Kitzbühel, Zell am See, and the Zugspitze. While I had seen many similar places in Switzerland, France, and Germany, I never seemed to tire of these "alpine treasures," complete with their exquisite views of the mountains, fresh air, wonderful gasthofs, aromas, weinstubes, quaint streets, alleyways, and splendid food.

When I was travelling in Austria enjoying everything this remarkable country has to offer, I received a frantic phone call from the head of the economics department at Acadia University in Wolfville, Nova Scotia. His request for a year off to undertake some post-doctoral studies he was anxious to complete had been granted at the very last moment. As a result, he was looking for someone to fill in for him for one academic year and wondered if I might be able to help out in this regard. After a great deal of thought and reflection, I decided to do this. Although I had to end my trip in Europe a little sooner than planned, I returned to Canada towards the end of August 1965. Fortunately I was expected to teach the same three courses I taught at Dalhousie University so there was not a lot of advance preparation to do.

I had been travelling in Europe for almost a year. I felt very privileged to be able to do this because Europe was generally regarded as a "Mecca" for people interested in the arts and culture. This was before a great deal was known in the west about the great artistic traditions and cultural accomplishments of Asia, Africa, Latin America, the Caribbean, and the Middle East, something which was to attract a great deal of my attention in the years to follow.

During my time in Europe and Morocco, I travelled through many countries and learned a great deal about them and from them. I had seen the economies of these countries at work and close up, thereby broadening and deepening my understanding of the way economies function in fact and not just in theory. What struck me most was how much these economies differed from one another. Some, like the German economy, were based primarily on industry and manufacturing. Others, such as the French and Swiss economies, were based more on agriculture and the land. While most of these economies were capitalistic and market-driven, some, like the Moroccan economy and certain parts of the Yugoslavian economy, were much more dependent on the barter system and "income in kind."

If the economies of these countries fascinated me, so did the towns and cities I visited. I discovered that the large majority of these towns and cities were as renowned for their artistic and cultural as for their economic and commercial accomplishments. Marx and the Marxists would say that this was because the economies of these places provided the "economic base" and "productive forces" that were necessary for the arts and other non-economic activities to thrive, thereby positing a kind of "dependency theory" for the arts and other non-economic activities. However, this is not the way things appeared to me. *The situation appeared much more interactive and interdependent than independent and separate.* In some cases, the arts and other non-economic activities did depend on the economies of these cities, true enough. But in other cases, the reverse was true – the economies of the cities depended on the arts and other non-economic activities. There was no general rule that covered all situations. This is consistent with virtually everything I have seen and experienced since that time. It is just as common to see developments in the arts and related activities trigger economic activity as it is for economic activity to trigger artistic and related activities.

When I first encountered this phenomenon during my stay in Europe and Morocco, I knew that I was on to something extremely powerful and profound here – something that I would have to analyze and write about in greater detail later in life. Doing so was imperative in my view because so many people and institutions accepted the Marxian theory of dependency and determinism, and with it the economic interpretation of history, without reservation or qualification. I couldn't accept this without analyzing these theories – *and they are theories, not facts* – in much greater detail, especially when they have such an enormous effect on the world situation.

Much as I was fascinated with the economies of the cities and countries I visited, I was far more fascinated with the ways of life I encountered there. There were many reasons for this. In the first place, they were very different from each other, even if they shared certain factors and features in common. There was a world of difference between the way of life I encountered in Germany compared to the one in Spain, just as there was a vast contrast between the way of life in France compared to the way people lived in Morocco or Yugoslavia. These ways of life also displayed many factors other than purely economic ones. This was instrumental in giving me a much more comprehensive understanding of what countries and people deem to be essential, as well as what is most important to them. Since these ways of life were concerned with ends as well as means, they resolved one of the most difficult problems I had with economics as a discipline and the direction it was headed in the future. I felt it was imperative to take all factors – and not just economic factors – into account when thinking about people's lives and how they might be improved. This was especially true with respect to the natural environment, which was to become such an important concern for me in life.

While I didn't realize it at the time, this was my first real encounter with the complexities of culture in general and cultures in particular that was to become such a quintessential part of my research and writing in the years to follow. It was also my first real encounter with the importance of perception and perspective, especially with regard to how we see the world and not just how we live in it – and therefore with what "worldview" and "worldviews" are all about – despite the fact that I was not able to articulate this fully at the time. Up to that point in my life, I had seen culture and cultures largely in terms of the arts. Following my far longer trip to Europe as well as to Morocco, I began to see culture and cultures in much more all-encompassing terms as "total ways of life" made up of many diverse elements or parts. This sense was strengthened substantially when I encountered the anthropological or holistic perception of culture.

However, more about this later. Much more. Here, I want to comment on another aspect of my travels that had a profound effect on my thinking about culture and cultures. It was the nature of the arts in the specific countries and cultures I visited during my two trips to Europe, as well as the way in which they seemed to epitomize the ways of life in these countries and cultures. This was especially true of music, but it was also true of other art forms.

English music, for instance, seemed to be very regal and majestic, especially the music of Sir William Walton and particularly Sir Edward Elgar and his Pomp and Circumstance Marches. Many other aspects of English culture also seemed majestic and regal, most obviously the monarchy and certain aspects of politics. German music, on the other hand, seemed to be much more pensive, ponderous, and heavy compared to English music, especially the music of Beethoven, Brahms, and Wagner. But then, so too was German food, philosophy, architecture, and the German language. Then there was French music and culture. French music seemed significantly lighter, more fluid, and delicate than either German or English music, particularly the music of Rameau, Debussy, Ravel, Chamanade, and others. But this was equally true of many other aspects of French culture and certainly for the French language and French food.

The more I reflected on this, the more I became intrigued with the role the arts play as "gateways" to cultures in an all-inclusive sense. It was not merely a case of understanding the intimate connection between economics and the arts. More fundamentally, it was a matter of understanding how the arts revealed the overall ways of life of cultures, and especially the differences between them. The paintings I saw, the music I heard, the crafts I enjoyed, and the architecture I encountered all helped to broaden and deepen my knowledge and understanding of all the various cultures I was exposed to during my trips.

Years later, I learned that the great Swiss cultural historian, Jacob Burckhardt, used the visual arts and architecture to illuminate our understanding of the Renaissance and Greek and Roman culture in classical times. It was unfortunate that I did not know about his ideas on this subject much earlier. All I knew was that there was an intimate connection between the arts and the ways of life in all the different cultures and countries I had visited up to that point in my life.

If my trip to Europe and Morocco was helpful in broadening and deepening my knowledge and understanding of culture, cultures, and the arts and the complex connection among them, it was also helpful in another very important way.

Despite the fact that I had agreed to teach economics at Acadia University for one academic year after returning to Canada, I decided while I was away that I would not pursue a Ph.D. in economics, even if was possible to work out a suitable arrangement with some university to write a thesis on the economics of the arts. I came to the conclusion that I had too many reservations about economics as a discipline, the direction it was headed in the future, and especially its treatment of the natural environment as a "given" and "externality" to make a commitment of this type.

What was I to do? Although I was still very interested in economics and many aspects of economies — especially the economics of the arts — something was tugging at the back of my neck and telling me that I should be in the arts, not economics. Although I didn't know where this was coming from or what was causing it, it was definitely there. Perhaps it was intuition, the long trip I had just completed to Europe and Morocco, the feeling that economics could not be transformed from the inside after the natural environment had been neglected for so many years, or the upbringing I had in the arts in my youth. All I knew was that it was real and manifesting itself very strongly in me.

But how could I make the transition to the arts happen? I had no formal training or academic credentials in this area, despite the fact that I loved the arts and had a great deal of exposure to them early in life. After a great deal of thought, I decided to design a practical study of the economics of the arts and see if there was an institution in Nova Scotia (where I would be teaching for an academic year) that might be interested in hiring me to undertake the study. This would enable me to capitalize on my training and teaching experience in economics while simultaneously opening up an opportunity for me to get involved in the arts in a more professional and intensive way.

As soon as I returned to Canada to commence the academic year teaching at Acadia University, I immediately set to work on this idea. I was told that the person to talk to about it was Don Wetmore. He was a specialist in drama who worked for the Department of Education at the Nova Scotia Government in Halifax and was responsible for arts education in the schools. After a great deal of discussion and several abortive attempts to convince authorities in the Nova Scotia Government they should hire me to undertake the study, Don suggested I expand the study to include New Brunswick and Prince Edward Island in the hope that the three Maritime governments in concert might be able to find the funds to finance the study. For more than a year, Don and I attempted to promote the study in the Maritime Provinces and find the necessary funding for it.

When our collective efforts in this area failed — not for lack of interest but lack of money — I decided to rewrite the proposed study and send it to governments and institutions in other parts of Canada. Fortunately, I was invited to attend a conference on the arts in Kingston, Ontario in 1965 that was organized by the Canadian Conference of the Arts. I was invited to attend this conference because I had given several speeches on the economics of the arts when I was living in Wolfville and teaching at Acadia University. When I was at this conference, I meet Milton Carman, executive director of The Province of Ontario Council for the Arts (hereafter referred to as the Ontario Arts Council, its present name), who had seen a copy of the proposed study. The council had been created in 1963 to promote the development of the arts in Ontario and Milton thought the study might be just the thing the council and the province required.

Milton and I hit it off immediately, so much so that he expressed interest in taking the proposed study to his board if I was willing to make a few small changes in it so that it would be applicable to Ontario, which I did. You can imagine my delight when Milton called me a few days later to say that the board had approved the study at its spring meeting in 1966 and wanted to hire me as an economic consultant to undertake it.

This was the break I was looking for and needed most. It was now possible to get into the arts on a full-time and professional basis, while at the same time retaining my interest in economics and its intimate connection to the arts. I was standing on the threshold of a whole new era in my life and was very excited about this. I knew that I would feel comfortable working in the arts, even if I did not have any formal credentials and academic qualifications in this field. I thanked God for the excellent education my parents had given me in the arts in my youth, as well as for "necessity being the mother of invention." I was on my way at last. A whole new stage was about to open up in my life and career. I couldn't have been happier.

CHAPTER FOUR

Embarking on a New Career Path

I was excited at the prospect of working at the Ontario Arts Council and undertaking the study on the economics of the arts. But my first year at the council proved to be much more difficult than I expected it would be.

Since I didn't have any academic credentials or professional qualifications in the arts, I was viewed with suspicion by some people at the council. It helped that my brother Murray was a well-known composer by this time, and that I had sung in a choir and taken some art classes and piano lessons in my youth. However, my lack of academic training or professional experience was deemed to be a serious drawback by several staff and board members. This was a time when a great deal of stress was put on these requirements and I had neither, despite the fact that I loved the arts and was totally committed to them.

It wasn't long before I realized that there was another reason why I was viewed with suspicion by some people at the council, particularly at the staff level. It had to do with the fact that I had been trained as an economist and had taught economics for several years. As a result, it was assumed that I would take an "economic approach" to the arts and expect them to be run like a business.

This was compounded by the fact that I had been hired to undertake an *economic* study of the arts, the very thing that several staff members feared the most. On the one hand, they thought I would want to market the arts like other commodities, expect them to make a profit, and focus on the bottom line. On the other hand, they thought I would hold artists and arts organizations accountable for their financial problems and be insensitive to their needs. While nothing could have been farther from the truth, it was assumed that I didn't really understand the arts and the reasons why artists and arts organizations seldom if ever make ends meet.

These views were not correct. I understood very well why I was at the council and it was definitely not to market the arts like other commodities, treat the arts like a business, or hold artists and arts organizations accountable for their financial problems. I was there to demonstrate that the arts produce economic benefits – and have economic consequences and implications – in the same way that virtually all activities do. For just as artists, arts organizations, and the arts make vital aesthetic, social, environmental, educational, and political contributions to the development of communities, societies, and countries, so, too, do they make vital economic contributions. However, this distinction didn't seem to matter to some people at the council. I was viewed with suspicion and seen as a symbol of everything that artists, arts organizations, arts administrators, and the arts community should guard against.

Not long after I joined the council, the theatrical situation in Toronto came to a head. The two major theatre companies that existed in the city at the time, Crest Theatre and Canadian Players, were experiencing severe financial and administrative problems and were on the verge of bankruptcy. This caused a great deal of consternation at the council because these two organizations had been experiencing difficulties like this for many years and the situation augured badly for the development of theatre in Toronto and generally throughout Ontario.

Since the council was providing grants to both organizations, the big question at the council was what to do about this. Should the council go on funding these organizations year after year despite their problems? Or should it discontinue its grants to these organizations and embark on a new course?

The implications of both options were artistically difficult, financially troublesome, and politically explosive. If the council continued to fund these organizations, it was highly likely that much of this funding would go to pay off past debts and creditors since both organizations were carrying huge debts. However, if the council discontinued its funding, it was likely that these organizations would go bankrupt and the council would be blamed for this, thereby tarnishing its reputation and the reputation of the arts.

Since the two companies were the only professional theatre companies in Toronto at the time – a fact that is hard to believe since Toronto now has more than a hundred professional theatre companies and is the second largest theatre centre in North America after New York – the collapse of the two companies would mean that there would be no professional theatre in a city of roughly one million people. Since the Canada Council, the federal agency charged with responsibility for the development of the arts, was also providing funding to these organizations, it was equally concerned about this situation and the potential artistic, financial, and political fallout. As a result, there were frequent and frantic telephone calls and many hastily arranged meetings between the boards and staffs of the two councils.

In the end, the Ontario Arts Council and the Canada Council decided not to fund the Crest Theatre and Canadian Players for another season, but rather set out in a very different direction. Since both organizations were heavily in debt and had severe and continuing financial and administrative problems, it was felt that they would probably be in a worse financial position at the end of the year than at the beginning if the councils sustained their funding, thus aggravating a highly undesirable and sensitive situation even more. This simply could not go on year after year. The time had come to take a new approach to the development of theatre in Ontario.

But what approach should this be? After a great deal of discussion and debate, it was decided that a comprehensive study of all aspects of theatre in Ontario should be launched with the Ontario Arts Council taking the lead. Since I had some experience with studies of this type and, when I was teaching at Dalhousie, designed and worked on a major study for the federal government on the feasibility of establishing a national park in Nova Scotia, I was asked to design "a study of all aspects and dimensions of theatre in Ontario" that could be discussed at the next board meetings of the two councils.

After several drafts and numerous revisions, the Ontario Theatre Study was finally approved by the boards of the two councils and launched in the fall of 1966. It was the first comprehensive study of theatre in North America and was subdivided into four basic parts: economics and administration; sociology and psychology; facilities and touring; and education and instruction. Work in each part was directed by a steering committee composed of highly respected authorities in the aforementioned areas. Moreover, a planning committee of distinguished representatives from the arts community in Ontario was established to oversee the entire study and take full responsibility for it. Fortunately, Mavor Moore, one of Canada's most respected and prolific theatrical talents, was able to act as director of the study. He was available to do this because he had been hired as the first director of the St. Lawrence Centre for the Arts — Toronto's centennial project in 1967 – which had yet to be built. As a result, he was able to spend a fair amount of time working on the Ontario Theatre Study while simultaneously attending to his duties as director of the soon-to-be-built St. Lawrence Centre.

Shortly after the theatre study commenced, I was appointed a research supervisor of it. As a result, I spent my mornings at the Ontario Arts Council and my afternoons in the St. Lawrence Centre's administrative offices, which were located in an historic flat-iron building on Wellington Street in downtown Toronto. It was very demanding work, since I had to travel from midtown to downtown Toronto every day, as well as travel to many other destinations in the city and other parts of Ontario for meetings, consultations, and research.

However, the rewards from this work were well worth it. During the two years I spent on the study, I learned an enormous amount about research and about all aspects of theatre in Toronto, Ontario, other parts of Canada, the United States, Europe, and the rest of the world. I also learned a great deal about writing and editing, since I worked closely on editing and proof-reading the final report with Mavor Moore, who was a very gifted author and editor in addition to being an outstanding director, actor, playwright, and producer.

The theatre study was published by Methuen Publishers in 1969 under the title *The Awkward Stage: The Ontario Theatre Study Report*. It continues to serve a valuable purpose today in terms of the state of theatre in Ontario during the 1960s, largely because it contains a wealth of information on theatre organizations, facilities, attendance patterns, financial conditions, and audience characteristics. As well, the report made many important recommendations that were implemented in the years to follow.

Due to the large volume of work associated with the Ontario Theatre Study, it was not possible for me to complete the study on the economics of the arts in Ontario as originally planned. However, since many aspects of this study were incorporated into the Ontario Theatre Study, the council decided that my original study was no longer required. This didn't pose a problem for me or the council because I was deeply involved in the work of the economics and administration committee of the Ontario Theatre Study and ended up writing a substantial section of the chapter on this matter for the final report. Moreover, I was involved in so many other activities at the council by this time that it would not have been possible to complete the study on the economics of the arts in Ontario even had I wanted to do so. In fact, I was appointed assistant director of the council in 1968, and this was accompanied by a major change in my work load, job description, and daily responsibilities.

The 1960s were exciting times to be involved in the arts and the work of the Ontario Arts Council. At the national level, the Canada Council was well established by this time and was providing valuable assistance to many artists and arts organizations across the country. Moreover, the centennial celebrations had taken place in 1967. This involved the creation of numerous organizations, activities, and facilities across Canada — art galleries, museums, concert halls, libraries, arts centers, community centres, and so forth — as well as the staging of many different projects, festivals, and events in small towns and large cities from the Atlantic to the Pacific and the Arctic. Of course, the centennial year also brought with it a huge celebration, Expo 67, in Montreal. This "world fair" provided a showcase for many of Canada's most distinguished artists and arts organizations, as well as those from other countries. It proved that Canada did not have to take a back seat to any country in the world in terms of excellence and creativity in the arts.

These unique events also led to a dramatic expansion of the size and character of arts audiences. Prior to Expo 67 and the centennial celebrations, arts audiences in Canada were small in size and elitist in nature. Not so after these unique and highly popular events. Many people who had not experienced the arts at all, or had only limited exposure to them, got their first real taste of the arts at this time. They must have liked what they saw and heard, since arts audiences in Canada have never been the same since.

Due to developments like these, and others, a real renaissance in the arts was starting to occur in Canada, and Ontario was at the very centre of it. Professional organizations like the Stratford Festival, the Toronto Symphony, the National Ballet of Canada, the Art Gallery of Ontario, the Royal Ontario Museum, and the Canadian Opera Company were growing rapidly in size and stature, as were many semi-professional and amateur organizations. There was a sense that Ontario was on the move artistically and the Ontario Arts Council was in the middle of this. This sense was manifested in the mood and morale at the council. It was felt that the council was there to "change the weather, not pass out rubber boots and raincoats," as stated in the council's fifth annual report in 1968. The report went on to say: "We've done the work of animals. We've done the work of machines. Now, please God, could we do the work of human beings." It was a feeling that was widely shared by many people in the arts in Ontario as well as other parts of Canada.

As my duties at the council expanded and intensified, I was able to delve much more deeply into the arts and the role the council was expected to play in their development. I had an enormous amount to learn in this area. This was especially true with respect to how arts councils execute their responsibilities, since most councils are intended to be quasi-independent agencies situated at arm's length from government and the political process. In the case of Ontario, the council's mandate was to develop *all* the arts in *all* parts of the province. What made this mandate especially difficult to implement was the fact that the council was given minuscule appropriations by the Ontario government in the early years — $300,000 in its first year of operation, for example — and then expected to stimulate arts development in all parts of Ontario and in all art forms.

It wasn't long before I began to realize how difficult this task was. Not only did the council have relatively little funding, but also the board and the staff had very different views about how the arts should be developed and how public funds should be disbursed for this purpose.

By and large, most board members favoured a "top-down approach." They were anxious to see most of the funds go to the big professional arts organizations in Toronto and other major cities in Ontario, perhaps because many of the council's board members also sat on the boards of the big organizations and were very committed to their development. In contrast, most staff members wanted a "bottom-up approach." They felt a much larger percentage of the funds should go to smaller arts organizations and individual artists, and that funding should go to all parts of the province, not just to Toronto and other large cities.

Fortunately, most of the tensions that resulted from these differing views and opinions were resolved in peaceful and constructive rather than hostile and confrontational ways. As a result, the council quickly earned the reputation for being one of the most advanced, sophisticated, and creative arts councils in North America. Not only was it at the forefront of many innovative developments in arts council administration at the time — such as getting creative artists into schools, providing grants to publishers, instituting some highly innovative film and video projects, bringing artists, presenters, and producers together, convening a number of future-directed and action-oriented conferences, and undertaking the Ontario Theatre Study — but also it was steadily expanding the nature, method, and scope of its operations. As a result, it became a model for other arts councils in Canada, the United States, and elsewhere in the world to emulate.

One of the biggest problems at the council in the early years was that of arts education. This issue was constantly being raised and debated at conferences, seminars, and meetings convened by the council and other arts organizations. There was virtually unanimous agreement in the arts community that vast improvements were required in arts education if the arts were to thrive and prosper in the future. This was especially true with respect to developing audiences, since "without audiences there are no artists," as the old saying goes.

Most people in the arts community felt that the "arts education problem" required immediate attention and forceful action. Not only were there far too few arts teachers and courses in Ontario schools, but the large majority of the teachers who were in place had little training in the arts because the arts were accorded a low priority in the educational system. Since the council received its annual appropriations from the Ministry of Education — and was accountable to the ministry for its grants, operations, actions, and administration — it was in a very difficult position with respect to dealing with this problem. It had no mandate to operate in the educational field, and there were no precedents to fall back on in connection with improving arts education in the schools.

What was the council to do? In the end, it decided to set up a Centre for Arts Research in Education — CARE — to tackle this problem and appointed me first director of it. While the centre had an extremely small budget ($50,000 in the first year), it was created to act as a catalyst in the educational field, largely by initiating projects the council felt were necessary to improve arts education and stimulate inventive approaches to teaching and learning about the arts in the Ontario school system.

Of immediate concern was the need to get creative artists into classrooms. This was imperative in order to expose students to the creative process, help students understand the way creative artists think, see, hear, and work, and initiate innovative solutions to arts educational problems. In order to do this, soon after the centre was created in 1968, it commissioned a number of highly creative artists — composers, poets, playwrights, actors, film-makers, and the like — to work in classrooms in Ontario. As expected, this did not sit well with the Ministry of Education, or with many arts teachers in the province's schools, who found this program threatening and wanted it discontinued.

These difficulties were eventually resolved to the mutual satisfaction of the ministry and the council and the program was greatly expanded in the years to follow, thereby confirming the fact that creative artists have a legitimate role to play in schools and the educational system. But this was not the only program that caused friction between the ministry, the centre, and teachers. CARE was also involved in a number of other highly innovative projects, such as the creation of multimedia music boxes and "perception bags," that caused controversy. This happened at a time when many new approaches were being taken to education in Ontario, largely as a result of the Hall-Dennis Report and the desire to break down the walls that separated different subjects and facilitate much more exploration, discovery, and research in the school system.

The music boxes and perception bags were filled with all sorts of audio, visual, verbal, and sensory materials related to various aspects of sound, music, vision, different types of aesthetic experiences, and pedagogical matters. They were designed to stimulate the imagination and creativity of students and encourage them to explore various ways of perceiving and creating in the visual, literary, musical, and theatrical arts. While these approaches were consistent with the more permissive view that was being taken of education in Ontario at the time, they raised the ire of officials at the Ministry of Education as well as that of many traditional teachers, because they were created by an institution that was working outside the educational system and had no real mandate to operate within it.

There is one final project that was initiated and funded by the Centre for Arts Research in Education that should be mentioned. It was the creation of a committee of distinguished authorities from the arts to examine the feasibility of establishing a comprehensive academic program for training arts administrators at a university in Ontario. Establishment of this committee had the full endorsement of the Ontario Arts Council because it had been a major recommendation of the Ontario Theatre Study. The recommendation came at a time when the demand for arts administrators was growing rapidly, yet there were no programs of this type in Canada, the United States, or elsewhere in the world.

Following a series of intensive meetings by the committee and a great deal of research, consultation, and information collection, a proposal was advanced to create a graduate program in arts administration at York University in Toronto in 1968. York University responded to this proposal by immediately creating the Program in Arts Administration — now the Program in Arts and Media Administration — in the Faculty of Administrative Studies in 1969, which has since become the Schulich School of Business. Dr. James Gillies, dean of the Faculty of Administrative Studies at the time, played a key role in the creation and development of this program.

He was very knowledgeable about administrative problems facing arts organizations since he was chairman of the Economics and Administrative Committee for the Ontario Theatre Study and had served on the boards of several arts organizations.

As director of the Centre for Research in Arts Education and a research supervisor of the Ontario Theatre Study, I was asked to chair the committee that led to the creation of the program at York. This enabled me to get a "bird's eye view" of the problems involved in training arts administrators in academic institutions, as well as to renew my acquaintance with academic life. Nevertheless, my responsibilities as the council's assistant director and director of CARE still consumed the bulk of my time and attention.

As my responsibilities at the council grew and diversified, I found myself getting more and more involved in the quest to create an effective "rationale for the arts." This was partly because I was interested in this matter in a personal and professional sense. However, in large measure, it was because the council was constantly being asked by the Ontario government to justify its annual appropriation and provide compelling reasons why its appropriation should be increased from year to year. Fortunately, I was working on a Five-Year Plan for the Development of the Ontario Arts Council at the time that had a direct bearing on this. The plan was being supervised by the Honourable J. Keiller MacKay, chairman of the council and a former Lieutenant-Governor of Ontario, from whom I learned an immense amount while I was working at the council.

Creating an effective rationale for the arts was undoubtedly the council's biggest challenge, just as it is the biggest challenge facing all arts organizations and the arts generally in all parts of the world. Without an effective rationale for the arts, the appropriation for the council would not be increased to any great extent from year to year and the council would not be able to execute its mandate and fulfill its responsibilities effectively. While I didn't realize it at the time, I would spend much of the next ten years of my life trying to develop an effective rationale for the arts — and after this much of the remainder of my life attempting to develop an effective rationale for culture — since I believed that the arts and culture deserve a central rather than marginal role in the world and it was imperative to make the case for this in the strongest possible terms.

I distinctly recall being motivated in this task by a statement I read in the Rockefeller Panel Report on the future of theatre, dance, and music in America. In its final report, entitled *The Performing Arts: Problems and*

Prospects, which was published by McGraw-Hill in 1965, the panel stated:

> The arts are not for a privileged few but for the many . . . . their place is not at the periphery of society but at its centre . . . . they are not just a form of recreation but are of central importance to our well-being and happiness.

This statement resonated strongly with me because I believed any rationale for the arts that is worth its salt must deal with the "artistic contribution" the arts make to people, societies, countries, and the world first and foremost. This meant recognizing the enormous amount of fulfillment and happiness that people derive from the arts and their ability to touch and move people in profound, fundamental, and very human ways. Walter Pater expressed this ability admirably when he said "the arts bring the highest quality to your moments as they pass." For regardless of whether people are watching a play, viewing a painting, listening to music, or participating in the creation or production of artistic works, there is something about the artistic experience that transports people to a very special place — a place created by the excellence, creativity, imagination, and ingenuity of artists and arts organizations.

Seen in this way, communication is the lifeblood of all artistic activity. The arts are a *shared experience*; the spark that ignites the intimate connection between artists and audiences. Both groups give something and receive something in return. Artists give much of themselves and their innermost thoughts and feelings. Audiences respond by taking the time and trouble to react to these courageous statements. What results is not always pleasant, but it is always productive. Artists benefit by getting a critical response to their work — a response that helps activate their creativity and strengthen their resolve. Audiences benefit by coming into contact with some of the most profound and moving expressions of feelings, emotions, ideas, insights, and perceptions imaginable. Consequently, both groups are essential to this highly interactive and intimate process. "To have great poets there must be great audiences" is how Walt Whitman expressed this requirement.

As essential as the "artistic contribution" is, it is not the only contribution the arts make to society. Far from it. They also make indispensable historical, environmental, educational, social, economic, and political contributions. The arts also provide a gateway to understanding all the diverse cultures and civilizations that have been created over the centuries. Moreover, they teach us a great deal about the natural environment, and help to conserve the natural environment because they are largely labour-intensive rather than capital- or material-intensive. They also stimulate creativity and imagination, make learning in other disciplines easier, help to convey our feelings and emotions more readily and express them more cogently, and bring people and groups together rather than split them apart.

While all these contributions were very valuable to the people of Ontario, staff and board members at the Ontario Arts Council were reluctant to make these arguments to the provincial government, especially the argument based on the artistic contributions. They felt the government would not respond positively to these arguments because it was obsessed with making "hard core arguments for the arts" – arguments that had much more to do with the economic contribution of the arts than anything else. For it was at a time when the Ontario government (like governments all around the world) viewed the economy as the centrepiece of society and development, and therefore felt bound to set out compelling economic arguments for virtually everything the government was involved in.

This obsession with justifying everything in economic terms and predicating support for the arts only on economic arguments was of great concern to me, both personally and professionally. While I was fully aware of the economic contributions the arts make to Ontario through their ability to generate jobs and income, stimulate consumption and investment activity, promote tourism, and produce multiplier and accelerator effects, I was reluctant to engage in any endeavour that justified the arts solely, firstly, or primarily in economic terms. I felt this should not be the principal reason for funding the arts since it was inconsistent with the real value, nature, and importance of the arts and treated the arts as means to other ends rather than ends in themselves. This was yet another confirmation of my conviction that economics was wrapping itself around everything, and that all things in the world and in life were being given an economic justification and orientation.

I was told by many people at the council and elsewhere in the arts community that my reluctance to justify the arts on economic grounds was short-sighted, naïve, and a mistake. Governments wanted hard economic arguments to convince citizens that spending taxpayers' money on the arts was justified and produced lucrative financial results. If I was really committed to the arts and wanted to help artists and arts organizations – so their argument went – I would tell the government what it wanted to hear and give them the concrete economic ammunition they wanted for funding the arts.

These were the professional and personal problems I was wrestling with at the Council when I was suddenly confronted with a major dilemma. Dr. James Gillies, whom I had worked intensively with on the Ontario Theatre Study, called me in the spring of 1970 to ask if I would be willing to come to York University to direct the graduate Program in Arts Administration that I had been actively involved in creating when I was at the council. The program had been in existence for a year and the university was looking for someone to replace Brian Dixon, who was director of the program in the first year but was assuming other duties in the Faculty of Administrative Studies.

Once more, I was confronted with an extremely difficult decision. Should I stay at the Ontario Arts Council, or should I go to York University? After a great deal of soul-searching, discussion, and debate, I finally decided to go to York University. I did this for a number of reasons. In the first place, I felt I had achieved just about everything I wanted to achieve at the council. Although I had only been there for four years, I had been involved in amassing a great deal of information about the contributions the arts make to society and had participated actively in the development of a rationale for the arts. I had also participated in many other activities and projects of crucial importance to the council, such as the Ontario Theatre Study, the creation and administration of the council's Centre for Arts Research in Education, writing the five-year plan for the development of the council, and many others.

I had also become deeply interested in, and committed to, training arts administrators at this time, especially as a result of my involvement in the Ontario Theatre Study. I was keen to see a major breakthrough in this area, and thought York University was the ideal place to realize it. I was convinced that the lack of qualified arts administrators would be a serious drawback to the development of the arts in Ontario and elsewhere in the world in the years and decades ahead. Undoubtedly this problem would exist as long as training programs for arts administrators were not available in academic institutions.

My interest in arts and cultural policies was also escalating rapidly at this time, so much so that I felt the position at York University would provide me with a perfect opportunity to delve much more deeply into this area. I sensed that the formulation and implementation of arts and cultural policies possessed the potential to draw governments more fully and forcefully into the development and funding of the arts and culture, primarily because "policy" was a word — and a process and activity — that governments, politicians, and civil servants understood and worked with on a daily basis. I hoped that development of sustainable arts and cultural policies would eventually provide an alternative to having to make the case for the arts (and later culture) on purely or primarily economic grounds.

Finally, I missed teaching and academic life very much, and was anxious to return to the classroom to discuss ideas about the development and administration of the arts and arts and cultural policies with students. This was reinforced by the fact that I had played a major role in bringing the arts administration program into existence and felt a strong personal commitment and professional obligation to be actively engaged in its future development.

Nevertheless, the decision to leave the council was not made without a great deal of pain and remorse. I was very committed to the work of the council and had cultivated many wonderful friendships there. Moreover, I was deeply indebted to the council for giving me an opportunity to commence my career in the arts when I didn't know where to go or what else to do. Regardless of how difficult the decision was, however, I mustered up all my courage and left the council in 1970.

This was an auspicious time to be assuming the duties as director of the Program in Arts Administration at York University. A number of events were happening at the time that were destined to have a profound effect on the development of the arts and culture in general, as well as the articulation of Canadian and international arts and cultural policies in particular.

In Canada, Gérard Pelletier, secretary of state in the federal cabinet and a close friend of Prime Minister Pierre Elliott Trudeau, made a seminal speech in 1970 on Canadian cultural policy to the Canadian Conference of the Arts. Not only did it provide the foundation for many developments that took place in the arts and culture at the national level and throughout the country over the next decade, but also it had a profound effect on me because Pelletier declared in his speech that "*cultural policy is nothing more or less than a plan for civilization.*" This statement resonated very strongly with me because I was searching for a broader and more inspiring way of looking at and thinking about culture in general and cultural policy in particular and Pelletier's statement provided it.

Nevertheless, it was at the international level that 1970 proved to be a particularly historic time as far as arts and cultural policy were concerned. For it was during this year that UNESCO convened the first world conference on cultural policy. For the first time in history, the Intergovernmental Conference on Institutional, Administrative, and Financial Aspects of Cultural Policies brought together people from the various governments of the world who were responsible for culture to discuss cultural matters. And what better place to convene this historic conference than Venice, which was universally recognized and embraced as one of the most outstanding cultural accomplishments in the world and a universal icon.

I have been told by people in the know that in order to convene and successfully conduct this conference, UNESCO had to obtain prior agreement from its member states that their representatives would abstain from discussing the meaning of the term culture for fear that the conference would degenerate into a vicious semantic debate. This was because there was (and still is) an enormous amount of confusion and controversy over the nature and meaning of culture.

This had been made abundantly clear in 1965 when two very distinguished American anthropologists, Alfred Kroeber and Clyde Kluckhohn, published a book called *Culture: A Critical Review of Concepts and Definition* that revealed that there were over 150 different perceptions and definitions of culture in use throughout the world. Perhaps this is why Raymond Williams, a very distinguished British cultural scholar, claimed a few years later that culture is one of the two or three most difficult words in the English language. While I didn't know it at the time, I would spend much of the rest of my life endeavouring to come to grips with this problem, largely in order to evolve a way of thinking about and understanding culture that was consistent with reality and the way culture and cultures manifest themselves in the world in fact.

But back to the Venice conference. As it turned out, the conference was a huge success, largely because people abstained from discussing the nature and meaning of culture and got on with the business of determining how culture should be dealt with in a governmental and public sense. While some delegates had reservations about whether governments should be involved in culture at all, what resulted in the end was a total endorsement and virtually unanimous agreement that every government in the world has a major responsibility for culture in general and cultural development and policy in particular. At long last, it was no longer a question of whether governments should be involved in the cultural affairs of countries, but rather what form this involvement should take.

This was the international and Canadian situation when I went to York University in the fall of 1970. I couldn't have been more excited, despite the fact that the training of arts administrators was non-existent in academic institutions at the time. There were a few "practical programs" in existence, but they were not academic or comprehensive in character. In England, for instance, the Arts Council of Great Britain was providing a program for practitioners in the field. In the United States, Yale University was offering a course in theatre management for its drama students; Harvard University had commenced a "summer institute" for practicing arts administrators based largely on the case method; and the University of Wisconsin had a student taking a Ph.D. in arts administration, but this was a unique situation achieved by combining a number of existing courses in the arts and business management with a thesis on an arts administration subject.

However, there were no academic programs in existence anywhere in the world at the time, with the exception of the program at York University and a similar program that was just beginning at the University of California at Los Angeles (UCLA). Interestingly, both programs were provided at the graduate level – this had been a major recommendation of the *Ontario Theatre Study Report* – although the program at York was designed to give equal attention to arts and cultural policy as well as arts administration, whereas the UCLA program was more specifically designed to focus on arts management. Of the hundreds of programs that have been created throughout the world in this area since the creation of the York and UCLA programs, most have both an arts administration component and an arts and cultural policy component like the York program.

Since arts administration was in a very embryonic state of development in the early 1970s, building the program at York University was fraught with difficulties from the outset. There were no models or prototypes to look to for guidance, and no precedents or historical experiences to fall back on. Moreover, there were almost no reading materials available for students, thereby making it essential to create virtually everything from scratch if the program was to be successful. This meant tracking down information from a variety of sources, creating a library of whatever reading materials were available, and undertaking a great deal of original research. It also meant finding first-class students, producing and distributing a great deal of promotional and informational literature, and raising funds for various activities.

Finding first-class students was a perpetual problem, especially as it was difficult to know where to find them. In some cases, they came from the arts, either because they wanted to have careers in the arts and decided to give arts administration a try, or because they had decided that they were unable to make it as professional artists but desperately wanted to stay in the artistic field. In other cases, they came from business, or some other area within the Faculty of Administrative Studies. Most of these students were either tired of business or didn't find business administration attractive and decided that a career in arts administration might provide a more exciting and viable alternative.

Fortunately, all the students who enrolled in the program in the early years were outstanding, thereby giving the program a terrific boost when it needed it the most. Many had been waiting for a program like this to come into existence and felt very fortunate when one had finally been established. All these students went on to have highly successful careers in arts administration and make valuable contributions to the field after they graduated. No matter where they came from or where they ended up, however, I always made a point of stressing the fact that arts administration is a very difficult profession. It would take a great deal of fortitude and persistence on their part to be successful in a field that was known for its low salaries, poor working conditions, non-existent fringe benefits, and few if any kudos for a great deal of hard work and long hours. This was because most of the recognition and attention went to the artists, not the administrators.

There was another difficult problem that had to be faced in the early years. There was considerable resistance to the program from people working in the field. In some cases, this was because they thought arts managers and administrators were born and not made, and therefore could not be trained in academic institutions. In other cases, it was because they felt arts administration was very different than business administration, and it was not a good idea for students in arts administration programs to be taught by business professors who were probably unaware of the intricacies and complexities of arts administration and insensitive to the needs of artists and arts organizations. This problem was compounded by the fact that students who graduated from the program received a Masters of *Business* Administration (MBA) with a concentration in arts administration, not a Masters of *Arts* Administration.

Concerns like this had to be taken very seriously because the success of the program in the early years depended on graduates getting jobs in the field once they graduated. As a result, the program was deliberately designed from the outset to provide students with practical experience in arts organizations in addition to their academic studies at the university, thereby making sure that they were exposed to the real problems artists, arts organizations, and arts administrators face. This was achieved by making internships in arts organizations compulsory between the first and second years of the program in order to receive the degree.

Of all the problems the program encountered in the early years, none was more difficult than developing an effective slate of courses in arts administration. In addition to the courses offered in the Faculty of Administrative Studies that all arts administration students were required to take – most notably accounting, finance, quantitative methods, organizational behaviour, and so forth – other courses had to be created from scratch to meet the specific needs of the program. Included here were four "core courses" that all arts administration students were compelled to take. They were Marketing the Arts, Legal Aspects of the Arts, Management of Cultural Resources, and Canadian and International Cultural Policy. Brian Dixon taught the course on Marketing the Arts, Donald Farber taught the course on Legal Aspects of the Arts, and I taught the two remaining courses. We had all worked in the arts and had close connections to many people in the field. Farber was an "arts lawyer" from New York who commuted to Toronto and the university once a week to teach his course, Dixon was a sculptor who worked closely with people at the Canadian Theatre Centre in addition to being a professor of marketing in the Faculty of Administrative Studies, and I had worked at the Ontario Arts Council.

As stated earlier, finding suitable reading materials for the core courses was a constant problem. Since virtually nothing had been written about the management of cultural resources, I had to rely on managers from the field coming to the university to provide some "course content" for that course. I myself had no experience in the management of theatre and dance companies, symphony orchestras, art galleries, and museums – and only limited experience in the management of arts councils – and therefore had to depend on friends, former colleagues, and people from the field to expose students to the rudiments, principles, and practicalities of arts administration in this area.

Things were somewhat better with respect to the course I taught on cultural policy. I was fortunate to have some booklets to give to the students on cultural policies for Great Britain, France, Czechoslovakia,

Japan, the USSR, and the United States that had been written for UNESCO's *Series of Studies and Documents on Cultural Policies for Member States*. Although they were only thirty or forty pages in length, I was delighted to have them. You can imagine my surprise when the students reacted to these booklets with what can only be described as incredulity. They were used to having textbooks running three or four hundred pages in length for other courses.

While the lack of suitable reading material was a perpetual problem, research fared much better. This was due to the fact that we were able to secure a grant of $40,000 from the Donner Canadian Foundation to underwrite the cost of a series of research studies on the administration of the arts and the formulation and implementation of arts and cultural policies. Included among these research studies were *Wooden Pennies: A Report on Cultural Funding Patterns in Canada*; *Who's Afraid of Canadian Culture: Report of a Study on the Diffusion of the Performing and Exhibiting Arts in Canada*; and *International Cultural Policy*. A fourth study — *Subsidy Patterns for the Performing Arts in Canada* — resulted from a commission the program received from the Canada Council. These studies were very useful in developing the core courses as well as for people working in the field. They were filled with valuable information on how the performing and exhibiting arts were funded at the municipal, provincial, and national level in Canada, how the arts were evolving across the country in response to a variety of touring and outreach requirements, and how Canada and other countries compared with respect to the formulation and implementation of arts and cultural policies.

As my work at the university intensified, I began to understand why arts administration and the training of arts administrators are so difficult. There are two major problems here that do not exist in most other fields at all, or do not exist to the same extent. The first emanates from the fact that there are two very different value systems at work in the arts; and the second from the fact that the arts, because they are labour-intensive rather than capital-intensive, can't take advantage of technological gains in the way most other fields can.

These two problems, and many others, were discussed at length at a Meeting of Experts on the Training of Arts Administrators and Cultural Activities Organizers in Europe that I attended in Amsterdam in 1971. The meeting was organized by UNESCO in preparation for the Intergovernmental Conference on Cultural Policies in Europe that took place in Helsinki in 1972. This was the follow-up to the historic Venice conference in 1970. Having convened that global conference on cultural policies first, UNESCO decided to divide the world up into parts and hold major conferences in each region, starting with Europe.

Although I was no "expert in arts administration," I was asked to be rapporteur for the aforementioned meeting, probably because I was involved in the development of one of the first academic programs in arts administration in the world, if not *the* first. The meeting provided an opportunity to talk about a whole series of problems related to the training of arts administrators and also to consider the different challenges arts administrators face in various types of institutions, such as art galleries, museums, theatre and dance companies, symphony orchestras, arts councils, service organizations, media agencies, governments, and so forth.

The meeting also provided an opportunity to talk about a group of people who are similar to arts administrators in some respects but different in others. Called *cultural animateurs* by the French – in English we would say "cultural animators" or, more likely, "cultural activities organizers" – these are people who are able to go into communities, get various types of artistic activities and experiences started, and get many people involved in the process. We have all seen people like this at work and they never cease to amaze us. They usually possess some basic artistic, administrative, and organizational skills, but much more importantly, they are able to "turn people on" and get them actively involved as participants rather than spectators. While the Program in Arts Administration at York University was not involved in training people of this type, I remember thinking that the world would benefit immensely from having many more cultural animators, especially if the arts and culture are to flourish in the future.

Not long after attending the UNESCO meeting in Amsterdam, I was asked to be the "general rapporteur" for another major event that had a direct bearing on the development of the arts and my work at York University. It was called Direction Canada. It was organized by the Canadian Conference of the Arts, and involved four regional conferences across Canada in 1972 and culminated with a national conference in Ottawa in 1973.

Over 2,000 people concerned about the arts – actors, painters, musicians, filmmakers, broadcasters, architects, arts administrators, corporate executives, citizens, and so forth – took part in this remarkable event. When I pulled all the recommendations emanating from the regional conferences together, classified them according to subject matter, and ranked them in order of priority, they produced a powerful statement of key priorities for the development of the arts in Canada in the decades to follow. In order of importance, these priorities were:

- to improve the status of artists;
- to increase funding for cultural development;
- to decentralize activity and policy;
- to improve cultural education;
- to democratize opportunities for exposure and participation;
- to distribute more information on domestic and international activities;
- to increase media support for cultural development; and
- to improve the administration of cultural resources.

When I wrote the final report on the regional conferences in preparation for the national conference in Ottawa – the report was titled *Direction Canada: A Declaration of Canadian Cultural Concern* – many government officials who attended the national conference expressed their displeasure with the report. There were two reasons for this. In the first place, most of the officials who attended the national conference in Ottawa had not been at the regional conferences across the country and were unaware of how much hostility there was in Canada's arts community over lack of public support for the arts. In the second place, most government officials saw the role of government in the development of the arts in Canada in a very different light than people working in this field. As noted earlier with respect to the intergovernmental conference in Venice, this was a time when most governments were just beginning to get involved in the arts and culture.

As a result, many government officials and politicians attending the conference in Ottawa viewed the arts primarily as "recreational" or "leisure-time" activities, and therefore of secondary rather than primary importance to Canada, Canadians, and Canadian development. They were inclined to think that the arts were doing quite well in terms of government support and that artists and arts organizations should be grateful for the financial assistance they were already receiving. In contrast, most people working in the arts community felt that the arts were of vital importance to the country and its citizenry and were not receiving nearly enough financial support from governments.

I wrote the report from the standpoint of the people who had attended the regional conferences because this is what I had been required to do by the Canadian Conference of the Arts. Not only was the report consistent with what I heard across the country, but also it was consistent with what the large majority of people who attended the regional conferences wanted me to communicate to political officials at the national conference in Ottawa. Despite this, the report did not sit well with many governmental and political officials at the national conference who seemed anxious to "shoot the messenger." As I look back on this experience now, it was clearly a harbinger of things to come, especially when I came to believe that the arts and culture should play a central rather than marginal role in governmental and political affairs.

This was not the only problem I had about this time with governments, politicians, and civil servants when it came to the importance of the arts and culture and governmental and political responsibility for them. In 1971, I had a similar experience when I was commissioned by the Government of British Columbia to undertake a cultural survey of that province on behalf of the government's Centennial Cultural Fund. The fund was established by the government in 1967 as a centennial project to provide support for the development of the arts in all parts of British Columbia.

Rather than providing the fund with a general appropriation out of operating revenues, as was most often the case, the B.C. government decided to create an endowment to provide the monies for the fund. In 1967, it made an initial contribution of $5 million to this endowment and added another $5 million in 1970. Since the fund used the interest on the endowment to provide support for the arts, this meant that roughly $700,000 was available to support all the arts in all parts of British Columbia in 1971. Decisions regarding the distribution of grants from the fund were made by politicians and civic servants in the provincial capital of Victoria, rather than by artists and people working in the arts as was the case for most arts councils in North America.

I felt the amount provided by the B.C. government to support the arts was woefully inadequate and said so in the final report. My thoughts on the matter were not based on wishful thinking, but rather on a careful and intensive assessment of needs as I encountered them during discussions I had with more than 300 people in the arts community over the course of visits to towns and cities all over British Columbia during the summer of 1971. It was the most comprehensive study of the arts ever undertaken in the province, and revealed an appalling lack of support for the many artists, arts organizations, and community arts councils I met with over the course of the study.

In specific terms, I recommended that the government increase the

Centennial Cultural Fund endowment by $5 million a year until the endowment reached a total of $30 million by 1975. In addition, I recommended that a general appropriation be made to the fund of $500,000 a year *out of operating revenues*, thereby ensuring that approximately $4 million a year would be available to support the arts in British Columbia by 1975. I also recommended that an Arts Panel be established of distinguished representatives from the province's arts community to oversee the operations and disbursements of the fund, and that an executive director be appointed to administer the fund on a full-time, professional basis. I felt these recommendations, and others that were contained in the report, were imperative if the needs I discovered across the province were to be met and the government's commitment to the arts was to be established at a level consistent with existing needs and future requirements.

The government responded to these recommendations — and indeed to the entire final report, which was entitled *A Cultural Survey of British Columbia* — by promptly shelving both the recommendations and the report. It was certainly the government's right to do this, as it had commissioned the report in the first place. However, some embarrassing questions began to emerge shortly after the report was turned over to the government. Was the report "too damaging"? "Too revolutionary"? "Too expensive to implement?" These were the tough and demanding questions Max Wyman, culture critic with the *Vancouver Sun*, asked when he mounted a campaign to put pressure on the government to release the report.

Wyman's campaign was eventually successful as pressure mounted steadily in the arts community throughout the province to have the report released. However, this did not happen until the Social Credit government that had commissioned the report was defeated in 1972 and was replaced by an NDP government which released the report in 1973. The new government promised to use the report as a guide to revamping the entire approach to the development of the arts in British Columbia in the years ahead.

Despite the problems I experienced with politicians and civil servants over the role of the arts and culture in society, I found myself getting more and more excited about the potential for governments to become more fully and actively involved in the development of the arts and culture at the community, regional, national, and international level. I was especially excited about the work UNESCO was doing in this area. My interest in its work was piqued by the Venice conference, the meeting in Amsterdam, the Helsinki conference, and the booklets on cultural policy. It was also piqued by the fact that UNESCO was struggling with the belief that culture had a much larger and more forceful role to play in the world than had heretofore been the case. While the bulk of its work was still focused on culture in the narrow sense — specifically the arts, humanities, heritage of history, and what came to be known as the "cultural industries" of publishing, radio, television, film, and sound recording — I was encouraged by the fact that this crucial organization was, like me, searching for a much broader understanding and perception of culture.

I desperately wanted to learn a great deal more about this, since I was beginning to feel that understanding culture in a much more expansive and profound way might enable me to make a stronger case for culture and the central role it is capable of playing in the world.

By this time, the program at York was "fully operational." The four core courses were much more developed than in 1970, several groups of students had graduated from the program and were working in the field, a library of books, articles, and other resource materials on arts administration and cultural policy had been created, and several seminal research studies had been completed and published. Moreover, the program was well respected across Canada and was now warmly accepted by the country's arts community.

But something was definitely lacking in my life in a professional and personal sense. I felt I had to get much more *practical* experience in arts administration and cultural policy than was possible at York University. While opportunities existed to get involved in a number of specific projects in my spare time, such as the UNESCO meeting in Amsterdam, Direction Canada, and the British Columbia report, I felt I would not be able to get enough practical experience in the artistic and cultural field if I remained at the university. The bulk of my work there centred on culture in the narrow, academic sense, rather than the broad, practical, and concrete sense. As a result, I decided to leave York University in 1974 and strike out on my own as a self-employed person. Once again, I had to go through a great deal of soul-searching and agony before making this decision.

Despite this, I felt within myself that the time had come to take the next great "leap of faith" in my journey to learn as much as I could about the arts and culture in general and arts and cultural policy in particular. It certainly was a leap of faith — one that would require a great deal of hard work and courage on my part — because I would be forced to rely on my own resources much more than ever before. Fortunately, I got a wonderful break in this regard when I needed it the most.

CHAPTER FIVE

Striking Out on My Own

Almost ten years had elapsed since I began working in the arts and cultural field. While I had learned an enormous amount at York University and the Ontario Arts Council, it was time to expand my knowledge and understanding of arts administration and cultural policy in a practical sense.

The fact that my wife Nancy was working at the time helped to make the decision to leave York University and strike out on my own easier. However, I no longer had a monthly pay cheque coming in and was compelled to depend much more on my own abilities. This was complicated by the fact that I didn't have to jump out of bed first thing in the morning, didn't have an institution to go to every day, and was not obliged to follow a daily and weekly routine. For the first time in my life, I was totally on my own in a professional sense and accountable to no one but myself. While a friend told me we are not really living until we are in this position — he was an artist — I quickly discovered that self-employment is much more difficult than it appears to be because one has to discipline oneself to a much greater extent, contracts are often sporadic and unpredictable, and payments for work completed are often neglected or delayed.

Shortly after leaving York University, however, I received a letter from Guy Métraux, editor of UNESCO's journal *Cultures*. I had sent Guy an article I had written on the need for a new world order based on culture—"Towards a New World Order: The Age of Culture" — and Guy had written to say that he wanted to publish the article in Volume II, Number 3 of *Cultures* in 1975. I felt very honoured by this, as the article was based on my belief that a major shift was required from a world system based on economics, science, politics, and economically and technologically developed countries, to a system based on culture, the arts, the humanities, ecology, and culturally and humanistically developed countries. Such a shift was necessary in my view in order to improve human welfare, environmental well-being, and global harmony. Since the article had been turned down by a number of journal editors in Canada, I was delighted to learn that it would be published in UNESCO's prestigious journal in English, French, and Spanish, and read by people in many different parts of the world and not just Canada.

Shortly after Guy Métraux accepted the article for publication, another stroke of good luck occurred. I was contacted by another official from UNESCO asking if I would be interested in undertaking an advisory mission to New Zealand. The objective of the mission, which was to be conducted under UNESCO's Programme of Participation in the Activities of Member States, was "to advise the authorities and institutions concerned, and notably the Queen Elizabeth II Arts Council of New Zealand, on the planning and administration of activities in the arts and the training of professional arts administrators and of those involved in administering amateur groups." I had been selected for this mission largely because of my experience at York University and the Ontario Arts Council, thereby confirming the fact that my decision to leave economics and get into the arts was starting to bear some fruit.

As is customary with UNESCO missions, I travelled to Paris after agreeing to undertake the mission to receive the usual briefing at UNESCO headquarters before departing for New Zealand. While I was there, I met with Guy Métraux to discuss the article he had decided to publish. You can imagine how thrilled I was when he told me that Jack Fobes, the deputy director general of UNESCO, had read the article and wanted to meet me when I was in Paris. Guy went on to say that Jack had ordered a special printing of the article for distribution to delegates attending the Round Table on Cultural and Intellectual Cooperation and the New International Economic Order that UNESCO was organizing for 1976.

I was even more surprised when Guy told me that he would like me to write a second article — this time on "The Age of Culture: Prospects and Implications" — for publication in the final issue of *Cultures* in 1975. In retrospect, this confirmation by Métraux and Fobes of the value of my writing on culture proved a defining factor in my life. It convinced me that I should spend the rest of my life trying to broaden and deepen knowledge and understanding of culture in general and cultures in particular, as well as making the case that culture and cultures have a central role to play in global development and human affairs.

Following my meetings with Métraux and Fobes, as well as the briefing at UNESCO headquarters, I set out for New Zealand. Since the trip was a long one — I was traveling halfway around the world and a long way south to boot — I decided to break the trip in Bangkok. Was I ever glad I did! Not only is Bangkok a very beautiful city — one that rivals many of the most beautiful cities in the world, surpassed only by Venice in my view — but also it was the perfect introduction to Asia. I was captivated by the people, architecture, and food I experienced there: the people were among the most beautiful I had ever seen or met; the architecture was exquisite, especially the temples with their conical shapes and golden domes; and the food was simply out of this world. It seemed to me to achieve the per-fect synthesis of Chinese and Indian food — not too hot, not too mild, not too sweet, not too sour — with many indigenous ingredients thrown in for good measure. I mention this because the western world has only begun its love affair with Thai food — indeed all things Thai — having long since enjoyed passionate love affairs with Chinese and Indian food.

When my stay in Bangkok was over, I flew to Sydney, Australia, and then on to Auckland, New Zealand. This experience proved to be a real shock. I knew very little about New Zealand, except what I had learned in school and studied in advance of my mission. In Canada, New Zealand and Australia are talked about in the same breath, largely because they are both Commonwealth countries and are situated in the far south of the Pacific Ocean. As a result, I had the impression that the two countries were almost side-by-side — so close, in fact, that it was possible to sail from Australia to New Zealand on a Sunday afternoon, do a little shopping and sightseeing, and then return home the same day. I was totally mistaken! You can imagine my surprise when I learned that the two countries are more than 2,000 kilometres apart. It took the better part of four hours to fly from Sydney to Auckland.

This made me fully aware of how isolated New Zealand is from the rest of the world, and what a challenge this situation poses for New Zealanders. Virtually every New Zealander I met during the mission asked me if there was some funding program I was aware of that would make it possible to get out of New Zealand for a time. I learned that there are difficult mental and psychological problems to address and overcome when people are living in a country that is isolated from the rest of the world and surrounded by water on all sides.

When I arrived in the capital of New Zealand, Wellington, to begin my mission, I had another shock. By the time my mission commenced, the group that originally requested the mission was out of power at the Queen

Elizabeth II Arts Council, and another group was in control. While this new group had not cancelled the mission, they made it clear from the outset that they were not enthusiastic about it. They felt it was unnecessary, and only grudgingly went along with it in order to avoid damaging New Zealand's reputation with UNESCO. While I did everything in my power to overcome their resistance to the mission — largely by working extremely hard on it and not allowing myself to get caught up in the battles between the two groups — I could never quite shake the feeling that the new regime was only paying lip service to the mission.

Nevertheless, the mission was a real success and accomplished a great deal in the end. Over the course of several months in late 1975, I travelled from the north end of the north island to the south end of the south island and visited virtually every town and city in between, from Kerikeri, Whangarei, and Auckland in the north to Wellington and Nelson in the centre and Christchurch, Queenstown, and Invercargill in the south. I also met with people from every walk of life — actors, musicians, playwrights, arts administrators, businesspeople, politicians, civic servants, mayors, volunteers, and so forth. More than once, I was told that I knew more about New Zealand and New Zealanders as a result of my travels there than New Zealanders knew about themselves and their country.

Since most people were interested in what I had to say about developing the arts in Canada as well as in New Zealand, it wasn't long before I found myself working day and night. During the day, I would meet with representatives from the arts community to discuss their problems and what could be done about them. In the evenings, I was expected to give a talk or speech at a local library, art gallery, museum, or community centre, which was invariably accompanied by a social reception of some type. While this was very exhausting, it was also exhilarating. I soon learned that New Zealanders are highly intelligent, informed, and knowledgeable people. They are keenly interested in other people and other countries, and certainly knew much more about Canada than I knew about New Zealand before my visit. On more than one occasion, I was corrected on something I said about Canada or Canadians. I learned that there is something about being thousands of kilometres away from everybody and everything that sharpens the mind and expands the appetite for knowledge and information about what is going on elsewhere in the world.

I valued these daily and evening meetings with New Zealanders immensely, since they provided me with keen insights into the arts and their administration in every part of that country. They also exposed me to many of the problems people in the arts community there were facing — problems that ranged from insufficient funding and lack of administrative resources to inadequate facilities, low salaries, poor working conditions, and few fringe benefits. These problems were not dissimilar to the problems people in the arts were experiencing in Canada, despite the fact that the two countries were half a world apart.

New Zealand, like Canada, was in the throes of a real renaissance in the arts when I was there. Not only was the number of artists and arts organizations expanding rapidly, but also standards were improving. Many organizations that were amateur or semi-professional only two or three decades earlier had become professional in their artistic and administrative operations. Moreover, symphony orchestras, theatre and dance companies, art galleries, and museums were springing up everywhere. The crafts were also on the move. Indeed, I learned that New Zealand has some of the finest craftspeople and craftwork in the world, especially gold, silver, and leather work. And jade! While much is made of jade from other countries, it pales by comparison to New Zealand jade.

A similar renaissance was occurring in the Maori community and Maori culture. This was especially true for wood carving, weaving, and the construction of carved and decorated meeting houses (*whare whakairo*). Maori songs and dances were also popular, as were Maori get-togethers, regardless of whether they were in "assemblies" (*hui*) or in "funeral gatherings" (*tangi*). Most of these get-togethers were conducted in the traditional style, with ancient customs, habits, and ceremonies strictly observed. Many of these developments were championed by Dame Kiri Te Kanawa and other Maori leaders in the decades to follow.

As my mission progressed, I discovered that there were countless other similarities between Canada and New Zealand. Although Canada is a huge country and New Zealand a small one, both countries share many geographical characteristics. It is not going too far to say that in a geographical sense New Zealand is a miniature replica of Canada in some ways. For instance, both countries have extensive plains — in the case of Canada, the Prairies; in the case of New Zealand, the Canterbury plain. Moreover, both countries have impressive mountain ranges. Canada has its Rocky Mountains and New Zealand has a rugged mountain range running down the spine of the south island around Milford Sound. Furthermore, both countries have a region whose climate is semi-tropical in nature. In Canada, it is the area stretching along the southwest coast of British Columbia, while in New Zealand, it is the area north of Auckland.

And the similarities do not end here. Both Canada and New Zealand have indigenous peoples who inhabited the countries for centuries prior to the arrival of the first Europeans. Moreover, both countries have evolved in economic terms largely through the exploitation and exportation of natural resources and basic staples. For Canada, it is fish, fur, timber, grain, oil, gas, and precious metals; for New Zealand, it is sheep, mutton, wool, gold, and coal. The periods of settlement and conflict are also very similar, with intense European settlement causing major upheavals and numerous conflicts between the European and indigenous peoples. The only difference is that New Zealand did not have a great deal of conflict between *two* European groups — French and English — as Canada did.

Despite the fact that New Zealand and Canada share much in common, I learned a great deal about culture and cultures in the broader, deeper, and more fundamental sense when I was in New Zealand. Whereas much of the knowledge I acquired about this in Europe and Morocco came from general observations, reading, and occasional discussions with local people, in New Zealand this changed dramatically. Suddenly, I had countless opportunities to talk to people at length about their country and their culture, enabling me to learn an enormous amount about the character, circumstances, and details of New Zealand culture in all its various forms and manifestations.

What I discovered was that New Zealand culture is highly creative, self-contained, self-sufficient, and independent. It could scarcely be otherwise. There is something about being so far away from everyone and everything else that makes New Zealanders realize that they cannot depend on anyone or anything else to a great extent. They must take their destiny in their own hands. I don't think I have ever been in a country — or a culture — where this stood out more clearly than in New Zealand. Regardless of whether it was finding the right balance between rural and urban development, establishing a sense of national identity and community pride, preserving cultural roots and traditions, or confronting the future, there was a sense that "going it alone" and "cooperating with one another" were imperative.

When my mission to New Zealand was over, I returned to Canada to write the final report. Shortly after the report was completed and sent to the appropriate authorities at UNESCO headquarters in Paris, I received a call from the secretary-general of the Canadian Commission for UNESCO indicating that the commission would like me to author Canada's contribution to UNESCO's series of *Studies and Documents on Cultural Policies* for member states — the very same series that I used to great advantage several years earlier when I taught at York University.

I eagerly accepted the commission's invitation. Not only did I feel honoured to do so, but the assignment provided an excellent opportunity to delve deeply into Canadian culture. It also provided an opportunity to make a major statement about Canadian cultural policy that would be disseminated to people in Canada and other parts of the world. The resulting publication, *Aspects of Canadian Cultural Policy*, was published by UNESCO in English and French in 1976. The choice of title was deliberate. It was designed to avoid the impression that Canada already had a cultural policy, which was not the case.

I established a broad perspective on Canadian culture at the beginning of the publication. This made it possible to identify some of the most important factors and themes that have dominated Canadian culture over the centuries. Included here were the diversity of regions and people; the dependence of Canadians on natural resources and basic staples such as fish, fur, timber, wheat, oil, and precious metals; the French-English situation; relations with Great Britain, France, and more recently the United States; bilingualism; multiculturalism; and the struggle between the conflicting forces of centralization and decentralization, individualism and collectivism. Following this overview, a framework was established that made it possible to differentiate between the many different perceptions of Canadian culture that exist throughout the country — artistic, humanistic, sociological, anthropological, ecological, and so on — as well as to identify the key players in Canadian cultural policy, namely the cultural community, the political community, and the general public.

With this overview and policy framework in place, it was possible to focus on three areas that were deemed to be most essential in terms of Canadian culture. These were *the arts*, *the mass media*, and *community and citizen initiatives*. The arts' importance stemmed from the fact that most Canadians think of the arts before anything else when they use the term "Canadian culture." Moreover, artists and arts organizations create many of the signs, symbols, myths, and metaphors that are fundamental to Canadian culture. The mass media are important because Canadians have always been very dependent on the media to link this vast country together. And community and citizen initiatives were seen as vital because communities and citizens play a powerful role in all dimensions of Canadian cultural life, to the degree that one Canadian prime minister claimed that the country was nothing less than "a community of communities."

In the final section of the book, I addressed what I felt were the main objectives and priorities that should govern Canadian cultural policy. These included high standards of creation and performance; equal access to opportunities; maximum participation in the process; creation of an indigenous rather than imported culture; increased domestic and international content; and adequate funding for Canada's future cultural development.

The publication ended with a statement that was telling in terms of how I was beginning to view culture and its relationship to economics, economies, and development. This statement went to the heart and soul of what I felt culture, cultural policy, and cultural development were all about, as well as why they were more important than economics, economies, and economic development. Little did I know that years later I would write an entire book on economics and culture and the relationship between them. However, here is how the UNESCO book ended:

> In the past, culture has been viewed largely as an extension of the economy. For the future, it may prove more profitable to treat a country's economy as an extension of its culture. Surely it is the culture of a country which determines the values, aspirations, hopes, dreams, and even the occupations of its citizens. . . . As soon as cultural policy is defined as an integrative process, it is immediately apparent that cultural development no longer constitutes an essential component of general development. On the contrary, it constitutes the quintessential essence of all development — the substance which determines both the shape and the structure of society.

Shortly after *Aspects of Canadian Cultural Policy* was published, I found myself getting very interested in communities, and especially in how communities should be viewed, understood, and developed from a cultural perspective.

There were many reasons for my interest in this matter. In the first place, I felt there was a great deal to be learned from culture at the community level that was relevant to culture at the regional, national, and international level. Not only is culture at the community level in many ways a microcosm of culture at these other, larger levels, but also it is more concrete and accessible there.

In the second place, culture as a "way of life" is easier to comprehend, experience, and trace at the community level. This way of life encompasses all the various activities in which people are engaged to form an organic and integrated whole. While culture in this sense can be felt at every level – unfortunately it is never possible to actually "see" culture in this way because of its infinite complexity and diversity – it is most apparent at the community level. There is an overall "way of life" or "organic and integrated whole" that exists in every community in the world that has a great deal to do with understanding what communities are all about when they are stripped to their essence and compared.

In the third place, communities were growing rapidly in importance all over the world and were obviously destined to play a very powerful role in the world of the future. This was true not only of colossal cities like London, Paris, New York, Hong Kong, Mexico City, Shanghai, and Istanbul, but also for countless smaller cities and towns.

Fourthly, culture was beginning to play a much more important role in communities and community development than it did in the past. I felt this required study, analysis, and documentation, as well as the creation of methods and techniques that could deal effectively with communities from a cultural and not just an economic or political perspective. What was needed more than anything else, in my view, was a *cultural* approach to community development, as well as the creation of an effective methodology that could focus on the way communities can be developed in a comprehensive, holistic sense.

Finally, my travels had convinced me that all communities in the world make cultural statements that vary greatly, primarily because they are based on different worldviews, values, beliefs, traditions, and customs. I found these "cultural statements" fascinating, and wanted to learn more about this.

Given this rapidly escalating interest in communities and community cultural development, I began to wonder if there was an institution in Canada that might also be interested in this matter. I immediately thought of the Ontario Ministry of Culture and Recreation. It had been created in 1974 to stimulate cultural and recreational development throughout the province and a significant part of its mandate involved development at the community or local level. So I decided to get in touch with authorities at the ministry to see if they might be interested in commissioning me to undertake a major project in this area.

As it turned out, they were! After a great deal of discussion and debate, the ministry commissioned me to undertake a highly exploratory study of community cultural development in Ontario. Since little was known about this topic at the time, we decided that what was required most was the creation of a methodology for community cultural development. It was felt that this methodology would be created most effectively by undertaking a series of "cultural probes" into several communities in the province.

Four communities were selected for this purpose. They were Don Vale and High Park in Toronto, and Hespeler and Markham in southern Ontario. They were selected because they represented different aspects of community life, living, and development. Don Vale and High Park, for example, were representative of life in large urban centres, although Don Vale was a newly emerging urban area and High Park was a more traditional area. In contrast, Hespeler and Markham were more representative of life in smaller, more distant communities. Nevertheless, there were some basic differences between these two communities that we felt were worth exploring in detail. For instance, Markham was typical of quasi-rural communities that were growing rapidly and quickly becoming urbanized. Located on the outskirts of Toronto, it was situated where rural and urban development were coming together, with new subdivisions on one side and farms on the other, thus posing difficult problems for municipal planners and policy-makers. Hespeler, on the other hand, was more typical of communities that were predominantly rural in character.

Through the cultural probes that were conducted in these four communities, a number of "strands" were identified and woven together to form the basis for a general methodology for community cultural development. Included among these strands were sensory profiles of the various sights, sounds, smells, textures, and tastes of communities; environmental and historical profiles that depicted different topographical, chronological, and ecological features; inventories of community cultural resources; maps, walks, and tours of many diverse types; photographs and pictures of unique features of community cultural life; itineraries of daily and weekly events and activities; and citizens' likes and dislikes of their communities.

What lay at the heart of this methodology was the community's *culturescape* or *cultural statement of itself*. Needless to say, this concept had an intimate connection with the notions of "landscape" and "soundscape." Whereas a landscape is a visual exposition of the many different natural and man-made features of an environment and a soundscape is an aural exposition of an environment's many different sounds, a culturescape is an exposition of *all* the different features — natural, historical, sensorial, social, economic, political, aesthetic, human, and so forth — of an environment. It is a community assaulted by all human faculties in concert – the infinite panorama of sights, sounds, smells, textures, tastes, institutions, events, activities, and historical and environmental features that exist in every community and constitute the core ingredients of community cultural life.

Landscapes and soundscapes cut down *into* communities. They are discrete notions designed to look at communities through the vertical lens of specialization. In contrast, culturescapes cut *across* communities. They are integrative notions designed to look at communities through the horizontal lens of holism. Whereas landscapes and soundscapes reveal similar features of community life, culturescapes reveal different features. They are structured to bring things together, not set things apart.

As the project for the Ministry of Culture and Recreation evolved and the culturescape methodology began to take shape, some key questions started to emerge: Should communities develop culturescapes or cultural statements of themselves? If so, what form should these culturescapes or cultural statements take? Where should these culturescapes or cultural statements be located? And what contributions can citizens make to this process?

Clearly every community has a great deal to gain from developing a culturescape or cultural statement of itself. For every community is like a shattered mirror. Every citizen possesses a piece large enough to see his or her own reflection; however, no citizen has a piece large enough to see the community *as a whole*. As a result, the culturescape is a tool for putting the shattered mirror of the community back together again. It is the glue needed to bind communities together and give them substance, character, identity, and solidarity in space and time.

Every citizen possesses something of value to contribute to the culturescape process. It may be information about a community's diverse features – environmental, social, economic, political, artistic, recreational, and the like. It may be objects – old photographs, artifacts, tapes of oral histories, stories, antiques, maps, records, or other memorabilia of local and historical interest. It may be itemized itineraries of daily or weekly events. Or it may be listings of people's likes and dislikes about their community.

These things can be pulled together, classified, and choreographed in different ways to produce different results. For example, information on the diverse features of a community can be classified according to the cultural area it represents – economic, social, educational, political, environmental, aesthetic, scientific, technological, and so forth — and used to prepare inventories of community cultural resources. These inventories can be useful in identifying gaps in a community's cultural resources, or as the foundation for time-budget studies, opinion polls, and attitudinal surveys. This information can also be used to prepare maps, tours, itineraries, exchanges, and probes into different facets of community life which may be helpful for planning purposes. Or it can be used to assemble citizens' impressions of the aesthetic state of communities, or the things they like most and least about their communities. It all depends on the task at hand and the nature of the information, objects, and artifacts collected.

When all this activity is added up, the most important factor may still be missing. This is a central place where citizens can bring their contributions, acquire information that has been orchestrated in different ways to produce different results, and become actively engaged in the planning and future development of their communities as dynamic and organic wholes. This makes it essential to create *community culturescape centres* that are devoted to the collection and presentation of all the most vital information about communities. When this happens, citizens will have an opportunity to weigh for themselves the costs and benefits of various courses of action. They will also have the means to express their concerns over certain types of developments, as well as possess the tools that are needed to participate actively in the process of community decision-making and change. This should help to ensure that community cultural development is shaped by citizens and community groups and not merely politicians, planners, bureaucrats, developers, and special interest groups.

If it is not possible to have a separate culturescape centre, space in a museum, art gallery, library, arts centre, or community hall should be provided for this purpose. However, given the enormous importance of a community's culturescape to the overall cultural development of the community, an independent home at or near the centre of the community is preferable, even if it is not specifically designed or created for this purpose. A deserted factory, an old warehouse, an abandoned building, a large, boarded-up shed, or a dilapidated railway station could all serve as ideal homes for piecing together the community's culturescape or cultural statement of itself.

When the project was completed, it was documented in detail in a final report — *Towards an Ontario Culturescape: A Probe into Community Cultural Development in the Province of Ontario* — and turned over to the Ministry of Culture and Recreation in 1976. Two additional publications resulted from the project. The first was a publication called *Explorations in Culturescapes: A Cultural Approach to Community Development*. It was published by the ministry in 1977 and made available through the Government of Ontario's bookstore in Toronto. The second was an article, "The Culturescape: Self-Awareness of Communities," that was written for UNESCO's *Cultures* and published in 1978. It described the culturescape process and methodology in detail and was designed to show their relevance for communities in all parts of the world.

Shortly after the culturescape project was completed, I received another letter from authorities at UNESCO. They were looking for someone to undertake an advisory mission to Sierra Leone to advise officials at that country's Ministry of Tourism and Cultural Affairs on cultural development, policy, planning, and administration. So by September 1976, once again I found myself packing my bags and heading off to UNESCO headquarters in Paris for the usual briefing before going to Sierra Leone.

This mission to Sierra Leone was very different — and much more difficult — than the one to New Zealand. For the first time in my life I was in a country where virtually everyone was a different skin colour than I was. While I found the experience exhilarating and learned a great deal when I was there, it was not without its problems because of major differences in worldviews, values, ways of life, and approaches to cultural development in general and the conduct of projects and meetings in particular.

Take meetings, for example. I was used to meetings that started on time, ended on time, and took place largely in boardrooms and conference rooms. These things seldom happened in Sierra Leone, as I discovered soon after my arrival. More often than not, people would arrive late for meetings, come and go frequently during meetings, leave early, and were clearly uncomfortable sitting in boardrooms and meeting rooms. I soon realized that the only way I could get everyone together at one time — and in one place — was when we were travelling in taxi cabs and buses from one location to another. So this is what we often did.

I also found it difficult to position myself properly for this mission. I soon realized that there was a real ambivalence towards westerners and the west generally among some of the people who worked at the Ministry of Tourism and Cultural Affairs. On the one hand, they admired the west and westerners for everything they had accomplished. On the other hand, they were suspicious of the west and westerners because of what they had done in Africa, especially in terms of how they had imposed their values and beliefs on many aspects of African life.

While it helped that I was from a "colonized country," and could identify with their concerns and frustrations with respect to British and American domination, I was nevertheless viewed by some people at the ministry, as well as in the cultural community, with a certain amount of mistrust. This was despite the fact that the last thing I wanted to do was impose on them my own views and thoughts on cultural development.

I desperately wanted to learn as much as I could about *their* thoughts and ideas on cultural development, since it was their country, culture, and way of life we were there to address. As a result, I kept saying, "Tell me how you would like *your* culture to be developed and I will tell you what I can do to assist you in this process based on my experiences in the cultural field." This caused a certain amount of consternation among some authorities at the ministry because they had applied to UNESCO to get an "expert" in cultural development to advise *them*. However, I persisted. Finally, it paid off. By constantly holding back and asking them how they would like to see their culture develop, I found that people started to come forward with interesting ideas of their own, rather than latching on to ideas that had been shaped in an entirely different cultural context or milieu.

The problems I encountered in Sierra Leone were very different than those New Zealand faced. By and large, the problems I encountered in New Zealand were similar to the ones I encountered in Canada: New Zealanders wanted to develop a group of highly professional artists and arts organizations that could perform and exhibit in different parts of the country on a sustained basis. While there was some interest in doing this in Sierra Leone, most people saw such a goal as an example of western cultural development and therefore a form of cultural imperialism. Generally speaking, there was much more interest in developing organizations that were indigenous rather than imported or imitative, and therefore more characteristic of African culture and especially Sierra Leonean culture.

A good example of this was the development of museums in Sierra Leone. Prior to my mission, a consultant from a western country had been sent to Sierra Leone to undertake an assessment of museums there and make recommendations concerning their future development and directions. Among many things, he recommended the creation of a "national museum of Sierra Leone" in Freetown, the country's capital. This museum would collect artifacts from all over the country to exhibit. While this proposal was very much in keeping with the western approach to cultural development in general and museum development in particular, many of the authorities with whom I spoke during the mission were strongly opposed to this plan. They believed that there was an intimate connection between an artifact and the environment in which it had been created. Consequently, any uprooting of objects from their original environments was deemed to be sacrilegious. This led to many discussions and debates about the differences between "western culture" and "African culture," as well as the implications of such differences for cultural development in Sierra Leone and generally throughout Africa.

Not long after my mission to Sierra Leone began, it became apparent that time did not permit intensive discussions with authorities at the Ministry of Tourism and Cultural Affairs and in the cultural community in Freetown, as well as with "the promoters and custodians of culture" – primarily the paramount chiefs – in the provinces. After a great deal of discussion, it was decided that my time was better spent working with officials at the ministry and elsewhere in Freetown to create a "cultural development plan for Sierra Leone," rather than undertaking a superficial treatment of both areas and dealing with neither in any real depth.

Through these in-depth discussions, as well as perusal of many documents and reports, we were able to piece together such a cultural development plan. Included among the main objectives of the plan were: achievement of national unity and identity through recognition of cultural diversity; attainment of a high level of cultural awareness among the citizenry through the harmonization and co-ordination of cultural policies and rehabilitation of cultural practices; realization of high standards of aesthetic excellence and economic viability for all cultural activities; development of a cultural system capable of protecting Sierra Leone's cultural heritage; respect for the cultural initiatives of citizens and making culture an integral part of national development; creation of domestic and international exchanges between the different peoples of Sierra Leone and between Sierra Leone and the rest of the world; and evolution of a unique culture that blends traditional, modern, African, and international elements together, but does so in a way that meets the needs and aspirations of the various peoples of Sierra Leone and the country as a whole.

In order to achieve these objectives, a number of programs were recommended. Included here were cultural education for the general public; a National Arts and Crafts Institute to train artists and craftspeople; establishment of a training program for arts administrators and cultural animators at the Institute for African Studies at Fourah Bay College in

Freetown; development of "cultural villages" devoted to solving the production, distribution, and consumption problems of creative workers; establishment of cultural centers in Freetown, Makeni, Bo, and Kenema; formation of a travelling cultural troupe; preparation of an inventory of cultural resources and a cultural atlas for Sierra Leone; key research studies and marketing initiatives; and creation of a National Media Development Fund to finance developments in publishing, radio, television, and film. Also included were programs to increase the number of cultural agreements between Sierra Leone and other countries; to make effective use of the National Dance Troupe to promote Sierra Leone's cultural interests at home and abroad; and to realize a much greater role for Sierra Leone in African cultural development through the affairs of the African Cultural Institute in Senegal and the harmonization of cultural policies throughout Africa.

Major changes were also recommended in the structure and functioning of the Ministry of Tourism and Cultural Affairs, the creation of a Sierra Leone Cultural Council as a quasi-governmental agency to promote the interests of the cultural community and coordinate the work of the various cultural associations in Sierra Leone, and a major increase in funding for cultural development. This last recommendation was particularly important, as the success of any plan depends on the financial and human resources provided for its implementation. As a result, year-by-year increases in funding for the component parts of the proposed plan were recommended for the five-year period beginning in 1976 and ending in 1981.

All these recommendations were set out in the final report I submitted to UNESCO after I returned to Canada at the termination of the mission. The report ended with the following appeal for a much greater role for culture in the national development of Sierra Leone:

> Cultural development never takes place in a vacuum or in isolation. This is due to the dynamic character of culture. Whenever there is change in society — or even vocal expression of the need for change — there is also culture. For ultimately, culture is merely a reflection of society's values, customs, habits, mores, and lifestyles. As such, culture acts as a kind of container in its own right — a container within which economic, social, political, environmental, and educational changes are always taking place. In consequence, it is inconceivable to talk about cultural development, and more importantly to plan national develop-

> ment, without taking into account the causes and consequences of cultural development.

In retrospect, this statement turned out to be prophetic, although it was impossible to know this at the time. When my mission was conducted in 1976, Sierra Leone was one of the most peaceful and orderly countries in Africa. While it had experienced its share of ups and downs, conflicts and tensions, and was exceedingly poor, it was one of the most stable countries in Africa, was well respected in other parts of the world, and was a member of the British Commonwealth.

No one could have predicted what happened next. Twenty years later, Sierra Leone was virtually in ruins, largely due to one of the most violent and oppressive civil wars in human history. Few people in the world suffered as much as Sierra Leone's five million inhabitants during this war, which lasted from 1991 to 2002. It drew fighters from all over West Africa, especially Liberia, and was one of the most brutal uprisings ever experienced in this region. The Revolutionary United Front, which claimed its goal was to liberate the people of Sierra Leone from a corrupt government, initiated the war by battling to take control of the diamond fields in eastern Sierra Leone. What made this war especially brutal was the fact that many of the fighters in the Revolutionary United Front were kidnapped children who were often forced to execute even their own parents as a sign of bravery and courage. They often went into battle under the influence of drugs, chopped off people's hands, legs, feet, arms, and ears, and mutilated the bodies of their opponents. Pro-government "hunting societies" responded in kind, setting the stage for an all-out blood bath before the war was brought to a halt by Nigerian-led military forces in 1998 and a United Nations peacekeeping force in the years that followed.

I found it hard to believe that such a war could ever take place given the state of affairs in Sierra Leone when I was there. But it taught me a valuable lesson. Regardless of how calm things appear on the surface and how settled things may be at any particular time, the potential for war, violence, and bloodshed is always present. There are often tensions smouldering under the surface that must be taken into account if the positive and negative sides of human nature and human life — and culture, cultures, and cultural development — are to be understood and dealt with effectively.

What happened in Sierra Leone could happen anywhere in the world at any time when people come from different ethnic groups, tribes, religious sects, and cultural backgrounds, or they lack the opportunities required for a decent standard of living and enjoyable quality of life. Subsequent developments in Afghanistan, Iraq, Syria, the Middle East generally, North Africa, and elsewhere in the world bear this out. In the case of Sierra Leone, this has been compounded by the severe Ebola outbreak that has devastated the country and its population and caused incredible suffering and hardship throughout 2014 with no end in sight.

My mission in Sierra Leone also taught me other valuable lessons, especially with respect to human interaction and communications. On the last day of the mission, authorities at the Ministry of Tourism and Cultural Affairs decided to throw a big party for me. I had the temerity to ask during the party how they thought the mission went. Very well in all respects except one was their reply. When I asked what this was, they laughed and said it was my obsession with punctuality and wanting to start and end meetings on time! However, we parted company on the best of terms, so much so that I was able to arrange for one of the officials I had worked closely with at the ministry to be awarded a UNESCO fellowship to come to Canada after my mission concluded in Sierra Leone to see how cultural development, policy, and administration were handled in Canada.

The official's name was Edward (Eddie) Kagbo. I arranged for him to stay with Nancy and myself for two weeks in Toronto, and then travel to Ottawa, Winnipeg, and a few other places in the country. During his time in Toronto, I arranged for him to spend a week at the Ontario Arts Council and a week at the Ontario Ministry of Culture and Recreation.

Eddie's stay in Toronto turned out to be a fascinating one. He had never been outside Sierra Leone, except for the few days he spent at UNESCO headquarters in Paris receiving his briefing before flying to Toronto. So his reaction to virtually everything he saw and experienced was enthusiastic to say the least: flying over the Atlantic Ocean; seeing snow for the first time (I believe he arrived in late April when there was still some snow on the ground, although I shudder to think what his reaction would have been like if he had arrived in January or February); travelling on the subway; going to a hockey game; cutting grass with a power lawnmower; and many other things. He marvelled at these things, and all the other technological devices, achievements, and developments he encountered. He would often mutter to himself, "A poto, a poto bonk," or words to this effect. When I asked him what this meant one day, he laughed and said, 'The white man is just the white man."

Nancy and I were intrigued by many things Eddie told us about his life in Sierra Leone, especially as he was the son of a paramount chief. Whenever he came home from a day at the Ontario Arts Council or the Ministry of Culture and Recreation, I would make a special point of asking him what he learned that day. He would usually say he had learned a great deal, and would go on to explain how useful this would be when he returned to Sierra Leone and the Ministry of Tourism and Cultural Affairs. I also asked him if anyone at the Ontario Arts Council or the Ministry of Culture and Recreation had asked him about *his* culture, and how the arts and culture are developed and administered in Sierra Leone. He always said "no" — no one had ever asked him about this. I found this disturbing because I felt people at the arts council and the ministry were missing an excellent opportunity to learn about the development of the arts and culture in a part of the world where activities of this type have been going on for countless centuries. I suspected this failure to ask questions was because these people thought Canada was light years ahead of Africa and Sierra Leone when it came to cultural development, or because they felt people working at Eddie's ministry had nothing to teach them. It was a huge mistake, since Sierra Leone has a rich artistic and cultural tradition dating back thousands of years.

Towards the end of Eddie's fellowship in Toronto, the Ministry of Culture and Recreation happened to be arranging a very special luncheon to honour its minister, Robert Welch, who had guided the ministry through its formative stages of development. As it turned out, Eddie was invited to the luncheon, as was I.

Eddie immediately asked what he should wear to this special function as he felt very honoured to be invited to such a prestigious event. Fortunately, he had brought with him an exquisite, hand-made hat and gown with beautiful designs, colours, and hues, as was befitting the son of a paramount chief. He asked me if I thought it would be proper for him to wear this hat and gown to the luncheon. I assured him it would.

After the lunch was over, a number of people got up to thank Welch for his remarkable accomplishments at the ministry. Someone must have spied Eddie in the audience in his exquisite hat and gown and thought it would be appropriate to ask him to say a few words, since he was from a different part of the world and his time at the ministry was coming to an end. I looked around the room and could see a number of people smiling. They probably thought Eddie would get up, stumble through a few sentences, and sit down. Were they ever surprised! Eddie got up and delivered one of the most passionate and eloquent speeches about the arts and culture and their role in development that I have ever heard. He spoke for about ten minutes, with no notes and no warning. In the process, he put all the other speakers, including the minister, to shame. People at the luncheon simply could not believe that Eddie was capable of getting up and delivering such a remarkable speech. It was so warm, heartfelt, and powerful that it stunned everybody in attendance.

And why not? While most westerners were sitting in front of their television sets becoming couch potatoes, most Africans were sitting on verandahs and porches telling stories. Not only do Africans have an oral tradition dating back countless centuries, but also they get a great deal of experience speaking in public and in groups. Small wonder Eddie was a real orator and had "the gift of the gab," as they say, as well as an ability to get up and speak "off the cuff" that few westerners could match. But I knew this all along. As soon as Eddie heard that I had been successful in arranging a UNESCO fellowship for him in Canada, he immediately started calling me "the architect of his dreams."

Given all the work I was doing for UNESCO travelling to other parts of the world and the various articles I was writing on the role of culture in the world, it is not surprising that I was growing more and more interested in international cultural affairs in general, and international cultural relations in particular.

This interest was also stimulated by two exciting and insightful statements I came across at the time. The first was by Rabindranath Tagore, the great Indian sage, who said, "We must prepare the field for the cooperation of all the cultures of the world where all will give and take from each other. This is the keynote of the coming age." The second was by Paul Braisted, an American expert on international cultural relations, who said, "Cultural cooperation is so directly a national interest that it should furnish the fundamental motivating principle in governmental foreign service, replacing or reordering all lesser motives. It should become the controlling principle in the establishment of new standards of service and fresh criteria of effectiveness."

With statements like this to inspire and motivate me, I began to study what was going on in this area in depth, both in Canada and in other parts of the world. This interest ultimately led to three specific projects. The first was a study of artistic exchanges and cultural agreements between Canada and a number of countries in western and eastern Europe that was facilitated through an Arts Grant I received from the Canada Council in 1977. The other two projects were for Canada's Department of External Affairs, now called the Department of Foreign Affairs, Trade, and Development.

The Arts Grant I received from the Canada Council made it possible to travel to several countries in eastern and western Europe, including Croatia and Serbia – part of Yugoslavia at the time – Bulgaria, Romania, Hungary, Austria, and France to interview individuals engaged in the creation and implementation of artistic exchanges and cultural agreements between Canada and these countries. The study included an examination of many different problems that officials encountered in the signing and execution of cultural exchanges and agreements. It also provided an opportunity to get to know many arts and cultural administrators in these countries and learn a great deal about their cultures and cultural development. This experience was very enriching, since cultural development was very different in eastern as opposed to western European countries, especially with respect to planning, decision-making, and the role of culture in community, regional, national, and international affairs. There was much more interest in eastern European countries in the scientific analysis of culture and a planned approach to cultural development, primarily because those countries were at the time still communist in principle if not always in practice.

The second project involved researching and writing a detailed publication on Canada's international cultural relations for the Department of External Affairs. I felt Canada's relations in this area were extremely important to the country and its citizenry, but were largely ignored because most individuals and organizations in Canada did not have the foggiest idea of what the department was doing in this area. Unfortunately, the department was not "telling its story" and acquainting Canadians with the constructive work it was carrying out in this field.

I decided to go to Ottawa at my own expense to see if I could convince authorities at the Department of External Affairs to hire me to research and write a major document on this subject. I felt such a publication could be used to excellent advantage to let Canadians and people in other parts of the world know in very specific and concrete terms what the department was doing. After numerous rejections and what can only be described as indifference on the part of officials at the department, I finally came across a senior official, Patrick Reid, who felt that the project should go ahead. This decision eventually led to the publication in 1979 (in both English and French) of *Canada's International Cultural Relations*. It was the first comprehensive document ever written and published on Canada's cultural relations with other countries.

The publication began with an in-depth analysis of how France, Great Britain, Germany, and Japan conducted their international cultural relations. These countries were deliberately chosen because they were recognized as the world leaders in this field. Not only had they been conducting international cultural relations for a very long time, but they had a great deal of experience and expertise to pass on to other countries with respect to how relations in this area should be conducted and developed in theoretical and practical terms. This analysis made it possible for me to show how Canada could benefit from international cultural relations in both the general and specific sense, as well as make the case that Canada should be doing much more in this field if it wanted to reap the profuse economic, political, commercial, educational, artistic, and diplomatic benefits that are available from enhancing the country's cultural relations with other countries.

For the purposes of this publication, international cultural relations were defined as the arts, education, the mass media, science, youth, recreation, the environment, sports, and multiculturalism. While this was a much less expansive way of defining international cultural relations — and especially the use of the term "cultural" — than those I was becoming more familiar with and attracted to, it was consistent with the Canadian government's definition, as well as the practice of putting any international relations that didn't fit into other areas into the cultural relations portfolio.

With this definition in place, I created a framework for Canada's international cultural relations that was subdivided into major public and private sector components. This made it possible to examine the historical development and contemporary state of Canada's international cultural relations in both public and private terms, as well as to lay the foundation for the creation of a dynamic and innovative policy for the development of the country's international cultural relations in the future. Included in this policy were a statement of aims and objectives; creation of the necessary infrastructure; examination of federal-provincial relations and relations with Canada's cultural community; marketing of Canadian cultural products aboard; selection of program countries and program repertoire; the need for publicity, promotion, program assessment, and program evaluation; and requisite levels of financial support.

Following a very detailed description and illustrations of the various programs the department was providing in this area, the publication ended with a statement about the importance of international cultural relations for Canada, as well as the need to view the country's international cultural relations in a new light:

> Just as we are beginning to understand the tremendous impact that culture has on our domestic development, so we must learn to understand the enormous influence that cultural relations have on our international development. For only then will we be able to reap the rich harvest which is available from cultural cooperation with the rest of the world.

The third project I embarked upon involved travelling across Canada with a group of officials from the Department of External Affairs in the fall of 1981. The purpose of the trip was to consult with provincial authorities engaged in international cultural relations, as well as to prepare a comprehensive policy statement on cooperation between federal and provincial governments in this area.

The document – entitled *A Working Document on Cooperation Between the Bureau of International Relations of the Department of External Affairs and the Provincial Governments on Canada's International Cultural Relations* – was composed of a series of very specific policy proposals dealing with areas of greatest concern as revealed through the consultative process. Foremost among these areas were the respective roles and responsibilities of the federal and provincial governments; selection criteria; eligibility of applications and applicants for financial support; selection procedures; the planning cycle for international cultural relations in general and bilateral and multilateral talks in particular; the need for an ongoing consultative mechanism and process; information collection and dissemination; long-term planning; funding arrangements and cost sharing commitments; publicity, promotion, and marketing; advisory services; program evaluation; and representation throughout the world.

I learned very quickly how complicated Canada's international cultural relations are, especially when there are major disagreements between the various levels of government over what should be sent abroad, why it should be sent, what individuals, organizations, and events should be brought to Canada from other countries, how activities in this area should be funded, and who has the right to make decisions about Canada's international cultural relations. This final matter was especially important because the federal government has always had a great deal of difficulty in this area, most notably with Quebec but also with the other provinces.

Despite these problems, I enjoyed working on this project very much because it was specific and practical in nature. Not only did it give me an enormous amount of personal satisfaction and professional pride to be involved in this project, but also it provided some relief from all the thought I was giving to trying to figure out what was meant by the evocative but elusive term culture.

There was another project I was involved in at the time that was very close to my heart. It was the international conference I attended in 1980 on "The Future of the Past." It began in Durango, Colorado and ended in Mexico City, and was co-sponsored by the Center for Integrative Studies at the State University of New York in Buffalo, the Center for Southwest Studies at Fort Lewis College in Durango, and the Center for Economic and Social Studies of the Third World in Mexico City. It was held to honour the work of John McHale, the famous futurist, sociologist, and artist who was captivated by the interdependence of the past, the present, and the future.

The conference provided a marvellous opportunity to learn a great deal about how authorities from different cultures and parts of the world viewed the past, and why they felt it exerted such a powerful effect on the present and the future. Included among the participants at the conference were Mochtar Lubis, a well-known journalist and social activist from Indonesia; Jorge Lozoya, academic coordinator for the Centre for Economic and Social Studies of the Third World in Mexico City; Janusz Ziolkowski, director of Cultural Development for UNESCO; Harlan Cleveland, a renowned American diplomat and Director of the Hubert H. Humphrey Institute of Public Affairs at the University of Minnesota; Aklilu Habte, director of education at the World Bank; and Abidin Dino, a Turkish artist. Three of my closest friends were also involved in the conference: Guy Métraux and Jack Fobes, who had worked at UNESCO; and Magda Cordell McHale, the widow of John McHale and a well-known futurist in her own right.

The conference provided me with an opportunity to make a major statement on the importance of interpretations of history in general and the cultural interpretation of history in particular. I was anxious to do this because I believed historical interpretations play a crucial role in determining how the world and world systems function. John McHale summed this up very nicely in his book *The Future of the Future* when he said, "People survive, uniquely, by their capacity to act in the present on the basis of past experiences considered in terms of future consequences."

Marshall McLuhan echoed these sentiments when he said "we see the future through a rear view mirror."

What makes interpretations of history so powerful is the fact that they are concerned with some of humanity's most pressing and profound questions: Where did we come from? Why have we evolved the way we have? Why do we behave the way we do? And perhaps most importantly, where do we go from here?

My own interest in this topic emanated from my belief that the world was securely locked in the economic interpretation of history. This had been true ever since Marx introduced this highly specialized way of looking at history. By the mid-nineteenth century, conditions were ripe for the economic interpretation of history to emerge as the predominant way of looking at the past and shaping the present and the future. The Industrial Revolution had given the world a highly economic and material orientation, and the Scientific Revolution had produced a strong backlash against metaphysics, spiritualism, romanticism, and humanism, thereby paving the way for a much more pragmatic, quantitative, and materialistic approach to life. Under these conditions, it did not take long for the economic interpretation of history to move from the wings to centre stage on the world scene. Although it was greatly simplified and popularized to enhance its mass appeal, it still bore the unmistakable stamp of Marx: the division of human life in general and human needs in particular into economic and non-economic components; the belief that all societies are composed of an economic base and a non-economic superstructure; the assumption that all historical change is the product of economic forces; and the conviction that economic activities should take precedence over all other activities because they are the cause of all other activities. So powerful had this interpretation of history become that it was taken for granted and seldom if ever questioned.

While I recognized that this particular interpretation of history had produced countless benefits, I felt it was fundamentally flawed because economic factors do not determine everything in life. Nor was it advisable to carry the economic interpretation of history forward into the future. I felt irrevocable harm would be done to the natural environment and people's lives if this occurred, primarily because it was encouraging unfettered consumption of the world's resources at an alarming rate and doing an incredible amount of damage to nature, not to mention sanctioning a way of life that was not in the best interests of people or the world in the years and decades ahead.

What was desperately needed in my view was a *cultural interpretation of history* to replace the economic one, since this new interpretation of history would be far more accurate, authentic, and consistent with the real nature of the human condition and global situation. This is because whenever and wherever people get together for the express purpose of living in the world and working out their association with the world, it is culture and cultures they create in the broader, deeper, and more fundamental sense. While economics and economies have played — and will continue to play — an extremely important role in this, culture and cultures in the all-encompassing, holistic sense as "dynamic and organic wholes" or "total ways of life" play the most important role of all. This results from the fact that culture and cultures are made up of many factors — environmental, economic, social, political, religious, recreational, technological, artistic, scientific, educational, and so forth — and not just economic factors. It follows from this that people have a variety of needs that must be attended to if they are to function effectively in society and survive.

Looked at from this perspective, the cultural interpretation of history is not an alternative to the economic interpretation of history; it does not deny the crucial importance of economic factors in the overall scheme of things. Rather, it *incorporates* economics, along with a great deal else, in a much more comprehensive and all-inclusive view of history, life, and the human condition. This is as it should be. For there is not a country, society, or group of people anywhere in the world, or at any time in history, that has preoccupied itself exclusively with economics, economies, and economic factors. While some countries have placed a much higher priority on these factors than others, all countries have endeavoured to address the totality of their needs — non-economic as well as economic — in this holistic sense.

Having expressed my conviction that humanity desperately needs a cultural interpretation of history to replace the economic one, I went on to explore some of the more essential implications and ramifications of this assertion. Particularly important in this regard were the impact a cultural interpretation of history would have on the way we see history, the world, the natural environment, and people's lives, as well as the theory and practice of development. Clearly we would see history and the world very differently than we do at present. Rather than focusing on the growth, development, and interaction of all the various economies of the world, we would concentrate on the expansion, cultivation, and interaction of all the diverse cultures of the world.

Does this not provide a more accurate and authentic view of history and the way the world has evolved to the present point? While we have become accustomed to seeing the world in terms of economies and countless interactions between them, the world is really made up of cultures and myriad interactions and interconnections among them. This is the "real" reality that exists in the world and we will pay a severe price in the future if we do not admit this and deal with the implications and consequences of it.

Nowhere is this more apparent than with respect to the natural environment. A cultural interpretation of history would place a much higher priority on activities like artistic creation, social interaction, spiritual renewal, recreational pursuits, and the like that are low in material inputs and outputs, and place a lower priority on activities like manufacturing, commerce, transportation, and technology that are high in material inputs and outputs. Not only would this have a favourable effect on the natural environment and bring about more effective conservation of the world's scarce resources, but also it would achieve a better balance between the material and non-material dimensions of people's lives.

What is true for the natural environment is also true for the theory and practice of development. Seen from the perspective of a cultural interpretation of history, development would no longer be understood in terms of ranking countries according to the level and rate of their economic growth, the use of economic indicators to measure a country's progress and performance, and the division of the world into unequal parts based on a few highly selective economic criteria. Viewed from a cultural perspective, all countries would be struggling to achieve an effective balance between the material and non-material (or quantitative and qualitative) dimensions of development. Development in this sense is much more an art than a science — an art that is concerned with achieving a judicious balance between all the diverse activities and factors that constitute development and life. Such an understanding of development is necessary to create the conditions for a more sustainable and harmonious world. It is hard to believe that peace and harmony will ever be achieved in the world as long as the economic interpretation of history reigns supreme, and the world is divided into different parts on the basis of a few highly selective and dominant economic criteria. These beliefs, like those of the other delegates, were included in a report, *The Future of the Past: Historical Identity? and Permanence and Change*, that was published shortly after the conference concluded.

While the conference provided me with an opportunity to make a major statement on the need for a cultural interpretation of history in a professional sense, some monumental changes were taking place in my life in a personal sense. A few months prior to attending the conference in the summer of 1980, Nancy and I got married. We had been living together for many years and had come to the conclusion that "tying the knot" was the next logical step in the development of our wonderful relationship together.

Despite exciting events and developments like these, culture was never far from my mind. I had the intuitive feeling that I would spend the rest of my life struggling to understand the complexities and intricacies of culture, as well as making the case that culture has a central rather than marginal role to play in the world. Everything I had done over the last ten years confirmed that this was my principal passion, *raison d'être*, and real mission in life.

There was only one problem. Virtually everything I had learned about culture and cultures up to this point in my life had come through practical experience, primarily as a result of the trips I had taken to other parts of the world, the work I had done for UNESCO and especially the missions in New Zealand and Sierra Leone, and the different projects I had conducted for various agencies and institutions in Canada and elsewhere in the world.

While all this was extremely helpful and extended from the municipal and regional level to the national and international level, I had never taken a course on culture and knew very little about it in the theoretical and scholarly sense. This shortcoming bothered me immensely, as I had come to believe that anyone whose main purpose in life is to deal with culture in depth and the central role it is capable of playing in the world should know far more about this subject than I did. As important as the practical experience was at every level in giving me a solid understanding of culture as a reality, I was beginning to realize that it was necessary to learn far more about the historical development and contemporary character of culture as an idea. I also had to acquaint myself with what generations of cultural scholars had to say about this matter. In order to do this, I had to find a place — and a job — where this goal could be realized.

Fortunately, another stroke of good luck occurred in my journey at just the right time, although it came about in a rather circuitous and unexpected way. At the same time that I was wrestling with the problem of finding a suitable place and job where I could study culture in depth in the theoretical and scholarly sense, a group of professors at Scarborough Campus of the University of Toronto were planning to start a program in arts administration. As fortune would have it, they called me one day to get my thoughts and advice on this matter, which eventually led to the creation of the Cooperative Program in Arts Administration. Shortly after this, I was asked if I would teach the two courses in arts administration and cultural policy that were compulsory for all students in the program, which I agreed to do.

As it turned out, the university was also looking for someone to be the half-time coordinator of this program and wondered if I might be willing to accept this responsibility as well, which I also did. They also happened to be looking for a half-time coordinator for a new Cooperative Program in International Development that was beginning there at the same time. Since I had a significant amount of international experience as a result of my work with UNESCO, and had taught a course on developing countries years earlier at Dalhousie University, they offered me this position as well. Since both positions were half-time, they amounted to the equivalent of a full-time job, which, in addition to the two courses I had agreed to teach in arts administration and cultural policy, meant that I had a job-and-a-half at the university.

While these responsibilities took up a great deal of time, working at the Scarborough campus of the University of Toronto brought with it two great advantages. For the first time in many years, I had a regular job and source of income. This enabled me to assume my family responsibilities effectively, especially as our first daughter, Charlene, was born in August 1982 and Nancy decided to stay home and look after her during her infancy and early years. Moreover, I was working in an institution that turned out to have an incredible collection of books, articles, and other documents dealing with culture, which I discovered soon after I arrived at the university. This was exactly what I needed. At long last, a fundamental gap in my knowledge and understanding of culture was about to come to an end.

CHAPTER SIX
Coming to Grips with Culture

It was wonderful to be back in an academic environment after working on my own for many years. I was especially grateful to be at the University of Toronto, where I had done my undergraduate and graduate work. I was looking forward to my association with students, faculty, and administrative staff immensely.

For some curious reason which I have never been able to understand, I have always preferred jobs where everything has to be created from scratch, rather than jobs where everything has already been done. This was certainly true for both the Cooperative Program in Arts Administration and the Cooperative Program in International Development. Everything had to be created from the beginning, since there was nothing to fall back on and no precedents to look to for guidance. While this did not pose a problem in the academic sense because I had already taught the two courses I was expected to teach, it did pose a problem in the administrative sense as coordinator of two new programs in embryonic stages of development.

Methods, procedures, and systems had to be created that made it possible to recruit students, evaluate applications, help with course selections, monitor academic programs and progress, develop newsletters and promotional materials, speak at high schools and other student gatherings, organize meetings and workshops, create two advisory councils, raise money for scholarships, and find placements for students.

Of these requirements, finding placements for the students was undoubtedly the most difficult. Since both programs were totally unknown in their fields and had no track records, it was difficult to find organizations willing to provide placements. In the case of the international development program, this problem was alleviated somewhat by the fact that the university had received a large grant from CIDA — the

Canadian International Development Agency — to put toward the cost of year-long placements for the students in Africa, Asia, or Latin America during their fourth year in the program. Nevertheless, many international development organizations were reluctant even with this funding to provide placements for the students in those parts of the world due to the high risks and dangers involved. However, finding placements for the students in the arts administration program was equally difficult, since arts organizations were expected to pay the salaries of the students during their placements and most organizations didn't have the funds to do this because they were strapped for funds themselves. It didn't help that the students had little or no experience in arts administration, making the search for placements in this area a perpetual problem.

Nevertheless, the two programs took shape and expanded rapidly. As they became better known, applications started to pour in from all parts of the country, as well as from other parts of the world. Since I established a policy to interview every prospective student, either in person or by telephone if necessary, the evaluative process took a great deal of time to complete. However, this policy paid off in the end. It wasn't long before the two programs were attracting some of the brightest and most capable students in Canada and other countries.

What was true for the interview and assessment process was also true for the creation of the two advisory councils and the quest to raise funds for scholarships. Both activities were very time-consuming, but the results were well worth it. Within a couple of years, strong advisory councils had been created for both programs composed of distinguished professionals in arts administration and international development from Canada and elsewhere in the world. Moreover, thousands of dollars were raised for scholarships, mostly from the Scarborough area. While these scholarships were limited in amount and number, they helped to defray the tuition and living expenses of some students, especially as many came from other parts of Canada and the world and had to live in residence. It was heartwarming to see organizations in Scarborough stepping up to the plate and providing financial assistance for programs in their own community.

While I enjoyed working on both programs immensely, I especially enjoyed working on the Cooperative Program in International Development. I was bowled over by the commitment of the students attracted to this program, which was the first of its type in Canada. Many of the students who applied for admission had some international experience already through organizations such as Canada World Youth, an organization created by Jacques Hébert (a close friend of Prime Minister Trudeau) that was designed to give young people practical experience in Africa, Asia, and Latin America during their late teens or early twenties. I have never encountered students as motivated, dedicated, and idealistic. They were so devoted to international development and creating a better world that their enthusiasm was infectious. It was a privilege to go to work every day and interact with these students, and doing so confirmed for me Confucius's sage advice to "find a job you love and you will never work a day in your life." The desire of the students to learn and their appreciation for what was done for them — and what they were anxious to do for others — were exemplary in every respect.

During the first few years I spent at Scarborough campus, it was impossible to do anything but work on the development of these two new programs. However, once the programs were up and running and things settled down a bit, I found myself once again thinking about culture and my desire to broaden and deepen knowledge and understanding of it in the theoretical and scholarly sense. While my efforts in this area were confined largely to my spare time — of which there was not a lot because I had the equivalent of a job-and-a-half! — I soon realized that I was in an ideal position to take advantage of the remarkable resources that existed at Scarborough campus in this area.

As soon as I began scouring the Bladen Library (which incidentally was named after Vincent Bladen, whose course on The History of Economic Thought I had taken years earlier), I realized that it had an unbelievable collection of books, articles, and other documents dealing with culture as mentioned earlier. For many years, various faculty members there had been teaching courses on different aspects of culture. As a result, the library was well stocked with literature on this subject. I was in "seventh heaven"! Whenever the opportunity presented itself, I headed off to the Bladen Library.

What I discovered immediately was that culture as an idea can be traced back to classical times, thereby making it one of the oldest ideas in the world with a history dating back some two thousand years. Interestingly, culture shares much in common with economics in this respect, since economics as an idea can also be traced back to classical times. Whereas economics as an idea was equated by the Greeks with "household management," however, the Romans associated the idea of culture with the practice of "cultivation." This is because the term "culture" derives from the Latin verb *colo* or *colere*, meaning "to plant," "to till," or "to cultivate." This is the way the great Roman poet and statesman, Cicero, used the term more than twenty centuries ago when he said, "*Cultura anima philosophica est,"* a passage which is usually translated as "Culture is the philosophy — or cultivation — of the soul."

This intimate connection between culture and cultivation shows that there has been a strong bond between culture and the natural environment stretching back to classical times. While this bond has been severed in the modern era, its existence explains why we have terms in our vocabulary such as agriculture, horticulture, silviculture, permaculture, and so on, all of which indicate that culture is not confined to the human species but exists in the realm of nature as well.

It wasn't long before I was in a state of euphoria over the cornucopia of books, articles, and other documents dealing with culture I had discovered. The problem was that this information was scattered all over the library rather than located in a single place. Scholars from many different disciplines — the arts, humanities, history, philosophy, psychology, sociology, anthropology, ecology, and biology — have all written about culture and set down their own impressions of what it is all about. As a result, I was compelled to search high and low, and in every nook and cranny of the library, to find information about culture and pull it all together. I wondered if anyone had done this before I did, since virtually every cultural scholar I came across had worked — or was working — in a specific area of culture, rather than across all areas.

As my investigations intensified, I became more familiar with the many different perceptions and definitions of culture. They ranged all the way from the arts, humanities, finer things in life, heritage of history, cultural industries, and leisure-time activity, to values and value systems, individual and collective behaviour, a state of mind, a way of life, a complex whole, the relationship between human beings and the natural environment, and the organizational forms and structures of different species. This also included everything in between.

This perceptional and definitional problem is exceedingly difficult because there are so many different uses of the term "culture" that it causes confusion, misunderstanding, and uncertainty for people. This makes it imperative to come to grips with the nature and meaning of culture, especially with respect to how the term is used in public and private discourse, before anything else is addressed. Whereas virtually unanimous agreement exists throughout the world about the nature and meaning of most activities and disciplines — it is generally agreed, for example, that economics is concerned with the production, distribution, and consumption of goods and services and creation of material and monetary wealth — this is certainly not the case for culture.

At the same time, while the many different perceptions and definitions of culture pose numerous difficulties, it was good to know where they came from originally, what cultural scholars had to say about them, and when they first appeared in the historical literature. Knowing these things gave me a much better understanding of the complexity, vastness, profundity, and potential of culture as an idea.

When I was young, I thought culture was the arts, pure and simple. By the time I had reached my late twenties and early thirties, however, I had expanded my understanding of culture to include the humanities, heritage of history, finer things in life, and the cultural industries of publishing, radio, television, film, and sound recording, since this was consistent with general practice in most parts of the world. Nevertheless, by the time I went to Scarborough campus in my mid-forties, largely as a result of my trips abroad and the work for UNESCO, I was beginning to think of culture in much more expansive terms as customs, traditions, beliefs, values, value systems, and even most broadly, an entire way of life. I continued to think that the arts played a crucial role in all this because they acted as a "gateway to culture," largely because artists create many of the signs, symbols, myths, legends, metaphors, paintings, plays, music, stories, and so forth that are required to understand culture in the all-inclusive sense.

However, all this posed a serious problem for me. As someone who was deeply committed to expanding knowledge and understanding of culture and making the case for the centrality of culture in global development and human affairs, it was not sufficient to say that it was unfortunate that there were many different perceptions and definitions of culture and let it go at that. I felt I had a professional duty and personal obligation to come to grips with this exceedingly difficult problem, primarily by evolving a way of thinking about and understanding culture that was consistent with how the idea of culture evolved historically, how culture manifests itself in the world, what different cultural scholars and practitioners have had to say about it, and what I myself believed culture was really all about. This required an in-depth analysis of the many different perceptions and definitions of culture, as well as a melding together of these perceptions and definitions to form an overall understanding of this elusive but evocative term.

It is often said that when a person is ready for something, it will appear. This was certainly true for me as far as perceptions and definitions of culture were concerned. I was working in the Bladen Library one day when I happened to come across a book by Sir Edward Burnett Tylor — one of the world's first anthropologists if not *the* first — entitled *The Origins of Culture* and published in 1871. No sooner had I opened the book to the first page than the following definition of culture was staring me in the face: "Culture is . . . that *complex whole* which includes knowledge, belief, art, morals, law, custom, and any other capabilities and habits acquired by man as a member of society" (emphasis mine).

This definition struck a responsive chord in me the moment I saw it. It seemed to sum up exactly what I had come to believe culture was all about and one of the principal ways it manifests itself in the world. It was also consistent with the way many cultural scholars used the term. This definition broke with the tradition of defining culture in terms of a part or parts of the whole — either as the arts taken separately or as the arts, humanities, heritage of history, finer things in life, and cultural industries taken together — and instead made a strong case for viewing culture in the holistic sense as a dynamic, organic, and complex *whole*.

It is important to emphasize here that Tylor did not reject the notion that culture is concerned with a part or parts of the whole, particularly as many of these parts are included in his definition. What he did, however, was incorporate those parts in a substantially broader, deeper, and more fundamental holistic perception.

This holistic perception evolved naturally when anthropologists began to study culture in general, and cultures in particular, in depth and in the field in the latter part of the nineteenth century. What they discovered was that people had all sorts of words to describe the specific activities in which they were engaged — agriculture, industry, recreation, economics, politics, science, sports, education, technology, the arts, religion, and so forth — as they went about the process of meeting their individual and collective needs. What they did *not* have was a word that described how all of these activities were woven together to form a whole.

Culture was the word anthropologists used to designate this phenomenon. This is why countless anthropologists since Tylor's time, including Franz Boas, Ruth Benedict, Margaret Mead, Ralph Linton, Bronislaw Malinowski, Alfred Kroeber, Clyde Kluckhohn, Edward T. Hall, and many others, defined culture as "the sum of *all* activities in a society," "*all* manifestations of a community," "the *totality* of material and non-material traits," "the *total body* of belief, behaviour, knowledge, sanctions, values, and goals that mark the way of life of any people," and so forth. Here, at long last, was a way of defining culture that placed the emphasis on the whole — and therefore the total way of life of people — and not just a part or parts of the whole.

This all-encompassing definition of culture solved a number of problems that had bothered me for years. In the first place, it focused attention on the whole and not just a part or parts of the whole, and therefore on "the big picture" rather than a specific part or parts of the big picture. Doing so was imperative in my view because humanity had lost sight of the big picture — and with it the whole — because of the tendency to break up the whole into parts in order to study the parts in detail. Nowhere was this more obvious than with respect to the natural environment and people's relationship to it, something which, as indicated earlier, is at the root of what culture was about in classical times.

In the second place, this definition was consistent with the nature of reality. Most things in the world, and the world itself, are wholes made up of many parts, not smorgasbords of disconnected and unrelated pieces. Here was a way of seeing and understanding the world that had "got it right" in my view because it was concerned with the way reality actually *is*, not the way it *appears* to us as a result of specialization.

In the third place, the definition made it clear that culture, and not economics or any other part of the whole, is ultimately the most important factor in society and the world system. This is because the whole is greater than the parts and the sum of the parts according to an age-old philosophical truth and fundamental ontological principle. Ruth Benedict, the distinguished American anthropologist and cultural scholar, illustrated this phenomenon very cleverly by using the example of gunpowder:

> The whole, as modern science is insisting in many fields, is not merely the sum of all its parts, but the result of a unique arrangement and inter-relation of the parts that has brought about a new entity. Gunpowder is not merely the sum of sulphur and charcoal and saltpeter, and no amount of knowledge even of all three of its elements in all the forms they take in the natural world will demonstrate the nature of gunpowder. New potentialities have come into being in the resulting compound that were not present in its elements, and its mode of behaviour is indefinitely changed from that of any of its elements in other combinations.

Finally, this all-encompassing, holistic definition of culture focused on the underlying unity that exists in the whole, and consequently on the forces that bring things together rather than split them apart. This was of crucial importance, in my opinion, because I felt much more attention should be given to factors that unite and unify rather than those that divide and separate.

It wasn't long before I discovered that this holistic way of defining culture was not limited to anthropologists and similar types of cultural scholars. It also included important institutions like UNESCO. After many years of perceiving and defining culture in terms of the parts — most notably as the arts, humanities, heritage of history, finer things in life, and more recently the cultural industries — UNESCO in the early 1980s began defining culture in the all-encompassing, holistic sense. This shift was confirmed when the member states of UNESCO unanimously adopted the following definition of culture at the Second World Conference on Cultural Policies in Mexico City in 1982, the same year I assumed my duties at the Scarborough campus of the University of Toronto:

> Culture may now be said to be the *whole* complex of distinctive spiritual, material, intellectual, and emotional features that characterize a society or social group. It includes not only the arts and letters, but also modes of life, the fundamental rights of the human being, value systems, traditions, and beliefs.

The impetus at this time for adopting such an all-encompassing understanding of culture was not coming only from UNESCO, anthropologists, and various other cultural scholars. It was also coming from other people and groups. As long as people are in no danger of losing their culture, it is easy to accept a definition of culture that is limited to the "parts," most frequently as the arts and humanities but sometimes other aspects as well. However, as soon as culture is threatened or there is a danger of losing it — as was the case in many countries in the latter decades of the twentieth century and even more so today — it is amazing how often there is a sudden realization of the holistic nature of culture as a complex whole or total way of life. There is nothing quite like the threat of cultural extinction or foreign domination to bring about a rapid realization of the all-encompassing character of culture.

It is impossible to perceive culture in holistic terms without extending it to *all* groups, classes, activities, people, and institutions. Culture is all-inclusive in this sense. It is the environment as well as economics, education as well as ethics, popular music as well as classical music, the arts as well as the sciences, business as well as religion, technology as well as sports, industry as well as agriculture, politics as well as social affairs, and "popular activities" as well as "elite activities."

This is what many people now mean when they say they are "products of their culture." They mean that they are products of everything that exists in their culture — or their culture *as a whole*. This includes environmental, economic, political, social, technological, communications, religious, scientific, educational and spiritual activities, as well as artistic, humanistic, and heritage activities. This is likely why Wole Soyinka, the Nobel Prize-winning African author, views culture as *source* — the source from which all things flow and to which all things return. As Soyinka states:

> We need therefore to constantly reinforce our awareness of the primacy of Source, and that source is the universal spring of Culture. It is nourished by its tributaries, which sink back into the earth, and thereby replenish that common source in an unending, creative cycle. That one tributary proves more aggressive, domineering, more seemingly nourished than others does not transform its egalitarian quotient. . . .

Sociologists also tend to think about culture in these terms, although their interest is more in things people share in common, and how people behave as members of groups, societies, and countries, than in culture in the all-encompassing, anthropological sense. Over time, these views have congealed to form the sociological definition of culture, as Paul Braisted pointed out in his book *Cultural Cooperation: Keynote of the Coming Age* (1945):

> Culture, a word of varied meanings, is here used in the more inclusive sociological sense, that is, to designate the artifacts, goods, technical processes, ideas, habits, and values which are the social heritage of a people. Thus, culture includes all learned behaviour, intellectual knowledge, social organization and language, systems of value — economic, moral, or spiritual. Fundamental to a particular culture are its law, economic structure, magic, religion, art, knowledge, and education.

Armed with these various definitions, I was in an ideal position to evolve a way of perceiving and defining culture that was consistent with one of the most essential ways culture manifests itself in the world, namely as a whole, as well as being consistent with my own convictions on the matter and what other scholars have had to say about this over the centuries. Based on these considerations, and others, I formed the following definition of culture, which I felt was consistent with everything I had learned about culture up to that point in my life: *Culture is a dynamic and organic whole that is concerned with the way people visualize and interpret the world, organize themselves, conduct their affairs, elevate and enrich life, and position themselves in the world.*

Since every component in this holistic perception and definition of culture is relevant to broadening and deepening one's knowledge of culture and making the case that culture has a central rather than marginal role to play in the world, it pays to examine each component in turn.

How people visualize and interpret the world involves all the cosmological, mythological, environmental, and ideological beliefs and convictions that people possess. These beliefs constitute the foundation of culture because they provide the axioms, assumptions, and premises on which culture in general and individual cultures in particular are based. These assumptions are like a huge iceberg, with the larger part submerged and hidden from view; while these assumptions are more invisible than visible — implicit than explicit — they are always there just lurking below the surface. As a result, they are of crucial importance to the overall understanding of culture.

How people organize themselves encompasses all the decisions people make with respect to economic systems, social processes, political procedures, government activities, technological and communications activities, and ecological practices. This includes all types of human settlements and collectivities — groups, institutions, neighbourhoods, communities, towns, cities, regions, countries, cultures, civilizations, and the world system. These entities are undergoing profound change at the present time, due to countless international developments, globalization, rapidly changing demographic conditions, as well as new economic, political, social, environmental, and technological realities.

How people conduct their affairs deals with the character of people's lives, including decisions about family life, child-rearing, consumer behaviour, living arrangements, gender relations, and personal preferences and practices.

How people elevate and enrich life takes in education and training, artistic and scientific preferences, spiritual practices, moral values, and all those things that make life deeper, richer, and more meaningful than it would otherwise be. It is in this domain that many of the signs, symbols, myths, legends, metaphors, similes, rituals, and stories are created that are needed to understand culture and cultures in the fundamental, holistic sense.

Finally, *how people position themselves in the world* involves geographic location, temporal situation, geopolitical processes, sense of place, and territorial maneuvering. These factors play a crucial role in determining the way distinct groups of people situate themselves in space and time and relate to the natural environment, each other, other species, and the world around them.

When culture is defined in this holistic sense, it is very much like a huge tree with roots, trunk, branches, leaves, flowers, and fruit. Metaphorically speaking, mythology, cosmology, ideology, and so forth constitute the roots; economic systems, technological practices, political and governmental processes, social structures, and the like constitute the trunk and branches; and artistic works, educational endeavours, moral codes, architectural edifices, spiritual activities, and ethical ideals constitute the leaves, flowers, and fruit.

This metaphor helps us to understand the nature and meaning of culture in the holistic sense. For just as every tree is an organic whole composed of many parts, so, too, is culture. And just as all the parts of a tree play an important role in the effective functioning of the tree as a dynamic and organic whole, so do all the many different components of culture play indispensable functions as well.

Interestingly, culture in this all-encompassing, holistic sense is concerned with three matters when it is stripped to its essence. The first is *worldview*; the second is *values*; and the third is *people*. It pays to examine each of these three matters in some detail because doing so reveals so much.

It is obvious why culture is concerned with worldview. Since how people see and interpret the world has a crucial impact on how they live in the world, act in the world, and value things in the world, worldview constitutes a quintessential factor in culture. Without a vastly improved understanding of worldview in general, and the specific worldviews people use in different cultures and parts of the world in particular, humanity could well experience higher levels of environmental deterioration, a great deal more poverty, pollution, violence, war, and terrorism, and increased conflict and confrontation among the diverse cultures and civilizations of the world. This is a chilling prospect but a likely one if much more attention is not given to the impact worldviews exert on every aspect of life.

Values also play a crucial role in culture. As Alfred Kroeber and Clyde Kluckhohn pointed out more than half a century ago:

> . . . values provide the only basis for the fully intelligible comprehension of culture, because the actual organization of all cultures is primarily in terms of their values. This becomes apparent as soon as one attempts to present the picture of a culture without reference to its values. The account becomes an unstructured, meaningless assemblage of items having relation to one another only through coexistence in locality and moment — an assemblage that might as profitably be arranged alphabetically as in any other order; a mere laundry list.

Values are important because they assign priorities or weights to the component parts of culture. How much emphasis is placed on the economy compared to the environment? How much emphasis is placed on products as opposed to people? How much emphasis is placed on the arts compared to the sciences? And where do politics, education, business, ethics, technology, and the like fit in? These are all crucial questions.

How values are determined in specific cultures varies greatly in accordance with people's needs, wants, preferences, circumstances, and practices. Whereas some people may prefer to place a great deal of emphasis on the economy, industry, the sciences, politics, and technology, others may prefer to place a great deal of emphasis on the environment, agriculture, ethics, people, religion, the arts, education, and the humanities. It all depends on how people decide to order the component parts of their cultural life.

Discussion of the intimate connection between culture, worldview, and values makes it apparent why culture is so concerned with people — the third and most fundamental factor since it is people who create worldviews and values. They do so as they go about the process of meeting their individual and collective needs and working out their complex relationship with the world. People have a variety of needs that must be attended to if they are to function effectively in society and live creative, constructive, and fulfilling lives. Fulfilling these needs gives rise to a complex set of social, economic, educational, artistic, religious, spiritual, recreational, technological, political, and environmental requirements as noted earlier. How these requirements are dealt with in specific situations is what culture in general — and cultures in particular — are all about.

For all these reasons, and others to be discussed later, I came to the conclusion that culture must play a central rather than marginal role in the world. My explorations of the meaning of culture also confirmed why it is so imperative to reach a general agreement on the nature of culture if firm foundations are to be created for the world system of the future. As the ancient Chinese proverb states, "The beginning of wisdom lies in calling things by their right names."

As my investigations in the Bladen Library intensified, I discovered that culture is not only a term that is used in the arts, humanities, history, philosophy, psychology, sociology, and anthropology. It is also used in ecology, zoology, botany, and biology, where it is applied not only to human beings but also to other species and indeed the entire realm of nature. Understood in this way, all species have cultures and manifest them through the various structures, systems, behavioural characteristics, traits, and preferences they create.

Consider the bee culture for example. Much like human culture, bee culture is intricately designed and highly complex, with its well-defined system of queen, drone, and worker bees, its rigid hierarchy and division of labour, its finely tuned communications network, and its extraordinary sensing capabilities and productive apparatus. While I didn't pay as much attention to the non-human aspects of culture as I should have when I was at the Scarborough campus, I did have the sense that I would return to this matter and write about it at some length later in life.

While the discoveries I made helped me to broaden and deepen my understanding of culture and work out an all-encompassing definition of culture that I was comfortable with, my knowledge was expanded even more when I discovered that cultural scholars have had an incredible amount to say not only about the meaning of culture, but also about how culture manifests itself at every level, from the individual, community, and regional level to the national, international, historical, civilizational, and environmental level.

At the individual level, I was particularly attracted to the writings of Matthew Arnold, Thomas Carlyle, Georg Simmel, John Cowper Powys, Johann Wolfgang von Goethe, Ruth Benedict, Margaret Mead, Ralph Linton, Gordon Allport, John Honigmann, Joseph Campbell, and others. Arnold, for instance, wrote about the need to attend to the harmonious development of all the faculties that comprise human nature. Powys expressed the belief that "the whole purpose and end of culture is a thrilling happiness of a particular sort — of the sort, in fact, that is caused by a response to life made by a harmony of the intellect, the imagination, and the senses." Carlyle even penned a great *Law of Culture*: "Let each man [or woman] become all that he [or she] was created capable of being; expand, if possible, to his [or her] full growth; resisting all impediments, casting off all foreign, especially all noxious adhesions, and show himself [or herself] at length in his [or her] own shape and stature, be these what they may" (inserts mine). Such ideas were very helpful to me in a personal sense because I was struggling hard to become a "whole person" and a "person in my own right."

But the cultural scholars who had the greatest impact on me in a personal sense were Joseph Campbell and Johann Wolfgang von Goethe. Campbell believed that all people should "follow their bliss," by which he meant that they should do the thing they are intended to do in life since this will bring them the greatest happiness and fulfillment in the end. And Goethe said, "Live in the whole, in the good, in the beautiful." These words had a profound effect on me because I felt they summed up what life and living were all about in the cultural sense and captured what I was trying to achieve in my own life. These words were never far from my mind after this, since they provided a great deal of inspiration in life.

At the community, city, and regional level, the writings of Lewis Mumford, Friedrich Ratzel, Fritz Graebner, Amos Rapoport, John Agnew, Richard Sennett, and others struck a responsive chord. Lewis Mumford was in a class by himself. His book, *The Culture of Cities*, proved especially interesting to me because I had visited many of the cities he referred to in his book. I also shared his conviction that "the city is both a physical utility for collective living and a symbol of those collective purposes and unanimities that arise under such favouring circumstance. With language itself, it is man's greatest work of art."

Amos Rapoport went even further than this. He was especially interested in "the character of cities," as well as the fact that different cities have different characteristics. He said: "Cities, among other things, are physical artifacts, experienced through all the senses by people who are in them. They are experienced sequentially as people follow different paths and use different modes through them. Cities look, smell, sound, and feel different; they have a different character or ambience. This is easily felt, but is very difficult to describe."

This observation made a great deal of sense to me. I had become convinced as a result of my travels, as well as all the work I had done on culturescapes, that every city and community in the world has a special character and identity all its own. Rapoport's work also put the emphasis on *place* as one of (if not *the*) most important factors in determining a community's specific nature and personality.

At the societal and national level, I was especially enamoured of the works of Edward Burnett Tylor, Franz Boas, Ruth Bunzel, Bronislaw Malinowski, Claude Levy Strauss, Alfred Kroeber, Pitirim Sorokin, and a constellation of other cultural scholars. Their work shed a great deal of light on the nature of societies, countries, and cultures, as well as the growth and development of these human collectivities in space and time. I appreciated their comprehensive approach to this subject, as well as their ability to show where the arts, humanities, history, and other aspects of culture fitted into the equation. The writings of Franz Boas especially captured my attention because Boas was concerned with the intimate connection between culture, cultures, and the arts, and how this connection plays itself out in history. The writings of Pitirim Sorokin also captivated me, especially his views on ideational, sensate, idealistic, and mixed systems of culture which he spelled out in great detail in his book, *Social and Cultural Dynamics*. He was a master at showing how these systems have different structures and evolve in different ways.

Sorokin also provided an excellent introduction to culture at the international level. In *Social and Cultural Dynamics*, he wrote: "If humanity mobilizes all its wisdom, knowledge, beauty, and especially the all-giving and all-forgiving love or reverence for life and if a strenuous and sustaining effort of this kind is made by everyone . . . then the crisis will certainly be ended and a most magnificent new era in human history ushered in." Statements like this inspired me as I became increasingly interested in what the French call "the dialogue of cultures and civilizations."

Oswald Spengler and F. S. C. Northrop were especially intriguing in this respect. Spengler led the way here because he had the courage to talk about "the decline of the west" at a time when no one wanted to hear about this. His book of the same title is a classic, and makes the case that civilizations rise and fall like all other forms of life because they experience internal and external pressures and tensions that make cycles inevitable. These cycles of growth and decline might well be called "a cultural fact of life."

At the historical and civilizational level, the writings of Arnold Toynbee, Johan Huizinga, Jacob Burckhardt, Fernand Braudel, and Karl

Weintraub were especially illuminating. These individuals were "big thinkers" who wrote about issues of fundamental importance to humanity, often from a long-term perspective. The writings of Karl Weintraub were especially valuable. Weintraub was keenly interested in the cultural interpretation of history, and saw the role of cultural historians as one of comprehending culture "not as a mere aggregate of traits but as forming an intricately interrelated pattern. In this delicately fashioned network the arts may have their ties to religion and economic values, morality may affect the constitutional arrangements and in turn be affected by political realities, a mood reflected in literature may also come to the fore in a social custom, and a scientific insight may work back upon a religious belief." This point of view resonated strongly with me because I felt it was much more in keeping with the real nature of historical development than the economic interpretation of history.

Finally, there was the environmental level. Ecologists, botanists, zoologists, and biologists such as Julian Steward, Gregory Bateson, and others have written a great deal about the cultures of plants and animals. Their observations make a great deal of sense, given the countless similarities between the cultures of human beings and the cultures of other species — far more than we are usually willing to admit. Nor should this be surprising. All species in the world are living organisms, and as such, obey the laws governing all living things.

When I began to reflect on all the information I collected on the nature and meaning of culture in general, and, in particular, culture at every level of human existence, I was *overwhelmed* by what I had discovered in the Bladen Library. There is simply no other word to describe it. And what was even more astonishing was that when I pulled all the ideas of these and many other cultural scholars together and thought about them collectively, they produced a very different picture of the world and virtually everything in it. I began to call this *the cultural way of looking at the world* or, for short, *the cultural worldview*.

Everything was contained in this worldview in one form or another: the nature and meaning of culture and cultures; the role of culture in the development of individuals, institutions, communities, cities, countries, the world, and the world system; the importance of culture in global development and human affairs; the connection between culture, human beings, nature, and other species; the origins and historical development of all the diverse cultures in the world; relations between the many various peoples, cultures, and civilizations of the world; the interpretation of history, and much more. I recall wishing that every person in the world could be exposed to the many different "*secrets of culture,*" and the valuable insights they provided into the human condition and world situation.

I also began to realize how different the cultural worldview was from the economic worldview. Whereas the economic worldview was concerned with products, profits, production, consumption, the marketplace, and economic growth, the cultural worldview was concerned with people, values, all activities in society, the relationship between human beings and the natural environment, humanity's greatest ideals and accomplishments, and much more. The problem was that this way of looking at the world was largely ignored because humanity was preoccupied with the economic worldview.

The contrast between these two different ways of looking at the world made me realize why I was so obsessed with culture and the role it was capable of playing in the world. What had long been a subconscious, intuitive, and subjective feeling was rapidly becoming a conscious, deliberate, and objective process. I was struggling so hard to expose the many different secrets of culture and capitalize on them because I was convinced that culture was the key to the future.

There was obviously something very profound and powerful going on here. Culture was too vitally important to the world of the future to downplay or ignore. While the cultural worldview was unknown at the time — and, for the most part, still is today — I was convinced that culture was destined to play a much greater role in the world of the future than economics, especially if that future was to be equitable, harmonious, sustainable, and humane. With this conviction came the belief that it was time to tackle the next great challenge in my journey. It was time to put down on paper everything I had learned about culture up to that point in my life and get it published.

CHAPTER SEVEN

Writing about Culture and Cultures

I had worked at the Scarborough campus of the University of Toronto for almost ten years. During that time, a great deal had been accomplished, especially the development of two new cooperative programs. However, I found myself becoming more and more obsessed with the need to write about culture and matters that were closest to my heart.

Unfortunately, this was not possible as long as I had a job-and-a-half at the university. So I began to cut back on my responsibilities, first by giving up the half-time position as coordinator of the Cooperative Program in Arts Administration in 1988, and then by giving up the half-time position as coordinator of the Cooperative Program in International Development in 1990. Fortunately, this did not pose a problem for me or for the university. I had made it clear to authorities at the university from the very beginning that my commitment was to getting the two new programs up and running, and this had been accomplished by the end of the 1980s. Giving up the coordinators' roles left me with only one responsibility – teaching the two courses in arts administration and cultural policy – which I did for several more years before giving this up as well. By the mid-1990s, I was back on my own as a self-employed person.

Many things were happening in the world at this time that were consistent with my desire to devote a great deal of time and attention to my writing. By far the most important in this respect was the declaration by the United Nations and UNESCO that the period from 1988 to 1997 would be officially designated the World Decade for Cultural Development. This designation sustained a commitment the United Nations had made in the 1960s to establish a series of "decades of development" that would, during each decade, focus on a specific developmental issue or problem.

The decision to designate the period from 1988 to 1997 the World

Decade for *Cultural* Development struck a responsive chord with me. It indicated that the United Nations was starting to view development from a broader perspective. (Further evidence of this shift in the UN's perspective was the fact that the immediately preceding ten year period had been designated the World Decade for *Environmental* Development.)

The World Decade for Cultural Development had four principal objectives: to ensure that the cultural dimension was taken into account in all economic development and planning; to assist in the preservation and enrichment of cultural identity, including promotion of the arts and safeguarding of the national heritage; to broaden participation in cultural activity; and to foster international cultural co-operation.

Although I had real concerns about the first objective, largely because I felt it subordinated culture to economics and ran counter to my conviction that culture is an essential factor in development in its own right and not just as a component part of economics, I was delighted to see that the United Nations was beginning to view culture as an important "dimension" of development. However, I subscribed fully to all the other objectives. I also recognized that the declaration of a World Decade for Cultural Development provided me with an excellent opportunity to connect my writing on culture to a specific activity, especially as I was anxious to do something to commemorate the Decade.

I was so excited by the opportunity provided by the Decade that I decided to create a World Culture Project. I visualized this Project from the outset as a long-term undertaking that would shed light on culture and cultures and the central role they are capable of playing in the world.

For purposes of the Project, I defined culture in the holistic sense as a "dynamic and organic whole" or "total way of life" that was concerned with the way people "visualize and interpret the world, organize themselves, conduct their affairs, elevate and embellish life, and position themselves in the world." This was consistent with the definition of culture I worked out in the Bladen Library, as well as the way I felt culture manifested itself most profoundly in the world.

My original intention was to limit the World Culture Project to the international level. However, the more I thought about it, the more I became convinced that I should include Canada in the Project because it would give me an opportunity to show how the holistic perception of culture could be applied to a specific culture in the world. I was also becoming very interested in Canadian culture, and felt that including Canada in the Project would enable me to focus on a culture that had much to contribute to the world of the future. Adding Canada to the World Culture Project made it necessary to divide the Project into an international component and a Canadian component. The international component was designed to examine the holistic understanding of culture and cultures in broad, general terms, as well as to apply it to a number of complex global issues and problems. The Canadian component was designed to examine the holistic understanding of Canadian culture in specific, practical terms, as well as apply it to a similar set of Canadian issues and problems.

My plan was to write and publish two monographs a year — one for the international component and one for the Canadian component — commencing with the nature and meaning of culture, cultures, and Canadian culture, and concluding with cultural visions of the future. I drew up a prospectus for the Project that outlined the specific topics that would be covered each year during the ten-year period. I also created two advisory groups for the Project — one for the international component and one for the Canadian component — composed of distinguished authorities from the cultural field. The role of the advisory groups was to provide input into the Project in their areas of expertise, as well as to provide feedback on the monographs in draft form. I let it be known wherever and whenever I could that the objective of the Project was to create a body of literature on the holistic understanding of culture, cultures, and Canadian culture — a body of literature that did not exist and was badly needed in my view.

Unfortunately, I was not able to acquire as much funding for the Project as I had hoped. This meant that I had to finance the development of the Project largely through my own limited financial resources. While UNESCO officially endorsed the Project as a World Decade for Cultural Development activity, it was in an exceedingly difficult position financially at the time and was not able to provide any funding. The Canadian Commission for UNESCO also decided not to fund the Project, largely because it didn't want to commit itself to a venture with such a long-term time horizon. Nevertheless, I did get a grant of $5,000 from the Government of Canada to get the Project started.

The foundations and corporations I approached were equally reluctant to fund the Project, primarily because they felt it was too abstract and theoretical, was not related to their goals and objectives, and was out of the mainstream. I did, however, manage to secure a grant of $6,000 from the Samuel and Saidye Bronfman Family Foundation to assist with the research, writing, publication, and distribution of one of the key monographs in the World Culture Project series, *The Challenge of Cultural Development*, which I will discuss in a moment. While lack of support for the Project was disappointing and discouraging, it taught me a valuable lesson. I learned that institutions and individuals who talk about the need to think "outside the box" and "long term" often provide little or no financial support for this.

Failure to generate much funding for the Project meant that I had to do most things on my own without a great deal of help. However, I was so committed to the Project and determined to do the best job I could with it that I decided to carry on, despite the many problems that would be encountered along the way. What motivated me was my belief that the world needed a much better understanding of culture, cultures, Canadian culture, and cultural development in the holistic sense. I felt humanity was rapidly losing sight of "the whole" in all its diverse aspects and manifestations as indicated earlier, due largely to preoccupation with the parts of the whole and especially specialization.

It wasn't that I was opposed to specialization. My training in economics had made me fully aware of the myriad benefits that were — and are — derived from specialization in every sector of society and area of cultural life. This process has been going on for centuries and probably from the beginning of time. However, it escalated rapidly after Adam Smith made a powerful case for specialization as the key to creating huge increases in material and monetary wealth. Smith did this through his famous example of the pin factory, showing that many more pins could be produced each day if people specialized in one or two production functions than if they generalized on many or all production functions.

As it was for pins, so it was (in Smith's view) for virtually every other activity in society. It is doubtful if specialization would be as pervasive and powerful as it is throughout the world today if Smith had not made such a compelling case for it.

The gains that have been realized from this in virtually every field of human endeavour have been and are enormous. I didn't have a problem with this, or with the multifarious benefits to be derived from it. What I *did* have a problem with — and a huge problem indeed — was the fact that specialization was causing humanity to lose sight of the whole and the importance of the whole as a result of preoccupation with the parts of the whole. Not only was this inconsistent with the true nature of reality in my view, but also it obscured things that were of utmost importance to the world of the future.

It was due to problems like this that I was so committed to the World Culture Project. I felt the Project's publications would illustrate that it is really culture in the holistic sense, not economics or any other activity in the partial or specialized sense, that is concerned with the whole and therefore of greatest importance to humanity. I was convinced that anthropologists had "got it right" when they created the holistic understanding of culture. The problem was that humanity was so preoccupied with subordinating everything to economics that this remarkable insight into the human condition and world situation was lost. Consequently, I was anxious to make the case that there were legitimate theoretical, practical, philosophical, and historical reasons for placing culture at the centre of global development and human affairs.

I decided to tackle this problem in *The Challenge of Cultural Development,* the second monograph in the international component of the World Culture Project. (The first international monograph, *The Character of Culture*, was concerned with shedding light on the many different perceptions and definitions of culture that have been advocated throughout history and are in use throughout the world today.) To me, *The Challenge of Cultural Development* was one of the most important monographs in the entire series. It explained what is meant by the holistic understanding of culture in both theoretical and practical terms, as well as how this all-encompassing understanding of culture can be applied to cultures and the evocative term *cultural development*.

Since the world was preoccupied with the idea of development at the time, I commenced *The Challenge of Cultural Development* by showing how this idea had evolved historically. As demonstrated earlier, Marx and the Marxists laid the foundations for this by defining development in economic terms through the economic interpretation of history. However, when President Truman promoted the idea of development as the key to improving living standards and the quality of life after the Second World War, the idea of development spread like wildfire throughout the world. This eventually led to the declaration of the series of "decades of development" by the United Nations in the 1960s. By this time, virtually every government in the world was using an "economic model of development" to make decisions about a variety of public and private matters.

This historical overview was followed by an intensive analysis of the strengths and shortcomings of development when it is perceived and dealt with in economic terms. Included among the numerous strengths were huge increases in the production, distribution, and consumption of goods and services, as well as major improvements in the standard of living and quality of life for millions of people throughout the world. It also included myriad advances in agriculture, industry, health care, transportation, communication, the arts, the sciences, education, and so forth.

Nevertheless, it was becoming increasingly apparent that development had its shortcomings as well as its strengths. Most of these shortcomings had to do with the fact that development was defined almost entirely in economic and material terms. Directly and indirectly, this was contributing to devastation of the natural environment, disappearance of many traditional identities, cultures, and ways of life, large inequalities in income and wealth between rich and poor people and rich and poor countries, a world divided into two unequal parts, lack of appreciation for the aesthetic, spiritual, and qualitative aspects of life, and preoccupation with products, profits, and power at the expense of people.

So apparent were these shortcomings that Wolfgang Sachs, an astute observer of the global scene, made the following statement in an article entitled "The Archaeology of the Development Idea" that was published in 1990:

> The idea of development was once a towering monument inspiring international enthusiasm. Today, the structure is falling apart and in danger of total collapse. But its imposing ruins still linger over everything and block the way out. The task, then, is to push the rubble aside to open new ground.

Leopold Senghor, former president of Senegal and a poet of international distinction, indicated how it was possible to "open new ground" when he said, "Culture is the alpha and omega of any sound development policy."

With statements like this to inspire me, I was convinced that I was on the right track by creating the World Culture Project. Since I believed culture and cultures are the most fundamental collectivities in the world, I felt it was the development of culture and cultures that was the real key to global well-being and human affairs in the future.

In order to develop culture in broad, deep, and general terms, it was necessary to expand knowledge and understanding of all the various perceptions of culture throughout the world and particularly the holistic perception. This meant fleshing out all the diverse perceptions of culture, as well as attempting to reach a general consensus on the holistic perception in all major public and private institutions. This was obviously a long-term undertaking and tall order, since there are many different perceptions of culture in use throughout the world and perceptions that focus on the arts and humanities tend to predominate, largely because they are more specific, concrete, and easier to use for planning and policy purposes.

As someone raised in an artistic and humanistic milieu and totally committed to the arts and humanities, I was not opposed to the artistic and humanistic perceptions of culture. In fact, I was very attached to them because they tend to place people before products and are very helpful in expanding knowledge and understanding of culture and cultures in the holistic sense. This is because culture and cultures cannot be known in their totality because of their complexity and vastness. As a result, knowledge and understanding of culture and cultures in the holistic sense can only be acquired through parts of the whole that *stand for the whole* and give us a *general sense of the whole*. The arts and humanities play a crucial role here, since they convey a great deal of information about culture and cultures in the holistic sense that can't be communicated as effectively in any other way.

Regardless of the importance of the arts and humanities, it is necessary to remember that they are still parts of the whole, even if they are extremely important parts. This is why I felt it was imperative to focus attention on the holistic perception of culture and convince authorities in business, government, education, and other areas that this all-embracing perception of culture should take precedence over the other perceptions at this particular juncture in human history because of its all-inclusive capability.

As difficult as it is to develop culture in broad, deep, and general terms, as well as win acceptance for it in its many different forms and particularly the holistic one, it is much more difficult to develop cultures in these terms. This is because cultures have to be *comprehensive, coherent, cohesive, humane,* and *properly situated in the natural, historical, and global environment* if they are to function effectively. While this goes to the heart and soul of what cultural development is really all about, it is obviously an ideal that can never fully be achieved in fact. However, it is an ideal worth striving for nonetheless, for in the process of striving to achieve it, much can be accomplished that is of crucial importance to the world of the future.

In order to develop cultures that are comprehensive, it is necessary to develop all the different parts of cultures and not just some parts. This includes artistic, scientific, recreational, educational, ethical, and spiritual activities in addition to economic, political, commercial, and technological activities. It also includes *all* individuals, groups, and institutions in society, not just some individuals, groups, and institutions.

Just as cultures need to be comprehensive, so they need to be coherent. In order to achieve this, it is necessary to blend all the various parts of cultures together to form an integrated whole. This is especially important with respect to the material and non-material — as well as quantitative and qualitative — dimensions of cultures. Activities that are devoted to the production, distribution, and consumption of material goods and services must be counterbalanced by activities that are devoted to the creation of non-material dimensions. The great Dutch cultural historian, Johan Huizinga, had this uppermost in mind when he declared that "the realities of economic life, of power, of technology, of everything conducive to man's material well-being, must be balanced by strongly developed spiritual, intellectual, moral and aesthetic values" following his examination of numerous cultures throughout the world. Despite his sage advice, humanity is far from achieving this, thereby making the creation of coherence in cultures one of the most essential requirements of all.

Cultures also have to be cohesive if they are to function effectively. In order to realize this, it is necessary to bind cultures together properly in space and time, as well as to create numerous bonds and connections between and among their many parts. Cultures that are not bound together properly run the risk of becoming unglued and splitting apart. They can easily fall prey to internal communications problems, especially when geographic scale or formidable terrain makes communication difficult or impossible. But they can also succumb to ethnic tensions and linguistic divides. This may occur when ethnic and linguistic groups visualize their futures in terms of isolation and separation rather than integration and inclusion, a situation that is not uncommon in many different areas of the world today and needs to be addressed fully in the future.

Many activities possess the potential to create cohesiveness in cultures. Language is the most important and obvious one. However, sports also perform this role; they are extremely popular in most cultures and serve to bring people together (although it must also be said that they can split people apart). The social media and cultural industries also create cohesiveness in cultures, as do cultural networks of many kinds and a variety of religious, spiritual, and recreational endeavours.

Nevertheless, the arts perform this function better than anything else, since, as indicated earlier, artists create many of the signs, symbols, myths, metaphors, and stories that give rise to a sense of identity, belonging, and cohesiveness. Think, for example, of what the music of Beethoven and Rodrigo, the paintings of Monet and van Gogh, the architecture of Florence, Venice, and Beijing, and the plays of Shakespeare and Molière do to create a sense of unity, identity, and cohesiveness in German, Spanish, French, Dutch, Italian, English, and Chinese cultures.

Cultures must also be humane if they are to be developed properly in the all-inclusive sense. This goal is achieved by infusing cultures with many of humanity's highest values and ideals. This includes the pursuit of knowledge, wisdom, beauty, and truth; the quest for excellence and creativity; the desire for order, stability, caring, sharing, and cooperation; commitment to peace, security, justice, equality, and diversity; and protection of the tangible and intangible cultural heritage. Without commitment to values and ideals such as these, cultures can easily fall prey to partisan interests, powerful lobbies, and corrupt elites, thereby becoming sources of oppression, injustice, and enslavement rather than joy, fulfillment, and liberation. History is full of examples where cultures have been misused for malicious and diabolical purposes, thereby making it imperative to be ever mindful of the actual and potential abuses of culture.

It is impossible for cultures to be humane without cultivating respect for the needs and rights of others. Initially, this respect will probably manifest itself most conspicuously in concern for other people through a desire to stamp out human rights abuses and various types of injustices and prejudices whenever and wherever they are encountered. Ultimately, however, it should manifest itself as well in concern for other generations, other cultures, other times, other places, other spaces, and other species. For humaneness in the all-embracing sense requires compassion, sensitivity, and care for the other as well as the self, the non-human as well as the human, the past and the future as well as the present, and the sublime as well as the mundane. In order words, it requires humanity, humility, and compassion in space and time.

This objective can't be realized without coming to grips with one of the greatest requirements of all in the development of cultures — the need to situate cultures effectively in the natural, historical, and global environment. For just as cultures as wholes provide the context within which their component parts are situated, so the natural, historical, and global environment provides the context within which cultures as wholes are situated. Careful attention to this matter is essential if human survival and ecological well-being are to be assured.

Clearly the natural environment in general, and climate, flora and fauna, geography, topography, and landscape in particular, play a crucial role in the development of all cultures in the world, as well as in every aspect of cultural life. They also provide the wherewithal required for survival of all the diverse species in the world. History, which has chronicled the decline of countless cultures, confirms — and confirms conclusively — that cultures that fail to give sufficient consideration to the environmental context in which they are situated run the risk of overextending themselves and collapsing entirely.

If the natural environment plays a crucial role in shaping cultures, so, too, does the historical environment. For temporal and historical factors, including the legacy from the past and especially the "baggage" that people carry from one generation to the next, have a profound effect on cultures. Once a way of life has been established, it is difficult to change it. It tends to perpetuate itself without a great deal of change in its structure, design, functions, and features.

Finally, there is the matter of situating cultures effectively in the global environment. Though a more recent requirement for most cultures, largely due to globalization, doing so is equally essential if cultures are to be developed properly. This need became apparent in the years after the Second World War.

Although I didn't ask myself when I was researching and writing *The Challenge of Cultural Development* which culture in the world comes closest to achieving the ideal of being comprehensive, coherent, cohesive, humane, and properly situated in the natural, historical, and global environment, I have often asked myself this question since.

Ultimately I would have to answer "the culture of France." There are many reasons for this answer. In the first place, France has always paid a great deal of attention to the various parts of its culture and not merely some parts. Doing so has helped France achieve a great deal of comprehensiveness and coherence in its culture, largely through the realization of an effective balance between the material and non-material dimensions of that culture. Moreover, the country has always placed a high priority on the arts and humanities and funded them accordingly, thereby achieving a great deal of cohesiveness in its culture as well.

Nor is this all. France has valued its history and myriad cultural accomplishments very highly, as is readily apparent in its long and distinguished tradition in international cultural relations and cultural diplomacy. This has enabled it to properly position itself and its culture in the historical and global environment. Moreover, and perhaps even more significantly, France has always placed an extremely high priority on "the land" and nature. Not only does France possess a long and distinguished tradition in agriculture, but citizens of the country love nature and the land in a way that is matched in few if any other countries. If one were looking for a "model" that best epitomizes the development of cultures in the holistic sense, then, one could do no better than to take a long, hard look at the culture of France, especially when France has made such a remarkable commitment and contribution to cultural development and policy and has long been recognized as a world leader in this field.

I often thought that my friend Jack Fobes, who lived in Paris for many years when he was the deputy director of UNESCO, must have had France and the culture of France in mind when, in a letter to me, he said: "The development of a culture starts with a base of cultural values and structures, builds according to processes that are native to the culture, and embodies goals and objectives (futures) which flow naturally from this culture." I have always felt that the culture of France does this better than any other culture that I am aware of, although I am quite prepared to admit that there may be many other cultures in the world that I am not familiar with that share this characteristic as well. I have often been told, for example, that Balinese culture achieves this, but I have no real knowledge or direct experience with this.

As I was writing *The Challenge of Cultural Development*, I was conscious of the fact that people might think I had created an understanding of culture in general, and cultures in particular, that was far too idealistic and theoretical; that I had, in effect, created a harness that was too heavy for the horse. However, I felt it was necessary to spell out in great detail what the holistic understanding of culture and cultures is really all about. I had not come across any detailed descriptions of this during the entire time I was working in the cultural field, and felt the aforementioned monograph should attempt to achieve this.

Everywhere I had travelled in the world, I was aware of the holistic character of culture and cultures. In each and every case, it was apparent that there was an underlying "whole" or "overall way of life" that was created by people as they went about the process of meeting their individual and collective needs and working out their complex association with the world. I also became aware of something else. People were constantly struggling to achieve this overall way of life, even if that struggle was not necessarily conscious or deliberate.

I felt much more attention should be paid to this matter if cultures were to be developed properly in the future. It was also necessary to develop some yardsticks against which the strengths and shortcomings of all the diverse cultures of the world could be measured, assessed, and compared, much as we presently have yardsticks to compare and asssess the strengths and shortcomings of all the diverse economies of the world.

This is particularly important with respect to the shortcomings of cultures. Unfortunately, the shortcomings are less evident than the strengths. This is because people tend to settle into a specific pattern or way of life and take it for granted, rather than constantly assessing it to determine where it is deficient and where it could be improved. Without much more attention to this matter, I felt the world was destined to pay a severe price, particularly in terms of increased pressure on the natural environment, growing shortages of natural resources, and heightened tensions between the diverse peoples, countries, and cultures of the world. The end result could well be the eventual breakdown of the entire global ecosystem if this does not happen.

Having put this theoretical ideal and practical framework in place in *The Challenge of Cultural Development* and the earlier monograph on *The Character of Culture*, I then turned my attention to the Canadian component of the World Culture Project. I was anxious to show how the holistic understanding of culture could be applied to a specific culture in the world, namely Canadian culture, as well as assess the implications of this for Canada, Canadians, and Canadian development. In doing so, I hoped that the monographs in the Canadian series might serve a useful purpose as "prototypes" for people and countries in other parts of the world that were interested in the holistic approach to the development of their cultures.

Four specific monographs were written and published on this matter: *The Character of Canadian Culture*; *Canadian Culture: Key to Canada's Future Development*; *Canada's International Cultural Relations: Key to Canada's Role in the World*; and *Culture and Politics in Canada: Towards a Culture for All Canadians*.

My first task in developing the Canadian component of the Project was to shed light on the holistic character of Canadian culture. In order to do this, I had to demonstrate how all the various parts of Canadian culture —

economic, social, political, technological, industrial, education, scientific, artistic, recreational, spiritual, and so forth — were combined to form a whole that was greater than the parts and the sum of the parts. Doing so necessitated explaining Canadian culture in detail, exposing some of its most fundamental features and characteristics, demonstrating its crucial importance to the country and its citizenry, and examining how it should be developed in the future.

These matters were addressed in the first two monographs in the Canadian component, namely *The Character of Canadian Culture* and *Canadian Culture: Key to Canada's Future Development*. Whereas the first monograph was concerned with the many different perceptions, definitions, and manifestations of Canadian culture — all of which are very relevant to the overall understanding of the country's culture as a whole or total way of life — the second monograph was concerned with the concept, content, reality, centrality, development, and future of Canadian culture.

This second monograph made it possible to create a portrait of Canadian culture as a *northern*, *resource*, *communications*, *diverse*, *dynamic*, and *creative* culture first and foremost.

It is a northern culture in the sense that much of Canada is covered with snow for a significant part of the year and the country is located in the northern half of the North American continent. It is a resource culture in the sense that Canadians have always had to rely heavily on the exploration, utilization, and exportation of natural resources, as best epitomized in Harold Innis's "staples thesis." It is a communications culture in the sense that Canadians have always been compelled to depend on various communications devices and networks to stay in touch with each other across the country's gigantic expanse. And it is a diverse, dynamic, and creative culture, since (apart from the aboriginal peoples) the Canadian population is composed largely of immigrants from other countries; Canadians have been compelled to make many fundamental changes in their lifestyles and overall way of life over the centuries in order to survive and prosper; and citizens of the country have had to be extremely creative in every domain of Canadian cultural life in order to come to grips with all the difficult challenges and take advantage of all the unique opportunities that have been presented to them.

I was especially anxious to show how knowledge of Canadian culture as a whole or total way of life can be achieved through exposure to works by the country's artists. Fortunately, I was able to use artistic works like plays, paintings, stories, and musical compositions to illustrate this point, largely because they have a great deal to say about Canada's natural environment, northern climate, immigrant experiences, social system, community celebrations, and, perhaps most importantly, sense of "place." Although artistic works demonstrated this better than anything else, they were not the only vehicles capable of doing this. It was also possible to illustrate this point through many other activities, including sports such as hockey, lacrosse, and curling, television programs like *This Hour Has 22 Minutes*, *The Rick Mercer Show*, and *Little Mosque on the Prairies*, films such as *Mon Oncle Antoine* and *Going Down the Road*, ethnic celebrations such as *Caravan,* and many others.

Once this holistic portrait of Canadian culture was in place, I made the case as emphatically as I could that Canadian culture, not the Canadian economy, should constitute the centrepiece and principal preoccupation of Canadian development. This was because the country's culture is concerned with the entire way of life of Canadians whereas the economy makes up only one part of this, albeit an extremely important part.

I wasn't opposed to placing a high priority on the Canadian economy. Nor was I opposed to building a strong economy in order to create jobs, income, and sources of livelihood. I knew how important these matters were if Canadians were to satisfy their material needs and enjoy reasonable standards of living and a decent quality of life. However, I believed that the Canadian economy was part of something much larger, as well as more fundamental and profound.

It was also important to make the case that successive generations of Canadians have struggled over the centuries to build a culture and not just an economy. They have done so for a very specific reason. It is the culture of the country that possesses the potential to meet the full range of Canadians' needs for survival, well-being, health, happiness, safety, security, and fulfillment in life. This is, always has been, and presumably always will be the principal purpose of Canadian development. It would be foolhardy and short-sighted to deny it.

These were not the only reasons for asserting the centrality of culture in Canadian development. Doing so placed a much higher priority on human well-being than on profits and the marketplace. This was of crucial importance because it shifted the priority from products to people, and consequently what was in the best interests of *all* Canadians, not just *some* Canadians. Without such a shift, it was not possible to evolve policies, programs, and practices that are designed to meet the needs of people rather than the needs of corporations, commerce, and elites.

I went on to point out that the real challenge facing Canada is the same as it is for all countries: to develop a culture that is comprehensive, coherent, cohesive, humane, and properly situated in the natural, historical, and global environment. It was necessary to make this point, and make it as emphatically as possible, if Canadians were to be successful in coming to grips with the rapidly changing nature of reality, an exceedingly complex world system, and the environmental crisis.

Having dealt with these matters in domestic terms, I turned to similar matters on the international front in the monograph, *Canada's International Cultural Relations: Key to Canada's Role in the World*. I was anxious to show that the principal challenge facing Canadians internationally was to project Canadian culture abroad in all its diverse aspects and manifestations, as well as to receive cultural projections from abroad in all *their* diverse aspects and manifestations.

Viewed from a cultural perspective, *all* relations that Canada had with other countries were obviously *cultural relations*, which is why I used this term in this monograph. This was much more than a play on words, or a theoretical necessity to be consistent with the way culture was defined for purposes of the World Culture Project. I truly believed (as I believe today) that all relations Canada had with other countries were cultural relations because they all had cultural implications and consequences in one form or another. This was as true for the country's economic and political relations as it was for its artistic, athletic, scientific, humanistic, social, and other relations.

Having made the case that there were legitimate reasons for deeming all relations Canada had with other countries to be cultural relations, I identified a number of fundamental principles that I felt should govern Canada's relations with other countries in the future. These principles were based on my conviction that the country's international cultural relations should constitute the foundation of the country's external development and the basis of its foreign policy; be balanced, diversified, equitable, and reciprocal; be predicated on caring, sharing, collaboration, and cooperation; and focus to a much greater extent on people and matters of human welfare and well-being.

These principles were designed to achieve a better balance — and much more harmony — between the material and non-material dimensions of Canada's foreign policy, as well as to provide parity between the country's social, artistic, scientific, and educational relations on the one hand, and economic and political relations on the other. This was imperative in order to position Canadian culture properly in the global environment, receive cultural projections from abroad effectively, and, in the long run, create a better Canada and a better world.

In order to achieve these goals, I felt a quantum leap was required in Canada's international cultural relations. The reason for this was not difficult to detect. Canada's external relations were severely underdeveloped. Canada had been dependent on Great Britain for so long, and Canadian foreign policy had been seen as an offshoot of British (and to a lesser degree French and more recently American) foreign policy to such an extent, that Canada was not master in its own home. A great deal more emphasis was needed on Canadian cultural sovereignty and developing Canada's own cultural relations in all areas of life in my opinion.

Once the country's international cultural relations had been deal with, I shifted my attention to one of the most complex and difficult problems of all in the development of Canadian culture — the relationship between culture and politics.

This was addressed in a monograph entitled *Culture and Politics in Canada: Towards a Culture for All Canadians*. My conviction was that Canadians needed to know much more about the complex connection between culture and politics, especially with respect to how this connection might affect the development of the country and its culture in the future.

In order to establish the proper perspective, I commenced the monograph by examining the historical development of the connection between culture and politics in Canada, particularly when culture was defined in the narrower sense as the arts and humanities. After all, this was how culture had been defined earlier in Canadian history and, for that matter, how it was still defined by many Canadians. Politics and culture in this narrower sense developed independently of one another during most of the country's history. In fact, a connection between these two areas did not really begin to emerge until the federal government got involved in a number of measures designed to preserve artworks, artifacts, monuments, and historic sites in the latter decades of the nineteenth century and first few decades of the twentieth. These actions were augmented by provincial and municipal governmental involvement about the same time in the creation of some of the country's first art galleries, museums, and libraries.

Even after the federal government created the Canadian Broadcasting Corporation (CBC) and the National Film Board (NFB) in the 1930s, established the Massey Commission in 1949 to undertake a comprehensive examination of the country's artistic and academic life, and created the Canada Council in 1957, the connection between culture and politics was still tenuous. This was because most public cultural institutions were created at arm's length from government and the political process, following a tradition well established in Great Britain to separate culture and politics.

Quebec was the only part of the country where there was a significant departure from this practice. There, the provincial government was deeply immersed in a whole series of issues related to protection of the French language and promotion of Quebec culture (in both the narrow and broad sense), largely to stave off strong pressures from Canada's rapidly expanding anglophone and non-francophone populations. Interestingly, Quebec's actions followed a tradition that was well established in France where, by contrast with Great Britain, the French government was directly and deeply involved in numerous cultural matters.

It was only in the 1970s and '80s that a stronger connection began to take shape between culture and politics in Canada. There were many reasons for this. One was the rapid growth in various types of cultural activities that were popular with Canadians and required governmental support, most notably the arts but also sports and many recreational endeavours. Another was Expo and the Centennial celebrations, which had profound cultural and political consequences in all parts of the country, largely because they were financed with public funds and a great deal of "cultural infrastructure" was created by the country's federal, provincial, and municipal governments. Yet another reason was the series of global and regional conferences convened by UNESCO in the 1970s and early 1980s to promote much greater involvement by governments in the cultural affairs of nations.

But the most important reason was surely that Canada was rapidly becoming a *multicultural country*, a fact which, needless to say, had profound cultural and political implications and overtones. The process by which this came about is informative. In the 1960s, the federal government established the Bilingual and Bicultural Commission to examine language and culture in Canada in detail. When the commission concluded that Canada was a bilingual and bicultural country, with English and French as the two principal languages and cultures, many groups that were neither English nor French reacted strongly. Although they were prepared to accept the fact that Canada was a bilingual country, they were *not* prepared to accept the conviction that Canada was bicultural. This was because many groups that were neither English nor French had made — and were making — valuable contributions to the country's cultural life. Consequently, the federal government was forced to back down and eventually declare that Canada would henceforth be designated a *bilingual, multicultural* country in the official, political sense. This declaration was made in 1971, and led to the creation of many institutions across Canada at all levels of government, as well as throughout the private sector, that were committed to translating this official designation into practice.

The resulting programs made it possible for all the diverse ethnic groups in Canada — and they were many since Canada was a "land of immigrants" — to develop and maintain their customs, traditions, identities, and cultures. Though efforts were made to promote the sharing of all the various cultures in the country, in practice a much higher priority was placed on preservation of these cultures than on sharing them. This eventually led to attempts to make the case that every ethnic group in Canada is entitled to preserve, protect, and develop its customs, traditions, identities, and culture, but not to the exclusion of others.

With this point of view came attempts to show that all Canadians shared a "common set of values and beliefs" despite their specific ethnic origins and differences. Included among these common values and beliefs were: dedication to a land of great beauty, size, and grandeur; commitment to equality, freedom, and democracy regardless of race, religion, age, gender, ability, or disability; devotion to social security and health care; recognition of the rights, freedoms, and traditions of others; willingness to consult, compromise, and make concessions; support for ethnic diversity; and commitment to peace, order, good government, and national unity. Many of these common values and beliefs — "commonalities of experience" as they were called at the Citizen's Forum on Canada's Future held in 1990 — were deeply entrenched in the country's history and culture.

Once I had dealt with these matters, I went on to establish a slate of requirements for culture and politics in Canada that I felt were imperative for the future. Five *fundamental necessities* stood heads and shoulders above the rest: commitment to a holistic rather than partial perception of Canadian culture; development of the requisite historical base; construction of an east-west cultural axis; creation of a global cultural system; and cultivation of a new political awareness. Time spent examining these five necessities is rewarding because it clarifies what is needed to ensure that Canadians are able to meet the complex challenges of the world of the future.

In my view, there was no better time to commit to a holistic perception of Canadian culture than in the final years of the twentieth century and first few years of the twenty-first. Not only would doing this help to expand awareness of the all-encompassing character of Canadian culture at a crucial time in the country's development, but also it would enable Canadians to come to grips with the nature and meaning of their culture and the reasons for protecting, preserving, and developing it. This was not only important for domestic reasons. It was also important for international reasons, due to the fact that Canada is located next door to the most powerful nation on earth and consequently Canadians are heavily dependent on American culture in many different ways.

Commitment to a holistic perception of the country's culture was also necessary to focus attention on how Canadian culture could be properly positioned in the natural, historical, and global environment, as well as to show how the component parts of this culture could be combined to form a dynamic and harmonious whole. Without more attention to matters like this, I felt Canada could easily experience higher levels of environmental pollution and ecological degradation, more social and political unrest, a declining rather than rising standard of living, and the risk of becoming unglued and splitting apart. These were unpleasant prospects, but ones which could be inevitable if the necessary precautions and actions were not taken to prevent them.

Next to a commitment to a holistic perception of Canadian culture, I was convinced that establishing the requisite historical base was an extremely high priority. It was necessary to confirm four historical facts without a shadow of a doubt: the origins and roots of Canadian culture are aboriginal, not European; the aboriginal peoples are the "founding peoples" of Canada in general and Canadian culture in particular; all of Canada's diverse peoples and ethnic groups have made — and continue to make — indispensable contributions to the development of the country's culture; and Canadian culture has a long and distinctive tradition.

There was also a dire need to create an east-west cultural axis in my view. I saw this as the key to overcoming many of the divisions that exist among the various provinces, regions, and peoples of Canada, as well as helping Canadian citizens to know and understand themselves, each other, the world around them, and the threads that bind them together as a people, a nation, and a culture. Not coincidentally, it was also the key to coming to grips with some of the country's most demanding and difficult problems, most notably the need for national unity and identity, which was threatened by too much reliance on American cultural programming, and especially by the tendency for things to flow north-south rather than east-west in North America.

I was quick to point out that Canadians were no strangers to building "axes" of one type or another. In the sixteenth, seventeenth, and eighteenth centuries, they created an east-west *exploration axis* which depended vitally on the fur trade in general and the canoe and the dogsled in particular. In the nineteenth century, they created an east-west *transportation axis* that depended initially on lake boats and steamers and later on railroads, highways, and eventually airplanes. In the twentieth century, they created an east-west *communications axis* that was dependent on the telephone, newspapers, radio, television, and, towards the end of the century, the Internet, the computer, and the rapidly emerging social media.

What I felt was needed in the twenty-first century — and needed badly — was an east-west *cultural axis*. Such an axis would have to prove capable of moving Canadian materials of all kinds — books, films, paintings, plays, musical works, radio and television programs, videos, products, natural resources, ideas, manufactured goods, and so forth — across the country in volumes and amounts hitherto unprecedented in Canadian history. In building this axis, maximum use would have to be made of materials that dealt with Canada's own cultural reality rather than the cultural reality of other countries, especially the United States, Great Britain, and France, important as these were.

There was an equally compelling need to create a global cultural system. This was required to achieve an effective balance between the component parts of this system, as well as the "inbound" and "outbound" dimensions of Canadian foreign policy. More than anything else, this necessitated achieving parity between the country's international artistic, humanistic, educational, and recreational relations on the other hand, and its international economic and political relations on the other as indicated earlier, as well as realizing a better balance between incoming and outgoing cultural activities.

This was also required to give Canada's global cultural system a more "human face," as well as to make it apparent that Canada was engaged in international relations for the purpose of improving the well-being of people and countries in other parts of the world and not just realizing economic benefits and commercial advantages for Canada and Canadians. For as John Ralston Saul, a prolific writer on Canada's historical and contemporary development, said:

> Canada's profile abroad is, for the most part, its culture. That is our image. That is what Canada becomes in people's imaginations around the world. When the time comes for non-Canadians to buy, to negotiate, to travel, Canada's chance or the attitude towards Canada will already have been determined to a surprising extent by the projection of our culture abroad.

It was for reasons such as this that I thought Canada and Canadians should pay much more attention to how people in other parts of the world view Canada and Canadians and benefit when representative aspects of Canadian culture are sent abroad. Obviously they benefit most when Canada's global cultural system is predicated on caring, sharing, and concern for others, not just on things that are of interest and importance to Canadians. In order to realize this more ideal state of affairs, it was necessary in my view to increase Canada's foreign aid and developmental assistance as a percentage of gross domestic product; develop policies and practices based on sending surplus food, clothing, building materials, supplies, and staples to less fortunate countries; share natural resources and material and monetary wealth more liberally and broadly; reduce international debts and debt loads, especially for African, Asian, Latin American, and Caribbean countries that required it; and contribute to improving social, medical, health care, and educational facilities and capabilities in the world.

The last "fundamental necessity" was to create a new political awareness. This was imperative because in the final analysis both culture and politics in Canada are concerned with "the whole" — albeit from very different perspectives — and consequently with ensuring that the parts of the whole are properly positioned in the whole and that balance and harmony are achieved and maintained between the parts and the whole. Making this a reality would give Canadian culture a stature in political affairs, and governmental policies, planning, and decision-making at home and abroad, that it has never had in the past.

The implications of all this were clear and unequivocal. Governments and politicians at all levels should abandon their penchant for thinking about Canadian culture in marginal and partial terms, and start thinking about it as the very heart and soul of the country's essence and existence.

To achieve this, political leaders and civil servants would have to devote much more time to developing Canadian culture in *all* its diverse forms and manifestations; ministries of cultural affairs would have to become the key departments in government; cultural models would have to become the main vehicles for making political and governmental decisions; and cultural policy would have to be accorded the highest priority in political affairs and public policy.

Ultimately, it was not a case of developing Canadian culture *or* developing the Canadian economy. Rather, it was a case of developing both, but developing them in such a way that the country's economy was positioned properly within the country's culture. Without proper positioning, the economy will serve economic, commercial, financial, and material interests far more than environmental, social, and human interests.

Positioning the economy properly in the country's culture was equally necessary to ensure that the economy was pointed in the right direction in the future. Not only would this yield multiple benefits, but also it would ensure that the more specific goals of the Canadian economy – production, consumption, investment, growth, profits, and so forth – were constrained and enriched by the broader and deeper goals of Canadian culture, most notably creativity, excellence, caring, sharing, respect for the natural environment and future generations, and commitment to people and the human factor in development. It would also reduce the strain Canadians were making on the natural environment, since more emphasis will be placed on the qualitative side of development and hence on activities like the arts, education, social interaction, lifelong learning, and spiritual renewal that make fewer demands on the resources of nature.

While researching, writing, and publishing the monographs in the international and Canadian components of the World Culture Project took up most of my time during this period (although I must confess not as many monographs were researched, written, and published as I had hoped), I was also involved in a number of other activities related to the quest to broaden and deepen knowledge and understanding of culture and cultures in general and Canadian culture in particular.

Most important in this regard was the close friendship and professional association I was developing with Walter Pitman. I had known Walter for many years and had the greatest admiration for him as a tireless promoter of education in Canada, a politician, a president of Ryerson University, an executive director of the Ontario Arts Council, and a director of the Ontario Institute for Studies in Education. He had retired from institutional life by this time in order to devote time to some research and writing that he was anxious to do.

We agreed to read each other's manuscripts in draft form and get together once a week to discuss this and other matters related to culture, Canadian culture, and the world situation. I found this extremely helpful, not only in terms of Walter's feedback on my draft manuscripts, but also because Walter was committed to writing books about what he called "Canada's cultural heroes." At the time, he was writing a book on Louis Applebaum and his contributions to Canadian music and Canadian culture. This eventually led to books on Harry Freedman and Mary Morrison and their contributions to Canadian music, and Elmer Iseler and Victor Feldbrill and their contributions to Canadian and international choral conducting and music.

Fortunately, I was also able to get a number of other documents and articles written and published during this time. Included here were "The Evolution and Character of the Concept of Culture" and "The Millennium Challenge: Making the Transition from an Economic Age to a Cultural Age," published in *World Futures: The Journal of General Evolution*; "Cultures and Economies: Irresistible Forces Encounter Immovable Objects" and "Towards a New World System: A Cultural Perspective," published in *Futures: The Journal of Forecasting, Planning and Policy*; and *Canada's Contribution to the International Practice of Arts Management*, published by the Centre for Cultural Management at the University of Waterloo. I was also fortunate to have another document — *The New World Order: A Contribution to the World Decade for Cultural Development* — published by UNESCO in its *Major Programme I. Reflection on World Problems and Future-Oriented Studies*.

All through this time, I was working on a book that was intended to pull all my thoughts, ideas, and research findings on culture together and make them available in one place. It seemed a fitting way to commemorate the World Decade for Cultural Development.

CHAPTER EIGHT

A New Beacon for the Future

I had been struggling to come to grips with the complexities and secrets of culture for more than thirty years. During this time, I had gained a great deal of practical experience through my work on cultural projects at the municipal, regional, national, and international level, as well as my missions for UNESCO. I had also acquired a significant amount of theoretical knowledge through my research at the Scarborough campus of the University of Toronto, the creation of the World Culture Project, and encounters with different cultures in the world.

While the journey up to this point in my life had been long and arduous, it was also extremely rewarding. I was beginning to see some light at the end of the tunnel. Things that seemed very murky several decades earlier were starting to become much clearer to me.

Nothing was clearer than the fact that humanity needed a new "beacon for the future." While economics had provided this beacon for more than two centuries, it was becoming increasingly apparent that economics did not possess the breadth of vision or depth of understanding that was needed to shine light on the way forward in the new century and new millennium.

My use of the term "beacon" was very deliberate here. I chose this word because a beacon must be able to perform two key functions if it is to do the job properly. In the first place, it must be able to warn of impending danger and ensure that the necessary safeguards and precautions are taken to prevent it. Secondly, it must be able to illuminate a clear, vital, viable, and safe path forward.

Of all the fields that might be able to perform these dual functions, culture headed the list in my view. But in order to achieve this, it was necessary to accord culture a central rather than marginal role in the world. Nothing was more imperative than this.

As I was searching for ammunition to make the case for the centrality of culture in the world of the future, I came across a statement that confirmed this belief better than anything I had even seen. It went straight to the heart of what culture is all about and why it is so essential. This statement was made by Bernard Ostry, a fellow Canadian who was working in the cultural field about the same time I was, in his book *The Cultural Connection*. Here is how Ostry's book began:

> Culture, however we define it, is central to everything we do and think. It is what we do and the reason why we do it, what we wish and why we imagine it, what we perceive and how we express it, how we live and in what manner we approach death. It is our environment and the patterns of our adaptation to it. It is the world we have created and are still creating: it is the way we see that world and the motives that urge us to change it. It is the way we know ourselves and each other; it is our web of personal relationships, it is the images and abstractions that allow us to live together in communities and nations. *It is the element in which we live.*

I was so enamoured of this statement that I decided to use it as the epigraph for the book I was working on throughout the entire World Decade for Cultural Development. I decided to call the book *Culture: Beacon of the Future*, in view of my belief culture could best perform the dual functions of a beacon. The book was published by Adamantine Press in Great Britain and Greenwood/Praeger in the United States in their *Twenty-first Century Series* in 1998. It was devoted to demonstrating in theoretical and practical terms why culture should be accorded a mainstream rather than marginal role in the world. The most important reason was that culture possesses many capabilities in general — and one very important capability in particular — that are of utmost importance to the world of the future.

Since these capabilities were inherent in the many different perceptions and manifestations of culture and there was so much confusion throughout the world over the nature and meaning of culture, I decided to tackle this problem at the very beginning of the book. No greater mistake could have been made in asserting the case for the centrality of culture than failing to be very specific about the way the term was used in the book.

It took four chapters at the beginning of *Culture:Beacon of the Future* to address this problem. However, the results were worth it. It made it possible to show how culture has evolved as an idea over a history spanning some two thousand years, shed light on the main perceptions and manifestations of culture – from the earlier artistic, humanistic, historical, and psychological ones to the later sociological, anthropological, ecological, and biological ones – and to illustrate when these many different understandings of culture first appeared in the historical literature. It also made it possible to show that every perception and manifestation of culture possesses a number of characteristics and capabilities that are of great importance to the world.

Consider the artistic perception and manifestation. When culture is seen and manifests itself in the world as the arts, it possesses the potential to bring an enormous amount of happiness and fulfillment into people's lives. It also acts as a gateway to a comprehensive understanding of all the different cultures in the world, as well as promoting the conservation of resources since artistic activities don't make as many demands on nature's resources as other activities. Or, to use an example drawn from the opposite end of the spectrum, when culture is seen and manifests itself in the biological sense as the organizational forms and structures of different species, it highlights the similarities and differences that exist between human beings and other species, as well as the multiplicity of relationships between and among all species.

Nor is this all. Many perceptions and manifestations of culture possess the potential to alert us to possible dangers. As a total way of life, for example, culture sheds light on why there are so many differences between the diverse cultures, countries, and peoples of the world. People see the world, act in the world, and value things in the world differently, thereby creating the potential for a great deal of conflict and confrontation if this matter is not dealt with effectively.

This is equally true (if not more so) when culture is seen as the legacy from the past. Culture in this sense focuses on the "cultural baggage" that people inherit from the past and carry with them from one generation to the next as noted earlier. This reminds us of the need to be ever mindful of the many different uses and abuses of culture, as well as to ensure that the necessary safeguards and precautions are created to ensure that differences in worldviews, values, customs, traditions, beliefs, and ways of life are dealt with fully. It also highlights the need to place a great deal of emphasis on cultural education – education committed to broadening and deepening knowledge and understanding of all the diverse cultures of the world and the many differences between them — as well as the need for many more intercultural and international cultural exchanges.

What is true for the aforementioned perceptions and manifestations of culture is equally true for all the others. Every one, from the artistic to the biological, possesses the potential to make crucial contributions to the world in a whole series of distinct, dynamic, and diverse ways, as will be demonstrated in detail later in the book

As difficult as this problem has been throughout my life, I was beginning to understand that the many different perceptions and manifestations of culture constitute a powerful asset to be capitalized on rather than a diabolical curse to be endured. While the many different perceptions and manifestations can cause a great deal of uncertainty and confusion, they also provide indispensable insights into virtually everything that exists in the world, from the human to the non-human, the individual to the collective, the local to the global, the material to the non-material, and the commonplace to the sublime.

Small wonder Bernard Ostry called culture "the element in which we live." Edward T. Hall, a well-known American cultural scholar, made this same point when he said:

> Culture is man's medium; there is not one aspect of human life that is not touched and altered by culture. This means personality, how people express themselves (including shows of emotion), the way they think, how they move, how problems are solved, how their cities and planned and laid out, how transportation systems function and are organized, as well as how economic and government systems are put together and function.

This is as it should be. For more than any other activity, culture possesses the potential to come to grips with the enormous amount of complexity and diversity in the world. We will never be able to deal effectively with this complexity and diversity until we recognize culture's remarkable capacity to come to grips with this.

While each perception and manifestation of culture has something of crucial importance to contribute, there was something of far greater importance that had to be identified and documented fully in the first few chapters of *Culture: Beacon of the Future*. It was the relentless trend throughout history towards a holistic understanding of culture. This holistic understanding is of quintessential importance to the world of the future because it possesses one key capability that the other understandings of culture do not, namely the capacity to see and deal with culture in terms of "the whole" rather than the parts. Here was the principal reason why I thought culture should be accorded a central role in the world and act as a beacon of the future. Humanity desperately needs an idea that makes it possible to see things in holistic rather than reductionist or specialized terms.

Having made this case in the first few chapters of *Culture: Beacon of the Future*, I set out to show how this all-encompassing understanding of culture could be applied to people, communities, the state, and the world. Just as economics had dealt with these four matters through the creation of a highly complex and elaborate system of thought and practice – largely through concepts like "economic man," municipal, regional, and national economies, the global economy, and the state as a generator of economic activity – so I felt culture had the potential to do this as well. As a result, I devoted a separate chapter to each of these matters.

Of these chapters, the one on culture and people was the most important. The world needed a "new prototype of the human personality" because of problems that were being encountered with the two existing prototypes –the "economic personality" and the "specialist personality."

The main problem with the economic personality (or "economic man" as it was called) was that people were viewed largely as consumers, commodities, and maximizers of consumer satisfaction in the marketplace. While this may have been an accurate depiction of the way people were (and are) treated in modern economic systems, such a view reflected only one dimension of the human personality, albeit an extremely important one.

The same problem was encountered in the specialist personality, or "specialized man." Just as contemporary economic systems relied heavily on specialization because it increased the production of goods and services and the productivity of workers, so people were encouraged to specialize in a very specific production function in order to secure a job and reliable source of income. While this practice produced benefits during the Industrial Revolution and for a long time thereafter, modern economic systems were changing so rapidly by the end of the twentieth century that highly specialized people were often redundant soon after they had acquired their specialization, due largely to rapid technological change and fundamental changes in economies and the marketplace.

These were not the only problems with these two prototypes. The economic personality emphasized consumption at a time when the natural environment was being destroyed at an alarming rate and demands were being made on the world's scarce resources that were difficult to justify or sustain. In much the same way, the specialist personality placed a great deal of emphasis on specialization at a time when more and more people were finding that they were "too specialized" and the trend was towards having many jobs over the course of a lifetime, rather than staying in one job forever.

What lay at the root of these problems was the fact that both these prototypes viewed people from a one-dimensional and partial rather than multi-dimensional and holistic perspective. Such a perspective was less and less relevant in a world that was in a state of dynamic change and continuous flux.

There was an urgent need for a new prototype of the human personality, which I called the *cultural personality*. For despite the importance of economics and specialization, the fact remained that every person lives a holistic life that (like culture itself) is composed of many parts — material and non-material, physical and mental, spiritual and emotional, earthly and sublime. Ultimately, these parts have to be combined in some way to form a harmonious whole.

I was reminded of Matthew Arnold's idea of the "whole person" that I had encountered years earlier in his book, *Culture and Anarchy*. In this book, Arnold talked about the need to attend to the "harmonious development of all the faculties that comprise human nature" as one of the principal keys to understanding how people should live their lives and develop their personalities. The fact that this was first and foremost a cultural and not an economic requirement could not be denied. John Cowper Powys expressed this same conviction, but in an even more compelling way, when he said:

> The whole purpose and end of culture is a thrilling happiness of a particular sort — of the sort, in fact, that is caused by a response to life made by a harmony of the intellect, the imagination, and the senses.

To achieve this sort of happiness is to be constantly striving to see, feel, experience, and comprehend the wholeness, oneness, and unity of all things, or, as Goethe said, "to live in the whole" and "will the whole" as one of the highest objectives in life. It matters little that holism in some ultimate, metaphysical sense may not be attainable. What is most important is to be continuously striving to achieve this, and to this end constantly fusing all the mental, physical, emotional, and spiritual dimensions of the human personality together to form a holistic and integrated entity.

Viewed from this perspective, the cultural personality is about perpetual acts of integration and synthesis aimed at melding together all the diverse fragments of being and personality development: internal and external; subjective and objective; material and non-material; self and other; and so forth. It is through this process that I felt the cultural personality would ultimately become *centred*, *authentic*, *creative*, *altruistic*, and *humane*.

These were obviously admirable qualities. But how can they be achieved? Surely by developing the mind, body, intellect, senses, emotions, and all the other faculties that comprise our personalities as fully and effectively as possible.

Of all the points of penetration into this process, cultivation of *the art of seeing* is by far the most essential. For how people see the world determines to a large extent how they act in the world, live in the world, and value things in the world. This is probably why Goethe said that it is with the eye more than any of the other sense organs that he learned to comprehend the world. Interestingly, Constantin Huysmans, Vincent van Gogh's art teacher in elementary school, possessed similar convictions. He felt that developing the powers of observation and cultivating the art of seeing are the principal keys to perspective, which in his opinion was the most essential aim of arts education.

All this made a great deal of sense to me because it was largely through the eye that I learned to see the world in cultural and holistic rather than partial and economic terms. Without cultivating the art of seeing, I doubted very much that I would have come to this understanding.

It followed from this that the art of seeing should be developed to the point where it acts as a window on the external world of reality and the internal world of the self. In order to do this, seeing must be extended in all directions: past, present, and future; spatial and temporal; spiritual and material; within and without. Not only should it be finely tuned to the larger world, but also it should be firmly focused on the mundane, the minute, and the minuscule. In other words, it should be concerned with the progressive enlargement of vision, as well as the perpetual refinement of vision.

As important as cultivating the art of seeing is to the development of the cultural personality, this is clearly not an end in itself, but rather the first step in cultivating all the other senses. For what is true for the art of seeing is also true for the art of hearing, touching, smelling, tasting, and intuiting. Cultivation and refinement of each of these senses must be undertaken with the same degree of care. For aural acuity, tactile sensitivity, olfactory capability, taste discrimination, and intuitive feeling are equally essential if the objective is to expand knowledge and understanding of the external world of reality and the internal world of the self. As John Cowper Powys said, "The very essence of culture is the conscious development of our awareness of existence."

It is difficult to see how cultivation of the senses can be attended to effectively without a comprehensive education in the arts. From music, there is exposure to sound, rhythm, harmony, counterpoint, and composition. From dance, there is exposure to touch, movement, balance, muscle control, and physical coordination. From the visual arts and architecture, there is exposure to mass, shape, texture, density, form, proportion, perception, and perspective. And from drama, there is exposure to emotions, feeling, tragedy, comedy, humour, pathos, and virtually every other aspect of the human personality and human society.

And this is not all. Every work of art is a whole made up of many parts, be it a painting, a play, a poem, a musical composition, an opera, or anything else. This means that there is an enormous amount to be learned about holism and the holistic perspective from the arts. While excesses and imbalances between the parts are permitted in a work of art — indeed, this is often what makes a work of art distinctive and unique — the parts are not allowed to dominate, overwhelm, or undermine the whole. The challenge is always to create a whole that achieves balance and harmony between and among the parts. Exactly the same is required of the cultural personality.

What education in the arts does for the development of the senses, physical fitness does for the development of the body. Without proper diet, good nutrition, health care, disease prevention, and a great deal of daily exercise, the body will not function effectively and will atrophy. This is why movement systems like tai chi, qi gong, yoga, calisthenics, and so forth, as well as walking, swimming, running, jogging, and other activities that require physical exercise, are so essential. They loosen up the limbs and lubricate the joints, thereby keeping the body in fine working order and good physical condition. This is especially important since many families and educational institutions presently pay little attention to this fundamental requirement of developing the whole person and consequently the cultural personality.

Cultivation of people's mental abilities is every bit as important as cultivation of their bodies and senses. Clearly, development of these abilities requires the capacity to use the mind and the intellect freely and fully, which is why subjects like philosophy, physics, chemistry, biology, mathematics, history, geography, and especially languages are so valuable. They enable people to cut through the shell of illusion in order to get at the key assumptions and premises underlying all things. Too often, too much time is focused on outward appearances and too little time is left to examine the fundamental essence of things. As a result, it is easy to end up dealing with secondary symptoms rather than primary causes.

It is through cultivation of all these diverse capabilities that the cultural personality is able to progress into some of the more profound areas of personality development. In much the same way that the art of seeing opens a window to the other senses, so the senses, body, intellect, and mind open a window to the heart, soul, spirit, and emotions. The development of these capabilities must be attended to with the same degree of rigour as the development of all other human faculties. This is what Jan Christiaan Smuts, an astute observer of personality development, prime minister of South Africa, and a philosopher of international renown, had to say about the importance of this and what may be expected in return:

> In proportion as a personality really becomes such, it acquires more of the character of wholeness; body and mind, intellect and heart, will and emotions, while not separately repressed but on the contrary fostered and developed, are yet all collectively harmonized and blended into one integral whole; . . . the wear and tear of internal struggle disappears; the friction and waste which accompany the warfare in the soul are replaced by peace and unity and strength; till at last Personality stands forth in its ideal purity, integrity, and wholeness.

It is difficult to see how the cultural personality can "stand forth in its ideal purity, integrity, and wholeness" without evolving a basic philosophy of life. In his book *Cosmic Understanding*, Milton Munitz explains why it is so essential to create and develop such a philosophy:

> When acquired, such a philosophy provides a framework of basic principles that helps guide a person's reactions to the cri-

> ses and opportunities of life, to the universal facts of human existence – being born and dying, being a member of society, being part of a wider universe. To have a set of basic guiding principles, whether accepted from some external source or worked out for oneself, is an inescapable requirement for a human being.

It follows from all this that the cultural personality is not a philosopher, artist, humanist, "cultured person," or "Renaissance man" in the conventional sense. On the contrary, he or she is a person who is concerned first and foremost with the way all the component parts of being are coalesced together to form a "total person" – a person who is fully integrated internally within the self as well as fully integrated externally in the world. This is what personality development is all about – blending together life's infinite ingredients and experiences to create a seamless web.

Smuts believed that this is the highest form of personality development. His thoughts on this matter resonated strongly with me as I was working on the chapter in *Culture: Beacon of the Future* on the cultural personality and still do so today:

> Personality then is a new whole, is the highest and completest of all wholes, is the most recent conspicuous mutation in the evolution of Holism . . . . [It is] the supreme embodiment of Holism both in its individual and its universal tendencies.

Whenever I scour my mind for people who best exemplify the cultural personality, I think of Albert Schweitzer, Pitirim Sorokin, Nelson Mandela, Mahatma Gandhi, Mother Theresa, and Dr. Martin Luther King Jr. Each of these individuals possessed many of the requisite qualities and characteristics; they also acted in ways that best exemplified what the cultural personality is all about.

Albert Schweitzer was an extremely gifted individual who abandoned an outstanding medical and musical career in Europe to work with lepers in Africa, risking his life and his health in the process in order to help others. A strong advocate of ethical conduct and reverential thinking and action as the keys to living a full, upright, and meaningful life, Schweitzer had this to say in a passage that is most revealing of many attributes of the cultural personality:

> The ripeness that our development must aim at is one which makes us simpler, more truthful, purer, more peace loving, meeker, kinder, more sympathetic. That is the only way in which we are able to sober down with age. That is the process in which the soft iron of youthful idealism hardens into the steel of a full-grown idealism which can never be lost.

Like Schweitzer, Pitirim Sorokin was a strong advocate of ethical conduct and the role that ethical conduct could — and should — play in people's development. As one of the strongest advocates for the centrality of culture in global development and people's lives, as well as one of the most prolific writers on the subject of culture and the intimate relationships between the component parts of cultures, Sorokin had this to say about the need for a heightened sense of consciousness in the human, cultural, and environmental sense:

> The most urgent need of our time is the man who can control himself and his lusts, who is compassionate of all his fellow men, who can see and seek for the eternal values of culture and society, and who deeply feels his unique responsibility to the universe.

What was true for Schweitzer and Sorokin was equally true for Nelson Mandela, Mahatma Gandhi, Mother Theresa, and Dr. Martin Luther King Jr. Whether Mandela, Gandhi, or Mother Theresa set out to change the world is impossible to say. What can be said, however, is that they had a profound effect on the world by staying largely in one location working with local people. They did not travel all over the world attempting to make it a better place for all. They remained in one place and hammered away at grassroots problems with deep-seated international implications and consequences, thereby allowing the force of their personalities and the strength of their convictions to speak for them. It was the same kind of dedication and commitment that Martin Luther King Jr. exhibited when he became the principal spokesperson for blacks in America. Towards the end of his life, which unfortunately ended too abruptly, King said he wanted nothing more than to be known as a person who devoted his entire life to a cause.

If the chapter on the cultural personality was one of the most important in *Culture: Beacon of the Future*, the chapter on community cultural development was not far behind. The reason for this was not difficult to see. By the time I was working on this book, urban communities of all types and sizes, from tiny towns and villages to colossal cities and megalopolises, had become as important — if not more important — than nation states. Half the world's population was living in urban centres by this time and that proportion was expected to grow rapidly.

This fact had major implications. For one thing, it exerted incredible pressure on municipal resources. Many of the problems resulting from this — over-utilization of facilities, inadequate waste disposal, increased water, air, and noise pollution, the appearance of ghettos, slums, and shanty towns, the loss of safety and security, and the spread of violence and conflict — could not be attended to properly because most municipalities lacked the financial resources, constitutional powers, and institutional mechanisms to do so.

Moreover, increasing numbers of people in the world were looking to various forms of urban agglomeration to solve their economic, social, artistic, and spiritual problems. With this desire came the realization that the quality of life in urban communities was a decisive factor. If urban centres lacked the basic necessities of life — good jobs, decent accommodation, fresh water, clean air, reliable food supplies, hospitals, health care, educational institutions, recreational facilities, artistic amenities, religious and spiritual possibilities, environmental conservation, and the like — no amount of industrial growth, technological innovation, or economic development would make up the difference.

As I began to research this matter more intensively, I began to realize that urban community development has almost always been approached from a partial rather than holistic perspective. As a result, it has almost always been dominated by specialized institutions and activities of one type or another.

Take Europe, for example. In classical times, many European towns and cities were dominated by amphitheatres, arenas, and monuments to the gods, of which the Parthenon in Athens and the Coliseum in Rome are only the best known examples. In medieval times, religious institutions and buildings played the dominant role. The church was the central institution and principal focal point in most European towns and cities. Not only did all roads lead to and from the church, but also it towered over the city in physical size and ideological grandeur. To live within sight of the church or the sound of the church bells was to live within the city.

During the Renaissance, social activities and institutions replaced religious activities, institutions, and buildings at the core of community life.

In a purely physical sense, the square replaced the church as the centrepiece in many European towns and cities. Not only were such squares as San Marco in Venice or the Palio in Siena *the* place to meet friends, conduct business, and idle away the time of day, but also, like the church, they were designed to inspire and uplift people. Through its use as a place to conduct business, communal celebrations, and community events, the square brought people together and strengthened the social bonds of the community.

In modern times, economic activities and institutions have replaced social and religious activities and institutions at the core of most European towns and cities, as well as in virtually all towns and cities in the world. The objective has been to satisfy the economic needs of people and the interests of trade, industry, and commerce. Even the terms used– industrial zone, business district, workers' tenement, middle-class neighbourhood, bourgeois area, and so forth – betray the economic shadow that hovers over most towns and cities. And what has replaced arenas, amphitheatres, churches, cathedrals, and squares at the heart of most urban centres in the world? In all likelihood a colossal office or bank tower, a factory, a mall, a smokestack, or a shopping centre.

While all these developments were legitimate for one reason or another in their own time, I kept wondering if the time had come to take a holistic approach to urban development. The reason was clear. Such an approach put the emphasis on communities as harmonious and integrated wholes, rather than smorgasbords of disconnected and unrelated parts, at a crucial time in municipal, regional, national, and international development.

It was at this point that I recalled my experiences with the Ontario Ministry of Culture and Recreation years earlier, when I was working on the development of the culturescape methodology. This methodology was very pertinent to urban development in all its diverse forms and manifestations.

As a device for developing an understanding of urban development that is total rather than specialized – cultural rather than religious, social, economic, or political – the culturescape methodology focused on bringing things together rather than splitting them apart, thereby dealing with one of the most difficult and dangers problems in urban development. The methodology was also designed to give people a strong sense of community identity and belonging, increase their awareness of their community as a dynamic, organic, and distinctive whole made up of many parts, and get people actively involved in the process of building their community in a comprehensive and collective sense. As noted earlier, much of this methodology depended on getting citizens and community groups actively involved in creating many different profiles of their communities — environmental, historical, scientific, economic, political, social, aesthetic, human, and so forth. These profiles were made up of many parts. For example, the aesthetic profile was made up of all the different sights, sounds, smells, textures, and tastes of communities; the historical profile of information on how communities were originally settled and how they evolved over time in response to the challenges and opportunities that confronted them.

When all these different profiles are added up, they produce a compelling portrait of communities as comprehensive entities and ordered wholes. Collectively, these profiles are concerned with the distinctive cultural imprint that communities make on a very specific piece of the world's geography as well as a very particular period in human history. As indicated earlier, they can be organized and orchestrated in different ways to produce maps, walks, inventories, tours, and so forth, and are very useful for planning and policy purposes because they convey the cultural statement that communities make to themselves and the rest of the world.

What could be said about community cultural development at the urban level in the final analysis? Surely this. Without a much higher priority on community exploration and discovery, cultural planning and decision-making, a holistic approach to community development, citizen participation in the process, and especially the development of people's pride of place, urban centres will not be able to respond to the demands that people will make on them in the future.

Once I had completed the chapter on community cultural development, I turned my attention to the cultural state. This was undoubtedly one of the most difficult chapters in the book to write. What I had in mind was the cultural state *at the national level* because I was moving progressively in the four chapters from the individual and community level to the national and international level. However, I recognized that this chapter was applicable to the cultural state at the municipal, regional, and other levels as well.

I commenced this chapter by documenting the fact that many different visions of the state have been advocated over the course of history. On the one hand, there have been utopian visions, such as those proposed by Plato, Saint Augustine, Robert Owen, Marx and Engels, and others. On the other hand, there have been theoretical and practical visions, such as those advocated by Machiavelli, military strategists, political theorists, economic authorities, religious leaders, and so forth.

These visions have produced a panorama of possibilities: the philosopher state, the religious state, the nation state, the industrial state, the authoritarian state, the growth state, the equilibrium state, the stationary state, the welfare state, the democratic state, and so on. All these visions, and others that have been proposed throughout history, have been idealistic in the sense that they have provided some ideal of the state that politicians, civil servants, religious leaders, and citizens can identify with and work towards in the realization of their roles, responsibilities, policies, and practices.

Despite the fact that all these visions have performed a valuable function at one time or another, the majority of them seemed ill-suited to the world of the future. They are either too discredited, outdated, or idealistic to merit serious attention — such as Plato's philosopher state and Marx and Engels' classless state — or are not relevant to a world that is dominated by groundbreaking developments in technology, economics, communications, the environment, and so forth. While considerable care must be exercised not to reject these visions out of hand since they all possess certain elements that are important — such as the welfare state with its emphasis on equitable distributions of income and wealth — it is not possible to adopt them as the basis for the ideal state of the future.

There are, however, a couple of visions of the state that have been advanced throughout history that do have some relevance to the world of the future. One of these is the *stationary state*. What makes this vision relevant to the world of the future is the fact that it arose out of fears in the nineteenth century over rapid population growth on the one hand and severe shortages of natural resources on the other. It is a situation not unlike that presently experienced in certain parts of the world, and that will likely be more common in the future.

Here is how the idea of the stationary state came about. According to classical economists, the stationary state was inevitable in the long run because the quantity of land (or the availability of natural resources, as we would say today) was fixed while population was growing. While the classical economists believed that improvements in "the state of technique" (or technology as we call it now) could make up for the fixity of land and resources and outstrip population growth for a time, ultimately the stationary state was inevitable in their view because improvements in technology would not be sufficient to ward off the law of diminishing returns indefinitely. When this day arrived, according to the classical economists, increases in the stock of capital and population growth from births would be offset by decreases in the stock of capital and deaths, thereby bringing about the stationary state. It was simply not possible to go on adding more of a variable factor of production — namely labour, which results from population growth — to a fixed factor of production — namely land or the natural environment — without eventually encountering the law of diminishing returns.

What is interesting to note about this particular vision of the state is not only its relevance to the present and prospective global situation, but also the way it was interpreted by the large majority of classical economists. While virtually all classical economists saw the stationary state as a diabolical curse that had to be endured because people's standards of living and quality of life would be decreased rather than increased as economic growth was curtailed, John Stuart Mill saw the stationary state in more optimistic terms. He felt it produced an opportunity that should be embraced rather than rejected:

> It is scarcely necessary to remark that a stationary condition of capital and population implies no stationary state in human improvement. There would be as much scope as ever for all kinds of mental culture, and moral and social progress; as much room for improving the Art of Living, and much more likelihood of its being improved.

Despite Mill's endorsement of the stationary state, it has received scant attention. There are many reasons for this. In the first place, the world has been much more concerned with economic growth than with the "art of living" over the last century-and-a-half. In the second place, the dominant belief throughout the world is that technology can continuously improve and therefore ward off the point of diminishing returns. Indeed, it has only recently been recognized that economic growth is being achieved at an incredible environmental cost, not only in terms of a great deal of human exploitation and suffering but also in terms of growing shortages of natural resources, climate change, and the deterioration of the globe's fragile ecosystem. The law of diminishing returns may not be dead after all! But the real reason for the lack of interest in Mill's interpretation of the stationary state is that it was a positive image erected on a negative base. Unfortunately, its inability to hold out a ray of hope for most people that the material circumstances of their lives could be improved accounts for the scant attention this concept has received.

The other vision of the state that has relevance for the world of the future is the *equilibrium state*. Unlike the stationary state, this concept holds out some hope for people that the material circumstances of their lives can be improved in the future, but only at a limited or sustainable rate. Consequently, there is a certain amount of flexibility, fluidity, and dynamism to the equilibrium state that does not exist in the stationary state.

In fact, the term "equilibrium" suggests that there is room for a certain amount of growth, movement, and development, but also that a great deal of balance is required between the opposing forces of economics and the environment, materialism and spiritualism. This is what makes the equilibrium state, or the *sustainable state* as it is often called following its advocacy by the Club of Rome and the Bruntland Commission on Environment and Development, so enticing today. Economic growth, technological development, and material advancement can occur, but not at an unmitigated rate. On the contrary, well-defined and carefully controlled limits are imposed on growth and development that are closely linked to the finite carrying capacity of the earth and the needs of future generations.

Having addressed two of the most relevant visions of the state in terms of the present situation and prospects for the future, I set out to address some of the main characteristics of the cultural state, just as I had identified some of the main characteristics of the cultural personality in the chapter dealing with that topic.

Viewed as a whole, the cultural state should be *authentic*, *indigenous*, *self-reliant*, *sovereign*, *civilized*, and *creative*. By this I meant that the cultural state should be true to its origins and roots, grow in a manner that is consistent with its own specific historical development and needs, depend on itself rather than other states to a significant extent, be master in its own home, be sophisticated and compassionate in dealing with people and all political procedures, policies and practices, and be innovative in its design and development. States that were too quick to embrace the worldviews and values of others, did not struggle to come to grips with their own circumstances, problems, and possibilities, allowed other countries to dominate their domestic and international development and decision-making processes, and acquiesced to ways of life inconsistent with their own interests and the interests of their citizens would never become cultural states in the all-encompassing sense.

Once the principal characteristics of the cultural state were examined, I analyzed some of the main similarities and differences between culture and politics when they are visualized in holistic terms, since these factors were of crucial importance to the administration and functioning of the cultural state.

The most important similarity by far was the fact that both culture and politics are concerned with "the whole," provided that culture is defined in the holistic sense and politics in terms of what is in the best interests of a country's citizens. The implications of this fact for political development and administration are clear and unequivocal. It is the first and foremost responsibility of politics in general, and governments, politicians, civil servants, and the political process in particular, to attend to the development of culture, cultures, and cultural development and policy in the all-embracing, holistic sense.

This is much more than a philosophical premise or theoretical device; it has profound implications for governments and politicians. The focus of attention in the future should be on achieving balance and harmony among all of the diverse components of the cultural state, rather than responding to the interests and concerns of certain components or some interests to the detriment of others. The consequences of this approach for the distribution of income and wealth, as well as the emphasis this approach places on the qualitative and quantitative dimensions of development, the material and non-material factors in life, and "soft" and "hard" activities, are monumental to say the least.

Despite the fact that both culture and politics are holistic, their objectives are not the same. Generally speaking, the objectives of politics are peace, order, stability, security, justice, the rule of law, and good government. The objectives of culture are creativity, excellence, diversity, beauty, truth, freedom of expression, and so forth. The potential for conflict between the two is readily apparent. Governments may be pursuing some objectives while citizens and community groups may be pursuing others.

A few examples of this should suffice. Citizens and community groups may be pursuing truth, while governments are prioritizing order, security, or the rule of law. While individuals may feel that freedom of expression is paramount, the state may feel that suppression or censorship are the best ways to ensure their priorities. Or, to cite another example from many, some citizens and community groups may be pursuing creativity while at the same time governments favour stability, thereby producing a great deal of conflict between the two goals. It follows from these two examples that there is a vast panorama of actual and potential points of conflict between culture and politics that must be resolved. In the cultural state, this is always resolved through dialogue, discussion, compromise, and concession rather than confrontation, suppression, oppression, and conflict.

Having examined the basic characteristics of the cultural state as a whole and some of the principal similarities and differences between politics and culture, it was necessary to examine the components of the cultural state. I emphasized that it was necessary to *reformulate* many of these components in order to keep them in tune with the dynamic nature of reality and rapidly changing world conditions, as well as to *reorder* them to ensure that they met the needs and interests of the cultural state, and not just the needs and interests of specific components of the state or specific individuals, groups, or institutions.

While I was deeply committed to the need to reformulate the components of the cultural state, since the world was changing so rapidly and most if not all of the components needed updating in some way, I was far more committed to the need to *reorder* these components. This was largely because the world was so deeply immersed in the economic age at the time that preference was accorded to the economic component over all others. As a result, there was a need to reorder priorities in such a way that much more attention was given to other key components, particularly the human, ethical, and environmental components.

In the case of the human component, it was essential to place a much higher priority on people, as well as the human factor in development. Here is what was said about this component:

> Failure to give sufficient consideration to the human component of the state accounts for many of the world's most difficult and debilitating problems: the division of the world into two unequal parts; the plight of the vast majority of inhabitants of the earth; the constant threat of nuclear war; the dehumanization of life; unacceptable levels of unemployment and pollution; and loss of personal identity and collective fulfillment. Many of these problems might have been reduced in severity, if not eliminated, if a higher priority had been awarded to the human factor in development.

If this problem was to be addressed successfully in the future, I felt a much higher priority had to be placed on the ethical component. In order to do this, it was essential to develop an ethical code that was capable of asserting the basic importance of people in general and ethical values and ideals in particular. For ethical values are buried deeply in the womb of the human condition and therefore the cultural state, regardless of whether it is viewed from a sacred, secular, religious, cultural, or any other perspective.

Development of this ethical code was essential in my view because ethical values are humane in nature and universal in scope. They are humane in the sense that they deal compassionately and sensitively with people's need for understanding, sympathy, empathy, equality, and trust. They are universal in the sense that they place the interests of humanity as a whole ahead of the interest of specific individuals, groups, and institutions. As a result, they yield that level of conscience and consciousness required to produce major redistributions of income, wealth, and resources on a more equitable basis. I believed deep down that ethics, rather than economics, is the key to overcoming hunger, poverty, starvation, income inequality, and human suffering in the world. The world situation will not change significantly until humanity makes a commitment to living life on a higher plane of ethical existence.

Reordering the components of the cultural state was also necessary to ensure that a much higher priority was placed on the environment component. I wasn't quite sure how this could be accomplished, but felt the first step in the process was to recognize that the natural environment plays a much greater role in people's lives and the world system than people are willing to admit. Without doubt, moving the environmental component closer to the core of the cultural state would achieve a great deal in terms of focusing on the need to reduce humans' huge ecological footprint. Whereas certain types of consumption practices make large demands on the natural environment, others make smaller demands. Many of culture's most cherished activities consume comparatively few resources, especially artistic, humanistic, educational, and social activities. Apart from the need for a limited supply of materials — paints, brushes, and canvases for the painter, stone, wood, or other natural elements for the carver, clay for the potter, musical instruments for the musician, books and computers for the scholar, and a park bench where people can sit, converse, and idle away the time of day — the arts, humanities, education, and social activities make much more modest demands on nature's precious resource legacy than many other activities.

The next task in *Culture: Beacon of the Future* was to examine culture at the global level. This chapter was titled "International Cultural Relations" and began with the following statement by Paul J. Braisted, an American authority on international cultural relations:

> Cultural cooperation . . . is the way in which the world's peoples can work together, voluntarily, constructively, and to mutual advantage, in building a progressive, orderly, and more kindly world society. . . . Cultural cooperation is so directly a national interest that it should furnish the fundamental motivating principle in governmental foreign service, replacing or reordering all lesser motives.

My commitment to cultural cooperation was accompanied by a corresponding commitment to other matters that were deeply entrenched in culture in general and international relations in particular, especially caring, sharing, equality, altruism, and collaboration. I felt focusing on these matters would do a great deal to increase foreign aid and developmental assistance as a percent of net disposable income, make it possible to renegotiate debt loads and the terms of trade on a more equitable basis, and facilitate much more sharing of income, employment, and resources throughout the world, particularly between rich and poor countries and rich and poor people. It would also contribute a great deal to creating a system of international relations based on the development of culture and cultures in the holistic sense.

Three priorities were essential in this regard. The first was to assert the importance of *the human family* in international relations. Despite the incredible complexity that exists in the world, all people are members of a human family in the sense that they share more similarities than differences. It was also necessary to make this case in order to assert the importance of people over things, especially in the myriad relationships that take place on a daily basis among the many diverse peoples, countries, and cultures of the world. Here again, Braisted had something very meaningful and relevant to say:

> The advancement of peoples and nations requires a radical subordination of profit-seeking motives to human impulses. The welfare of people must gradually become the primary concern, and the manifold activities of commerce and business, hasty or careless industrialization, competition for natural resources, labor, and markets, must be adjusted accordingly. . . . Clearly,

> subordination of economic motives to the humane interests of people is essential to world order, and to preparation for more fruitful cooperation.

The second priority was to assert the importance of the cultural heritage of humankind in the development of this new system of international relations. For just as all people are members of one human family, so they are all inheritors of a priceless legacy from the past.

What stands out most clearly when the cultural heritage of humankind is looked at in totality is its vastness, diversity, and universality. Not only is it made up of countless contributions from every part of the world, but also there is hardly a group of people, community, region, or country in any part of the world that has not made a crucial contribution to it. Since this heritage is the product of all people, countries, and cultures, it is on this undeniable fact that humanity should seek to build a more just, equitable, and viable system of international relations. As the real indicator of humanity's greatest accomplishments down through the ages, this priceless treasure-trove of objects, artifacts, ideas, and so forth is discernible amidst the rise and fall of different countries, cultures, and civilizations.

And this brings us to the third and final priority in the creation of this new system of international relations. It is the need to place a much higher priority on the arts, humanities, and education in this system. This was in marked contrast to the system that was in vogue when I was writing *Culture: Beacon of the Future* and still is today. In the existing system, economic, commercial, technological, political, and financial interests are accorded top priority as indicated earlier. Despite the vast importance of these interests, what must be recognized is that these interests are cold and impersonal, since they deal with products rather than people and matters of material and monetary gain rather than the heart, the soul, and the spirit. Because the human element is missing, the potential for war, aggression, conflict, confrontation, and terrorism is high and ever-present.

But this is precisely where the arts, humanities, and education come in. Human expression is their very nature. Whether it is the sonorous melodies of the musician, the passionate pleas of the priest, rabbi, or imam, the curiosity of the scholar, or the teaching of the educator, the human element glows through every artistic, humanistic, and academic act. As the true purveyors of a country's most human and humane expression, these activities expose the real heart and soul of nations. In doing so, they communicate across geographical frontiers and political divides in profound and moving ways, revealing most clearly what countries, cultures, and civilizations are all about, how they have evolved over time, and what they hold most dear to themselves.

Bringing countries, cultures, and civilizations into intimate contact in this way is not the only reason for advocating a massive build-up of international relations in the aforementioned areas. There are other reasons as well. When economic, commercial, military, and political relations are turbulent, relations in these other areas provide a strong stabilizing and countervailing force. They help to cushion the shocks that can easily arise from erratic swings in the pendulum of economic, political, military, commercial, and financial power. They also help to eradicate fears, suspicions, mistrust, and misunderstanding that often result from the inability to understand the beliefs, behaviour, values, and worldviews of others. As a result, a massive build-up of artistic, humanistic, and educational relations provides an opportunity to bring the whole of humanity into intimate and personal contact — an opportunity that is far too important to pass up.

Maximum use should be made of the latest and most sophisticated forms of technology and communications in the development of this new system of international relations. It is now possible to transmit knowledge, information, ideas, and expertise from one part of the world to another in the flash of a second. Not only are such technologies helpful in conserving resources, but also they possess the potential to bring the very best humanity has to offer within reach of virtually every member of the human family.

Once I completed the four chapters on people, the community, the state, and the world viewed from a cultural perspective, I turned my attention to how these lofty ideals could be translated into concrete realities. Since this aim was achieved most effectively through "the art of cultural development and policy," I wrote a separate chapter on this subject.

This chapter was designed to show how cultural development and policy are the vehicles that are needed to achieve the aforementioned objectives and ideals. This is particularly true for cultural policy, since it possesses the potential to focus public and private attention on the many different strategies, tactics, procedures, and processes that are needed by governments in general — and ministries of cultural development in particular — to produce concrete results. As noted earlier, Gerard Pelletier summed up this potential most effectively when he said "cultural policy is nothing more or less than a plan for civilization." This is exactly what I believed was most essential for the world of the future. I believed the world needed a new plan for civilization — a new beacon of the future, as I put it — that was predicated on the holistic understanding of culture and the effective development of culture and cultures in all parts of the world.

I ended *Culture: Beacon of the Future* with a chapter entitled "Towards a Cultural Age." As I was writing this chapter, my thoughts harkened back to 1975 when Guy Métraux published two of my articles on this subject in UNESCO's journal *Cultures*.

Although much had transpired in the intervening years, my thinking on this matter had not changed. While my understanding of the complexities of culture had broadened, deepened, and intensified considerably through all my theoretical discoveries and practical experiences, I was still deeply committed to the idea that the world needed to pass out of the existing economic age and into a future cultural age if human welfare and environmental well-being were to be achieved. Consequently, this is how *Culture: Beacon of the Future* ended:

> . . . when culture is conceived and defined in holistic terms, it possesses the potential to combine all the parts of the whole in a more coherent, compelling, and harmonious rendering of the whole. Here the challenge is not to downplay or disregard the powerful forces of the present age, but rather to blend these forces with other forces in the creation of a more integrated and humane approach to the human condition. . . . Ultimately this is what crossing over the threshold to a cultural age and viewing culture as a beacon of the future is all about.

Shortly after *Culture: Beacon of the Future* was published, I received a letter from Professor Gao Xian in Beijing, China. We were both members of an international organization called CULTURELINK that had its headquarters in Zagreb, Croatia. This remarkable organization was brought into existence by UNESCO and the Government of Croatia in 1989 to commemorate the World Decade for Cultural Development, much as I created the World Culture Project at the same time for a similar purpose.

Gao informed me that he had been asked by the Social Sciences Academic Press in China to recommend a few books in other languages that he felt should be translated into Chinese and made available to Chinese readers. He had read an article of mine — also called "Culture: Beacon of the Future" because it was related to the subject matter of the book I was working on — that had been published in an issue of CULTURELINK's *Newsletter*. Gao learned that I had a book published on this subject, and wondered if I could send him a copy, which I did.

I didn't hear anything more about this matter for several months. Then, one day, a second letter arrived from Gao saying that he had read the book and had recommended its translation into Chinese and publication in China by the Social Sciences Academic Press and they had decided to do this. Talk about making my day! I had long admired Chinese culture — indeed, ever since the time when I presented the project on Marco Polo in public school, as described in the first chapter of this book — and now one of my books on culture was about to be translated into Chinese and published in China. I couldn't have felt more honoured. I had worked on *Culture: Beacon of the Future* for the better part of ten years on a part-time basis and four years on a full-time basis. I had fervently hoped that the book would help to shine the spotlight squarely on culture — and with it cultures and cultural development and policy — and now it was going to be translated into Chinese and published in a country that had one of the oldest and most distinguished cultures in the world. I felt blessed.

CHAPTER NINE

Assessing the Economic Age

By the time *Culture: Beacon of the Future* was published, the twentieth century was coming to an end, and the twenty-first century and the third millennium were beginning. There was a great deal of excitement in the air. It stemmed from the belief that humanity may well be standing on the threshold of a new age in global development and human affairs.

Many books were coming out about this time that discussed what kind of age this should be. For some, it should be an information, technological, scientific, or environmental age. For others, it should be a social, humanistic, artistic, or spiritual age. Such thoughts were understandable in view of the fact that many people felt the dawning of a new century and new millennium provided a unique opportunity to strike out in a bold new direction. As a result, the market was flooded with all sorts of books dealing with this matter.

Culture: Beacon of the Future was one of these books. I was hoping that the book would resonate strongly with people who felt the future age should be a cultural age. I had made a concerted effort in the book to show that culture and cultures should play a central rather than marginal role in the world, and had even called the last chapter of the book "Towards a Cultural Age" in the hope that this type of age might be realized in the future. The fact that the book was published by Adamantine Press and Praeger/Greenwood in their *Twenty-first Century Series* augured well in this regard. The timing couldn't have been better. People seemed to be tired of the existing situation and were looking for new visions of the future.

While I was hoping *Culture: Beacon of the Future* would generate some fruitful discussion, interest, and debate, I was not so naïve as to think that a cultural age could be realized any time soon. My training in economics had taught me that the world was securely locked in an economic age, and that economics was the most powerful force in the world. The reason for this was not difficult to discern. Since economics is concerned with the production, distribution, and consumption of goods and services and creation of material and monetary wealth, it is concerned with people's jobs, income, and sources of livelihood on the one hand and power, money, and materialism on the other hand. On these grounds alone, a compelling case could be made for the fact that the world was securely locked in an economic age.

And this was only half of it. By the end of the twentieth century, most people and institutions believed economics was the key to everything in life, and therefore fundamental improvements in all sectors of society, and not just the economic sector. In fact, Marx had even gone as far as to contend that humanity is *always* locked in an economic age as indicated earlier. This view was endorsed and embraced by most countries and governments in the world, regardless of whether they were capitalist, communist, socialist, liberal, or conservative in nature.

I found myself growing ever more concerned about this view of the human condition and global situation as the twentieth century ended and the twenty-first began. Was humanity really destined to live in an economic age forever? If so, what were the implications and consequences of this? If not, what kind of age should follow the prevailing economic age? Should it be a cultural age as I hoped? Or should it be some other kind of age?

What slowly but surely began to emerge in my mind was a book that would subject the economic age — and the possibility of a cultural age in the future — to a vigorous and detailed analysis. The book would begin by examining the origins, evolution, mechanics, and most powerful forces of the economic age, and then go on to assess its various strengths and shortcomings and compose a "balance sheet" on it. This would make it possible to show in concrete terms why the economic age was not viable going forward, despite the fact that it has produced an enormous amount of material and monetary wealth and improved standards of living and the quality of life for billions of people since it was first created in the eighteenth century. It was not viable because it was incapable of coming to grips with the problems that had loomed up on the global horizon.

Compiling such a balance sheet would also make it possible to show why it was so essential to pass out of the existing economic age and into a future cultural age. This would be followed by a detailed examination of how a cultural age could be created and how it would function, as well as what the basic aims, objectives, and ideals of such an age would be. What I was doing, in effect, was subjecting two of the oldest and most powerful forces in the world — economics, which can be traced back to the Greeks, and culture, which can be traced back to the Romans — to an intensive analysis that was intended to show that they both possessed numerous qualities, capabilities, and characteristics, but that the qualities, capabilities, and characteristics possessed by culture were more relevant to the world of the future than those of economics. With these thoughts in mind, I set out to do the research and writing necessary to create the book.

While economics has constituted a fundamental part of human development from the very beginning, humanity did not really enter an economic age until 1776, when Adam Smith's *The Wealth of Nations* was published. Smith was the first person to make a comprehensive and compelling case for the centrality of economics and economies in global development and human affairs. He did so because he was convinced that this was the key to creating material and monetary wealth, higher standards of living, and a better quality of life. Those goals were to be accomplished by means of an elaborate theoretical and practical *system*. It is clear in retrospect that the system he created provided the foundation needed to usher in the economic age as documented earlier.

Once I had fleshed out the origins of the economic age through a detailed examination of Adam Smith's evocative theories and famous book, I turned my attention to how the economic age had evolved from that time through the end of the twentieth century. I considered powerful theoretical contributions from classical, Marxian, neoclassical, Keynesian, and developmental economists, as well as equally powerful practical contributions from corporations, governments, and individuals. By the end of the twentieth century, the western world was fully ensconced in the economic age. Economics and economies had become the centrepiece of western societies and the cornerstone of the world system, which was dominated almost entirely by the western world.

Underlying all this was an *economic worldview* that was undoubtedly the most powerful worldview in the world. It was based on the belief that people's needs and wants *in all areas of life* can be satisfied most effectively by making economics, economies, and economic growth the principal preoccupation of life in general and municipal, regional, national, and international development in particular.

Susan Hunt, an astute observer of the world situation and rapidly emerging global trends, summed this situation up best when she said:

> The economic ideology, the dominant intellectual framework in the world today, has reduced practically every human value to the categories of economics: production and consumption, basic needs and satisfiers, human rights, scarcity, nature, energy, systems, Cartesian time and space, the assumption that all things are measurable and comparable. One example is the expression "Third World," now used in an exclusively economic sense, which overlooks all the other significant differences between the industrialized world and alternatives to it.

Having demonstrated how the economic age had evolved from the publication of Adam Smith's *The Wealth of Nations* to the end of the twentieth century, I proceeded to document how this age — like all ages — was based on a number of forces that had come to dominate society. In the case of the economic age, these forces were specialization; production and consumption; the interaction of producers and consumers; capital accumulation; profits, profit maximization, and the profit motive; competition; technology; consumerism; materialism; the marketplace; and monetization.

Once these forces had become firmly established in the west, it was only a matter of time before pressure would build to extend the economic age to other parts of the world. As discussed earlier, this commenced shortly after the Second World War, when President Truman made his inaugural speech to Congress and the American people about the importance of *development* for the United States and the world as a whole. Momentum gathered quickly after this as a result of the transmission of the idea of development to countries in Asia, Africa, Latin America, the Caribbean, and the Middle East, largely through the work of developmental economists, western countries, many international organizations, and world leaders who were committed to this objective.

These trends received a major boost at the very end of the twentieth century through major advances in technology and communications in general, and *globalization* in particular. With the cold war and twentieth century concluded and a new century and new millennium beginning, it was believed that the "miracle of development and economic growth" could be extended, albeit with far greater difficulty, to Africa, Asia, Latin America, the Caribbean, and the Middle East. Globalization would ensure that people in all parts of the world, not just in the west, would be able to enjoy higher standards of living and a better quality of life. Globalization would also enable huge markets to be opened up in China, India, Brazil, and other eastern and southern countries, more effective development to be realized through the efforts of the World Bank, the International Monetary Fund, the World Trade Organization, and especially the United Nations through its "development goals," and a much stronger commitment to western values and the western way of life to be achieved in other parts of the world. Many felt it was only a matter of time before poverty would be significantly reduced, if not eliminated, through economic growth. Once these developments took place, the entire world would be living in an economic age. There was a sense of optimism that the economic age was finally beginning to fulfill its full potential.

Such was the situation that existed when I completed my examination of the economic age and began to undertake a rigorous assessment of it. Why was this assessment so essential? It was essential, in short, because there is a tendency in *any* age to get so caught up in the strengths of the age that sight is lost of the shortcomings. This fact alone makes it imperative to stand well back from every age and examine it with a critical eye in order to expose both its strengths and its shortcomings.

Doing so was particularly important with respect to the economic age because it had become so powerful and pervasive throughout the world by the end of the twentieth century — and individuals, institutions, and governments in all parts of the world had become so caught up in it — that its continuation was now taken for granted and accepted without reservation or qualification everywhere in the world. This was all the more reason why it was essential to undertake a vigorous assessment of the economic age's basic strengths and fundamental shortcomings, in order to determine whether it should be perpetuated in the future.

In undertaking this assessment, I was exceedingly grateful for the training I had in economics and the social sciences, as well as the many years I spent wrestling with the complexities and secrets of culture, and most especially the holistic understanding of culture. The training I had in economics and the social sciences enabled me to assess the economic age with a great deal of detachment. In fact, it led me to undertake the assessment in the first place, since one of the principal premises of social scientific training — like training in all the sciences — is to examine everything with an impartial and critical eye.

I was equally grateful for the struggle I had waged over the years to come to grips with the complexities and secrets of culture and particularly the holistic rendering of it. I had learned an enormous amount from this struggle about how necessary it is to focus on the "big picture" and not merely its component parts, as well as on the importance of examining the complex interconnections and interrelationships that exist — ***or do not exist*** — among the component parts.

With these thoughts in mind, I set out to examine the many strengths of the economic age. What stood out most clearly was how much had been achieved since the publication of Adam Smith's *The Wealth of Nations*. In Smith's day, substantial material and monetary wealth was limited to a few countries in western Europe, such as England, France, Germany, and to a lesser degree Portugal and Spain, as well as to a very small percentage of people in those countries — and an incredibly smaller percentage of people in other parts of the world. The overwhelming majority of people in the world lived in abject poverty, with few prospects for enjoying even "the basic necessities and conveniences of life" (as Smith put it). When Thomas Hobbes, writing half-a-century before Smith, declared that life was "nasty, brutish, and short," he captured the essence of what life was like for the large majority of the world's inhabitants, then and for a long time thereafter.

Contrast this with the situation at the end of the twentieth and beginning of the twenty-first century. While many people throughout the world continued to live in abject poverty and had little hope that their standard of living and quality of life would improve, a large and increasing percentage of the world's population was enjoying living standards, quality of life, and per capita incomes that were immensely greater than those of people living three centuries earlier. This change was due largely to enormous increases in production, productivity, and productive capacity, increases which would not have been possible without the economic age's commitment to the centrality of economics, economies, and economic growth. Not only had levels of production increased astronomically in many parts of the world, but they had done so in every sector and segment of public and private life, from agriculture, industry, business, government, education, and health care to social affairs, the arts, the sciences, politics, and technology. Substantially more of everything was being produced compared to previous centuries. The fact that a substantial percentage of the world's population was still not much better off had far more to do with problems related to the *distribution* of wealth than problems related to the *production* of wealth.

What was true for production was also true for productivity, the amount of goods produced per worker. This increase in productivity was due primarily to specialization, but also to capital accumulation, improvements in labour-management relations, education, and vast increases in the size and character of markets. While conditions were far from ideal in most parts of the world for millions of workers, there is no doubt that workers in virtually all parts of the world were producing more of everything in per capita terms than they had a decade or two earlier, let alone a century or two earlier.

Productive capacity had also grown exponentially during this time and was many times greater than in the past, despite the fact that many companies were operating at far less than full capacity. Rather like the issue of distribution as opposed to the production of wealth, this was far more a problem of demand than supply. Whenever there was enough effective demand — demand backed up by the money to pay for it — supply increased quickly to take advantage of it.

These advances would not have been possible without phenomenal improvements in science and technology. Not only did these improvements prove capable of circumventing the law of diminishing returns and thwarting the arrival of the stationary state — prospects that were of such grave concern to the classical economists — but also they made life less physically strenuous for millions of people throughout the world.

The entire way agriculture and industry were perceived and practiced was totally transformed, due largely to the agricultural and industrial revolutions, incredible breakthroughs in science and engineering, and substantial advances in "the state of technique." These advances were matched by major improvements in disease control and prevention, health care, sanitation, life expectancy, birth rates, death rates, and incredible achievements in transportation and communications.

These developments were matched by a tremendous expansion in the realm of choice, as well as the creation and availability of millions of new and better products. There were also many more opportunities for education and training, travel and tourism, and recreation and entertainment, particularly in the west but increasingly in other parts of the world. For all these reasons, people in every part of the world were keen to enjoy the fruits of the economic age. While some may have lamented the passing of bygone eras, few would have exchanged the existing situation for life in the past, especially if it meant substantially shorter lives, much higher mortality rates — especially child mortality rates — premature death, destitution, a great deal more poverty, disease, and suffering, sixty- to eighty-hour work weeks, and vastly more squalor, misery, and starvation.

Nor were these the only strengths of the economic age. The economic age also demonstrated a remarkable capacity for dealing with many of the difficult, demanding, and unexpected problems that arose during its evolution. When preoccupation with production was getting out of hand in the early part of the nineteenth century, for instance, Thomas Malthus, John Stuart Mill, and especially Karl Marx were able to shift the focus from the production of wealth to the distribution of wealth. While this did not solve the distribution problem once and for all — in fact, it is worse today than ever before in many ways, because a tiny percentage of the world's population now owns or controls most of the world's income, resources, and wealth — the efforts of Malthus, Mill, Marx, and others were instrumental in creating a better balance between the production and distribution of wealth in their own time and for a considerable time thereafter.

This same responsive capacity was evident a century later when there was excessive preoccupation with economic growth and *laissez faire* economics. In this case, welfare economics, which was aimed at taking the needs and interests of all classes in society and not just the rich and privileged into account, grew rapidly. Thanks to theoretical contributions from economists like A. C. Pigou, John Hicks, Gunnar Myrdal, John Kenneth Galbraith, and many others — as well as practical contributions like medicare, workers' compensation, pension plans, progressive taxation, labour unions, better labour-management relations, and a variety of redistribution schemes — the economic age demonstrated a remarkable capacity for responding to the problems and inequalities that it was confronted with at that time.

More recently, there has been the international spread of the idea of *sustainable development* — or development that takes the natural environment and future generations into account — that resulted from the World Commission on Environment and Development, or Bruntland Commission, of 1982. While the capacity of the economic age to respond to the environmental crisis has not resolved the crisis — indeed, many would argue that matters are worse than ever before — there is no doubt that the idea of sustainable development has helped to mitigate some of the adverse features of the crisis. The environmental crisis would have been far worse by the end of the twentieth century had the concept of sustainable development not been created.

This capacity of the economic age to respond to many different and demanding problems was also accompanied by advances in the ability of governments and financial authorities to manage highly complex economic systems. This ability should never be underestimated or taken for granted, since economic forces capable of having devastating effects can hit at any time. This fact has been repeatedly demonstrated, from the stock market crash of 1929 and the financial "meltdown" of the 1990s, to the various financial catastrophes that have erupted since that time, especially towards the end of the first decade of the twenty-first century.

Despite these problems, corporate and governmental officials have a better understanding of complex economic systems and how they can be managed than they did when the economic age began. They also have a much better understanding of how the various monetary and fiscal tools at their disposal can be used to control fluctuations in economic activity and address difficult economic, commercial, and financial problems. While there is still an enormous amount to be learned, many of these advances grew out of experiences with the Great Depression and the New Deal, the management of business cycles, Keynesian economics, refinements in economic science, and major advances in monetary and fiscal policy.

Yet another strength of the economic age that was crystal clear by the end of the twentieth century was the favourable effect this age was having on population growth. While it is difficult to determine which is cause and which is effect, there was no doubt by the end of the last century that there was a high correlation between improvements in people's standards of living and reductions in population growth. People who enjoyed higher standards of living needed fewer children to look after them in old age. They also needed more income to educate their children and their grandchildren, thereby causing them to limit the number of children they were likely to have.

As a result, population growth slowed significantly in the final decades of the twentieth century in those parts of the world where economic growth was most rapid — most notably Europe, North America, Australia, New Zealand, and Japan — thereby providing an effective alternative to the kinds of population controls that had to be instituted in China. While the world's population continued to increase in *absolute* terms, there were significant improvements in the *rate* of population growth. While population growth remains a major problem in the world today, it (like the environmental crisis) would be a much greater cause for concern had it not been for the impact of the economic age.

There is one final factor that must be examined if the strengths of the economic age are to be dealt with effectively. It is the creation of a set of goals and objectives that people, governments, and countries in all parts of the world could identify with, work towards, and endeavour to achieve. While this is a less obvious strength than the others, it must also be included if the list of strengths of the economic age is to be complete.

Think what the world would have been like by the end of the twentieth century if most people, countries, and governments did not share the conviction that economics, economies, and economic growth should be the centrepiece of global development, human affairs, and the world system. This belief provided an inexorable bond between peoples, countries, and governments. There would have been much more instability, conflict, and chaos in the world if different countries and governments had been committed to divergent agendas and different courses of action rather than sharing this common ground.

By the time I had completed the examination of the many strengths of the economic age, the twentieth century had ended and the twenty-first century had commenced. Unfortunately, the sense of optimism and excitement that ushered in this new century was not maintained. The vicious attacks on the World Trade Center and Pentagon on September 11, 2001, without doubt one of the most horrific events in human history, sent shock waves through the entire world community. They signalled that there was something seriously wrong in the world. While most people still believed that the economic age was "the way to go," it was obvious that there were groups of people — and possibly even entire countries — that did not agree with this.

The fact that the attacks occurred in the United States and were directed at the World Trade Center did not go unnoticed. For the United States and the World Trade Center epitomized everything the economic age stood for and was predicated on: money, power, materialism, consumption, consumerism, capitalism, corporatism, economics, and unfettered economic growth. When the Twin Towers collapsed before the eyes of the world, it confirmed that not everyone was "on side" with the economic age and that many had concerns and reservations about it.

Like most people in the world, I was struggling to understand this horrific event and make sense of it. My immediate concern was for the many people who had lost their lives or loved ones in these vicious attacks, as well as for their families that would be compelled to endure the pain and suffering of this "dark day in history" forever. However, I knew from my travels in different parts of the world that there were some people, especially in those parts of the world that had not benefited greatly from the economic age and felt marginalized, exploited, and oppressed, who opposed the continuation of the economic age if it meant imposing values and ways of life that were prevalent in the United States and the west upon the rest of the world. Clearly there were some fundamental shortcomings of the economic age that also had to be identified and addressed.

The most obvious shortcoming was the devastating effect the economic age was having on the natural environment. As economic demands and expectations escalated everywhere in the world, more and more pressure was exerted on the natural environment and a great deal more damage was done to it. Countless environmental problems were manifesting themselves throughout the world, most notably climate change as a result of global warming, the spread of greenhouse gases and toxic substances, and especially pollution. These problems were so pronounced that many environmentalists were predicting that the entire global ecosystem could collapse at some point in the not-too-distant future if aggressive action was not taken to prevent it.

If devastation of the natural environment was one shortcoming of the economic age, promotion of a highly materialistic way of life and exploitation of the world's scarce resources at an alarming rate were others. These shortcomings were all connected, of course. Not only was everyday life becoming highly dependent on the ever-increasing production and consumption of goods and services, but also there was a vast increase in demand for products that were high in material inputs and outputs, such as seemingly endless quantities of consumer goods. This demand entailed an exponential increase in consumption of natural resources, thereby exerting enormous pressures on the world's finite resource base and limited carrying capacity.

These problems were exacerbated by the fact that the large majority of economists, business leaders, and government officials continued to treat the natural environment as a "given" and pay little attention to it. They persisted in the belief that the natural environment should be treated as an "externality" that exists outside the realm of economics.

While this was bad enough in itself, it was far worse when considered in relation to population growth. While growth of world population had slowed significantly in relative terms as noted earlier, the world's population was still expected to increase substantially in absolute terms in the years and decades ahead. If at the turn of the century six billion people were making incredible demands on the natural environment, what would the situation be like when the population of the world was eight billion, ten billion, fifteen billion, or possibly twenty billion? The mind boggled at the mere thought of this.

Major inequalities in income and wealth were another serious shortcoming of the economic age. While some impressive gains had been achieved in the distribution of income and wealth in the final decades of the twentieth century, largely through rapid rates of economic growth and higher standards of living in China, India, Brazil, and other Asian, African, Latin American, Caribbean, and Middle Eastern countries, many disturbing problems and trends remained.

Average income in the world's richest countries — primarily countries in the west — was still many times greater than average income in the poorest countries. And what was true *for* countries was also true *within* many countries. Income of the richest people in the rich countries was many times greater, and growing far more rapidly, than income of the poorest people in these countries. The same was true in virtually all the world's poorer countries. It was as if the middle class was being "hollowed out" in many parts of the world and the situation was reverting back to the old "two-class society" made up of a few rich people and everyone else. This problem was worsening substantially as the twenty-first century progressed, so much so that it led to the creation of the Occupy Wall Street Movement and many other activist initiatives that were concerned first and foremost with the fact that a tiny minority of people owned or controlled the bulk of the world's wealth. It was a problem that augured badly for the future.

A related problem was the high human cost of increased production and economic growth. While wealth creation was recognized as one of the greatest strengths of the economic age, it did not come without a price. Many of the increases in production and productivity would not have been possible without a great deal of oppression in the form of low wages, deplorable working conditions, and the exploitation of labour — particularly female and child labour — in the "less developed" parts of the world. When this was combined with poverty, hunger, unfair labour practices, non-existent social benefits, and high unemployment and underemployment rates, it was evident why there was so much hostility, anger, and resentment in certain parts of the world. This was without doubt an important factor in contributing to the horrific events of 9/11.

While valiant and influential efforts were being made by the United

Nations through its "development goals," as well as other international organizations, governments, and countless aid workers and welfare agencies to come to grips with these problems, the economic age was proving to be much more effective at producing and consuming wealth than at distributing it. There seemed to be an inherent tendency in the economic age to produce huge disparities in income and wealth – and with this a great deal of unemployment, underemployment, and exploitation – regardless of what type of economic system prevailed in the world and whether governments were capitalist, communist, socialist, liberal, or conservative. Recent developments have confirmed this trend since many of these problems have become more acute over the last few years.

Another serious shortcoming of the economic age was the high priority that was placed on products, profits, capital accumulation, and the marketplace as opposed to people and human welfare and well-being. While this had not been the intention when the economic age began, it was certainly a conspicuous feature of this age by the first few years of the twenty-first century.

One consequence of this was that governments were much more immersed in the economic affairs of nations, so much so that their principal role had become economic rather than political. This shift in roles was accompanied by concerted efforts to "force-feed" economies and economic growth by spending much more public money than governments were bringing in, thereby causing many governments to go deeper and deeper into debt. Unfortunately, governments failed to heed the sage advice of John Maynard Keynes in this respect – that they should accumulate budgetary surpluses in good times in order to have the funds necessary to expend on public works and other projects in bad times. It was as though governments felt they could go on accumulating debts and deficits forever without having to pay a severe price at some point. This became painfully apparent midway through the first decade of the twenty-first century, when the financial bubble burst and many governments were forced to deal with colossal debts and deficits by introducing stringent austerity measures.

What was true of governments was also true of ordinary people. Many people, caught up in the economic age, were going deeper into debt in order to acquire more and more material possessions. One consequence was that people were being treated more as commodities and objects than as human beings. The exclusive focus on how people were expected to behave in economic terms had turned them into little more than consumers whose principal (if not their only) function was to purchase ever increasing amounts of goods and services in order to maximize their consumer satisfaction and keep economies growing.

The problem here, as became painfully apparent in the first decade of the twenty-first century, was that people were buying more and more on credit and accumulating larger and larger debts, much as governments were. This was not significantly different from the situation that occurred during the stock market crash of 1929, which triggered the Great Depression, except that consumers were buying commodities on credit rather than stocks and bonds on margin. However, the consequences were the same. When the financial bubble broke, many consumers lost their homes and other possessions, just as people did in the thirties when their stocks and bonds became worthless.

This created countless problems. It made it impossible for people to realize their potential in a human sense because their lives were defined almost exclusively in economic terms. Some called this "the crisis of maldevelopment," or "spiritual poverty in the midst of plenty." People in the developed parts of the world were discovering that consumption and materialism did not provide a guarantee of happiness and fulfillment in life. In fact, the more consumer goods and material commodities they acquired — and the more they participated in the economy and the marketplace — the more they found they were lacking the spiritual and emotional resources required to live happy and fulfilling lives. As Oscar Wilde once said, it is possible to know "the price of everything and value of nothing."

A concomitant problem here was the high level of stress and anxiety that many people were experiencing as a result of living in the economic age. For some, this was because contemporary economic systems were robbing them of their jobs, due in large measure to the rapidity of technological change which brought with it a great deal of corporate downsizing and outsourcing. For others, it was because the economic age was destroying their traditions, identities, customs, cultures, and ways of life, as well as eroding cherished institutions like the family, the neighbourhood, the community, and religious institutions. And for still others, it was because life had become so speeded up that it was impossible to escape from the economic system's constant demands in order to get some badly needed rest and relaxation. While it would be a mistake to blame the economic age entirely for these problems, there is no doubt it was a major contributor to them.

And this brings us to the final shortcoming of the economic age — the tendency to destroy the sense of community and social bonds necessary to hold people, organizations, societies, countries, and cultures together when other forces are splitting them apart. Karl Polanyi focused attention on this problem many years earlier in his book, *The Great Transformation: The Political and Economic Origins of Our Time*. In this book, Polanyi described in detail the transition that occurred from a "market economy" to a "market society" in the nineteenth and early twentieth centuries. He demonstrated how, through the development of markets for land, labour, capital, and commodities, everything had become individualized and atomized, thus severing the bonds that existed in most societies and in the various social collectivities that were to be found within them.

Once I had addressed the strengths and the shortcomings of the economic age, I was confronted with the most difficult task of all — drawing up a balance sheet for the economic age.

This necessitated much more than adding up all the various strengths and shortcomings of the economic age, prioritizing them in some way, and awarding the outcome to the winner. While this was part of the assessment process, what was really needed was to evaluate the economic age at a much deeper and more profound level. This is what my training in the social sciences and research in culture encouraged me to do and what my intuition and inner convictions drove me to do. Regardless of how difficult this task was, they compelled me to assess the economic age as objectively and impartially as possible.

Examining the economic age in this way was imperative because the population of the world was continuing to increase rapidly, albeit at a slower pace than before, a fact that had profound implications for human beings in all parts of the world as well as other species in the future. It was also imperative because there were many problems at the core of the economic age that had to be confronted and overcome if human survival and environmental well-being were to be assured. Most prominent among these problems were:

- Huge inequalities in income and wealth;
- Treating economics as "the whole" rather than a part of the whole; and
- The potential collapse of the natural environment.

As I was thinking about the huge inequalities in income and wealth, I kept going back to John Stuart Mill and the distinction he made between the laws governing the production of wealth and the laws governing the distribution of wealth.

According to Mill, the laws governing the production of wealth are largely physical, mechanical, and technical in nature, and therefore cannot be changed to any great extent. However, the laws governing the distribution of wealth are very different. They are primarily human and social in character, and consequently can be changed — and changed significantly. Mill concluded from this that it was possible to do something practical and concrete about the distribution of wealth. He attempted to do this in his own society by advocating policies that were liberal and socialist rather than capitalist and conservative in nature, as well as by focusing on the potential that education possessed to change people's beliefs and attitudes about how wealth *should be* distributed as opposed to how it *is* distributed. In Mill's opinion, once wealth is created, people can distribute it in any way they like.

Thinking about Mill's approach to this issue focused my attention on how political systems and governments deal with the distribution of wealth. Unfortunately, by the end of the twentieth century, the world seemed to be moving farther away from liberal and socialist approaches to this problem, as well as closer to conservative approaches. With this shift, distributions of income and wealth were becoming *more* unequal, not less so. Study after study revealed that the bulk of the world's income and wealth was owned and controlled by a small percentage of the world's population. Not only was this imbalance contributing to the explosive political and social situations that existed in some parts of the world; those situations were likely to become much more explosive in the future if nothing was done to alleviate and correct this problem.

What had become crystal clear by the beginning of the twenty-first century was that the "trickle-down effect" — the scenario by which, as the economy grows, wealth and income "trickle down" from the richer classes of society to the poorer classes — was not working as expected. At the same time, the problem of whether or not more equitable distributions of wealth could ever be lastingly achieved in the economic age was moot. Clearly a much higher priority would have to be placed on social and humanistic policies and practices, as well as on the emotional, sensorial, and spiritual sides of life, if more equitable distributions of wealth were to be realized to any significant extent.

This was something that seemed very unlikely, if not impossible, as long as humanity was locked in the prevailing economic age. There was an inherent tendency in this age to produce huge inequalities in income and wealth regardless of what policies, practices, governments, programs, and political parties were in existence. As a result, the only way standards of living and quality of life could be improved for billions of people throughout the world was through higher rates of economic growth, something that was clearly unacceptable because it would mean exerting even more pressure on the finite carrying capacity of the earth and the world's scarce resources. Ultimately, this course of action could make everyone worse off rather than better off if it destroyed the capacity of the earth to support a huge human (and non-human) population.

As difficult as this distribution problem was, the second problem was equally difficult. Just as there is an inherent tendency in the economic age to produce huge inequalities in income and wealth, so there is an inherent tendency in this age to treat economics as "the whole" and everything else as "a part of the whole." As we have seen, this point of view is not justified in philosophical, theoretical, or practical terms. What makes it particularly acute is the fact that when economics is looked at in this way, everything is justified in economic terms. If activities don't deliver "economic impact" and contribute to economic growth and development in some concrete and measurable way, they are deemed to be unimportant.

By the end of the twentieth century, signs of this way of looking at things could be found everywhere. As noted earlier, people were treated as "human resources" or "economic assets," and valued according to the contributions they make to the economy and the marketplace. The arts and cultural industries were valued far more for their ability to generate economic growth than their capacity to bring happiness, fulfillment, and contentment into people's lives. The same was true of most sports, recreational, and entertainment activities. Even religious activities and institutions were beginning to be valued for the economic benefits they produced in the neighbourhoods and communities in which they were situated. While this practice was most prevalent in the west, it was spreading rapidly to other parts of the world. This spread was inevitable in a world dominated by an economic worldview, model of development, and age.

Especially troublesome in this respect were the implications of this for the world of the future. It meant treating virtually all "non-economic activities" as means to economic ends, rather than ends in themselves. This was true for artistic, humanistic, social, educational, and spiritual activities, and especially true for culture. The economic age was robbing culture of its real value, purpose, and capabilities, and in doing so, negated the huge contributions culture is capable of making to communities, societies, countries, and the world at large.

And this brings me to the final problem that had to be confronted in creating a balance sheet for the economic age — the potential breakdown of the natural environment.

This possibility was undoubtedly the most troublesome of all. The roots of this problem can be traced back to the time when economics was evolving and gathering momentum as a discipline. During this time, the natural environment was treated as a "given" provided by God or by nature and therefore ignored by most economists and the economics profession as a whole.

I had been bothered by this fact for decades, indeed, ever since I taught economics in the early 1960s. I simply couldn't accept the premise that the most important factor of all — the natural environment on which everyone and everything depends — should be treated as a "given" and "externality." This premise was one of the main factors that eventually drove me to the conclusion that economics could not be transformed from the inside, and therefore caused me to commence the search for a field where I didn't have to sacrifice my own personal beliefs and convictions in order to remain faithful to the foundations of the discipline.

But what exactly was and still is the problem here? *The problem is that it is not possible to insert the natural environment into a system of theory and practice that has evolved progressively and relentlessly over the last two hundred and fifty years* ***after the fact***. Whereas the natural environment should have provided the foundation for this system, or at least occupied a very prominent position near the centre of it, it was not to be found anywhere. This would be tantamount to building a huge skyscraper without a foundation, or an elaborate theory of the solar system without the sun in it.

During the entire the time the economic system was evolving, gathering momentum, and extending its influence throughout the world — from the individual, local, and community level to the national and international level — the natural environment was taken for granted and ignored. While this was not a major problem in 1776 when the economic age was beginning and the population of the world was roughly 800 million, it had become a very serious problem at the beginning of the twenty-first century when the population of the world was well over six billion. The problem is even more acute today, now that the population of the world is over seven billion, and promises to be far more acute still in the future, when the population of the world is likely to reach twelve or fifteen billion by the end of the twenty-first century.

This explains why it has been so difficult to make any real progress on the environmental front. Environmental issues are almost always subordinated to economic issues whenever there is conflict between the two. The most that can be expected is to open up a place for considering environmental issues in selected parts of the economic system, but never at its centre where the natural environment rightfully belongs. Even climate change, which was receiving more attention at the beginning of the twenty-first century and is receiving far more attention today as documented fully in Naomi Klein's latest book, *This Changes Everything*, cannot alter the fact that the natural environment exists largely outside the realm of economics because it was never included in it.

Taking all these problems into account, I concluded following the creation of the balance sheet on the economic age that the risks involved of perpetuating the economic age in the future were much too great. Regardless of the myriad benefits the economic age had produced and was producing, there were some fundamental flaws in the philosophical, theoretical, practical, and historical underpinnings and foundations of the economic age that simply could not be corrected or ignored. Indeed, if the economic age *was* perpetuated for much longer in the future, a total breakdown was likely to occur in the entire global ecosystem.

Clearly people will not sit idly by while the natural environment is decimated, higher and higher prices are charged for fewer and fewer resources and basic foodstuffs, and living standards are decreased rather than increased. This is a recipe for environmental catastrophe and global revolution — a catastrophe and revolution whose only benefit would be to reduce the size of the world's population and rein in the economic age's excesses and imbalances, but likely at the cost of millions if not billions of lives. Violent outcomes could be in store for humanity if it persists on this course. As Ruth Benedict, the renowned American cultural scholar, put it years earlier in talking about humanity's past experiences with excesses and indulgences of one kind of another:

> Revision comes, but it comes by way of revolution or of breakdown. The possibility of orderly progress is shut off because the generation in question could not make any appraisal of its overgrown institutions. It could not cast them up in terms of profit and loss because it had lost its power to look at them objectively.

> The situation had to reach the breaking point before relief was possible.

This didn't need to happen in my view. In order to prevent it, however, I felt that it was necessary to pass out of the prevailing economic age and into a future cultural age. This was best achieved by realizing a renaissance rather than a revolution in global development and human affairs. Javier Pérez de Cuéllar, former Secretary-General of the United Nations and president of the World Commission of Cultural Development, expressed this same viewpoint, but somewhat differently, when he said:

> Today, rethinking development is necessary on a global scale. . . . It was believed, not so long ago, that the economy was the base, the infrastructure. That is wrong, the historians of the "long history" have shown that the decisive element is culture. . . . Without a large cultural transformation, development is doomed to the destiny of ghost towns.

The key to this "large cultural transformation" — or renaissance as I liked to call it — was not to reject the economic age, but rather to incorporate it (and a great deal else) into a broader, deeper, more fundamental way of looking at life, living, reality, the human condition, and world system. The world needs strong economies and the strengths of the economic age if things are to improve in the future, *but it needs them constrained and enriched by the broader, deeper, and more fundamental concerns and capabilities of culture in general and a cultural age in particular*.

This is where composing a balance sheet for the economic age proved very helpful. Not only did it make it possible to identify the underlying problems with the economic age, but also it made it possible to ascertain what was required to address its problems and set things right.

In thinking about the type of renaissance that was needed for the future, I didn't think it was necessary to go back to classical times, the way the Italian Renaissance did in drawing its inspiration from Greek and Roman culture. What was necessary, however, was to make maximum use of culture and the many different capabilities and secrets it possessed. Here was the key that was required to overcome the fundamental flaws of the economic age, as well as to usher in a new, and more exhilarating, cultural age.

No sooner did I reach this conclusion than I realized I had uncovered the clue that was required to solve the final problem connected to the book

I was working on. I would call the book *Revolution or Renaissance: Making the Transition from an Economic Age to a Cultural Age* and divide it into two parts.

Part I would be called *The Age of Economics* and deal with the origins, evolution, mechanics, and assessment of the economic age. Part II would be called *The Age of Culture*, and would deal with the signs, foundations, functioning, priorities, and flourishing of a cultural age. Having completed the first part of the book, I was anxious to plunge into the second part. I was bursting with ideas about how a cultural age could be realized, as well as how a renaissance rather than a revolution could be achieved throughout the world. Here is how Part I of the book ended:

> . . . what can be said in conclusion about the economic age that is relevant to a future age? Surely this. While the economic age has made countless contributions to global development and human affairs, it is not capable of carrying humanity forward into the next great epoch in human history. For this a different type of age is required. This age must flow from a different set of foundations, principles, practices, policies, and priorities, as well as a different worldview, value system, and model of development. The key to this age lies in the realm of culture rather than in the realm of economics.

CHAPTER TEN

Entering a Cultural Age

I was excited at the prospect of working on the second part of *Revolution or Renaissance* on a cultural age. Underlying all my thoughts on this matter was a concern that had bothered me for years and driven much of my interest in culture. It was this. How can we create an age where all people and all countries enjoy reasonable standards of living and a decent quality of life without straining the globe's fragile eco-systems and limited resources to the breaking point? Doing so was necessary to prevent the global situation from spinning out of control, as well as to transport humanity into the next great epoch in history.

Since culture lay at the core of this requirement, it was clear that firm foundations would have to be created for a cultural age. Foremost among these foundations were achieving a general agreement on the holistic nature of culture; broadening and deepening understanding of the comprehensive character of cultures; interpreting history from a cultural perspective; and capitalizing on culture's rich theoretical and practical tradition. Although much has already been said about these matters, it is necessary to strengthen and solidify their importance here.

Of these foundations, achieving a general agreement on the holistic nature of culture was the most essential, as well as the most difficult to achieve. This is because there are many different perceptions and manifestations of culture, and most people do not view culture as "the whole" or the "total way of life of people." However, it was necessary to persevere with the quest to realize this objective, not only to take advantage of the rich potential culture possesses in the holistic sense to understand and come to grips with the world's diversity and complexity, but also to emphasize that culture is concerned with three matters when stripped to its essence — worldview, values, and people.

As noted earlier, Wole Soyinka, the great Nigerian writer and Nobel laureate, provided a valuable step in the right direction when he described culture as "*source*" — the source from which all things flow and to which all things return.

Treating culture as "source" — or the whole, or total way of life of people — was necessary because it made it possible to focus on the "big picture" and not merely component parts of that picture. This was particularly important with respect to the devastating effect human beings were having on the natural environment, but it was also important with respect to the enormous amount of hunger, poverty, starvation, inequality, and unemployment that still existed in the world. Unfortunately, these matters were not receiving the priority they needed in the economic age, something I felt had to be changed in the future.

Nor was this all. Culture in the holistic sense also focused on the many different relationships that exist *between* and *among* the component parts of the whole. In addition to the relationship between human beings and the natural environment and that between rich and poor people and rich and poor countries, other relationships of crucial importance were the ones between economics and ethics, women and men, religion and politics, technology and society, the arts and the sciences, materialism and spiritualism, and the quantitative and qualitative dimensions of life. Asserting the fundamental importance of these relationships, as well as the priorities that should be assigned to them, was imperative if the pressures, tensions, and conflicts that existed in the world were to be reduced or overcome.

What was required more than anything else in this area was to achieve balance and harmony between the component parts of these relationships. This was necessary in order to deal with the many imbalances and excesses that existed in the world system and people's lives. While increasing material and monetary wealth was essential and required a high priority — it would be foolhardy to deny this or contend otherwise — what was needed far more was to realize balance and harmony between the component parts of global development and human affairs, especially between human beings and the natural environment as well as between the material and non-material dimensions of development.

While it was apparent that achieving a general agreement on the holistic nature of culture would not be realized any time soon, and not without a great deal of difficulty, I felt there were some promising signs on the global horizon. After several centuries of being preoccupied with specialization and the parts of the whole, a "holistic transformation" was beginning to take place in the world that was manifesting itself in many areas of public and private life. This transformation was most evident in medicine and education, especially in terms of the trend towards "holistic medicine" and the escalating interest in interdisciplinary and multi-disciplinary studies in many educational systems. However, it was also evident in other areas, such as the Human Genome Project and the need to see the world as "all of a piece" as a result of globalization and other developments. This augured well for the eventual acceptance of the holistic nature of culture. It was clear that humanity needed an all-encompassing way of looking at the world and everything in it if it was to come to grips with the most debilitating and difficult problems of modern times.

If achieving a general agreement on the holistic nature of culture was one foundation that had to be put in place, broadening and deepening understanding of the comprehensive character of cultures was another. There were many reasons for this, but four in particular were essential.

In the first place, cultures are *the* most important human collectivities in the world when they are dealt with in comprehensive terms. This is because they are concerned with the entire way people, groups, and countries visualize and interpret the world, organize themselves, conduct their affairs, elevate and embellish life, and position themselves in the world.

Furthermore, all the various cultures in the world are different in the comprehensive sense because they are based on different worldviews, values, customs, traditions, beliefs, and ways of life. Without a much better understanding of this fact, as well as creation of the necessary safeguards, precautions, and mechanisms to deal with the implications and consequences of it, the potential for violence, conflict, confrontation, terrorism, and war is always present and likely to increase.

This underscores the need to transform existing cultures and create new ones that are more open, heterogeneous, diverse, and inclusive, rather than closed, uniform, homogeneous, and exclusive. This is necessary both *within* and *between* cultures, especially given the fact that more and more cross-cultural interaction, mixing, and borrowing are going on and required between and among all the various cultures and civilizations of the world. Mahatma Gandhi set us on the right path in this respect when he said, "I do not want my house to be walled in on all sides and my windows to be stuffed. I want the culture of all the lands to be blown about my house as freely as possible. But I refuse to be blown off my feet by any."

Broadening and deepening understanding of the comprehensive character of cultures is also necessary if existing cultures are not to break up. To prevent this, it is necessary to understand how cultures are bound together and the crucial role that artists, scholars, and other types of creative people — as well as artistic works, scholarly endeavours, signs and symbols such as flags, national anthems, and community celebrations, languages, stories, the cultural industries, the Internet, modern communications technologies, and the social media — play in this process. For these are the people and forms of expression, communication, and sharing that are required to tie all the different parts of cultures together and maintain them as distinct, dynamic, and organic entities as well as overall and exciting ways of life. Without this, the existence of *every* culture in the world is threatened — not just the existence of esoteric, isolated, or traditional cultures.

If the aforementioned people and forms of expression and communication are needed to bind cultures together, they are also needed for another reason. They help to ensure the distinctiveness, uniqueness, and identity of cultures. Whereas some cultures are best known for their customs, cuisines, traditions, regional variations, or linguistic capabilities, others are best known for their architectural achievements, athletic prowess, philosophical accomplishments, and creative capabilities. Clearly a rich reservoir exists here that is capable of providing people with a great deal of happiness and fulfillment, as well as myriad opportunities for education, learning, and enrichment. Appreciating and preserving these cultures is of utmost importance if human well-being is to be assured.

Finally, and perhaps most importantly, broadening and deepening understanding of the comprehensive character of cultures is imperative if humanity is to be successful in understanding the changes that are required in people's behaviour, habits, attitudes, beliefs, and ways of life to overcome the world's most pressing and debilitating problems. That this is a cultural requirement more than any other type of requirement cannot be denied, especially when people's behaviour, habits, attitudes, beliefs, and ways of life are deeply entrenched in the sociological manifestation of culture in general and all the cultures of the world in particular.

Just as "peace begins in the minds of men," according to the founding charter of UNESCO, so creating the conditions for a better world begins with recognizing that changes in people's behaviour, habits, attitudes, beliefs, and ways of life are first and foremost *cultural* requirements. The environmental crisis, the poverty crisis, the unemployment crisis, and all other crises in the world will not be overcome until people make a commitment to making fundamental changes in this area.

Then there is the need for a cultural interpretation of history. This third foundation for a cultural age will also have to be put into place. This is particularly important if humanity is to be successful in realizing a renaissance rather than a revolution in global development and human affairs.

As I was working on the second half of *Revolution or Renaissance*, it was popular in academic and professional circles to talk about "the end of history." Indeed, one scholar, Francis Fukuyama, had even written a very successful book on this subject. Entitled *The End of History and the Last Man*, it was predicated on the conviction that with modern capitalist democracy, humanity had reached the last stage in socio-cultural evolution and the ultimate form of government. Arguments like this were popular at this time because a great deal had been achieved since the end of the Second World War in many areas of public and private life, and things were changing so rapidly as a result of developments in science, technology, and communications that many scholars and international leaders felt that the past and history had little or no relevance to the present and the future.

I did not share this belief. I believe that humanity is — and always will be — locked in the web of history and for one very good reason. History is concerned with some of humanity's most pressing and profound questions as noted earlier, especially where we came from, why we have evolved the way we have, and where we are going in the future.

What is true for history was equally true for interpretations of history. I was convinced that humanity is always locked in the web of one interpretation of history or another. As indicated earlier, this is currently true for the economic interpretation of history, and has been ever since Marx formulated it more than a century ago. While I understood why Marx had interpreted the world in which he was living in economic terms — he was, after all, living at the height of the Industrial Revolution when everything was taking on a highly materialistic and physical orientation — it was one thing to interpret his world in economic terms but quite another to claim that this is always true.

I was strongly opposed to this highly deterministic way of interpreting history, largely because I felt that different periods in history have been dominated by different themes, ideas, and factors and not always the same themes, ideas, and factors. Clearly free will rather than determinism lies at the core of history in general and interpretations of history in particular, since history is always an open book that is charted in accordance with humanity's ever-changing needs, wants, preferences, aspirations, and circumstances. Viewed from this perspective, the economic interpretation of history, regardless of how powerful and pervasive it is in the world today, is not the most accurate and authentic interpretation of history. Moreover, it will be fatal to carry it forward into the future as a result of the devastating effect this will have on the natural environment and people's lives.

Clearly the cultural interpretation of history is far more accurate and authentic than the economic interpretation of history when it is understood and dealt with in holistic terms. There is not a country or society anywhere in the world that has failed to address the totality of people's needs, from work to play and materialism to spiritualism, and do this simultaneously and fully rather than sequentially and partially.

Acceptance of the cultural interpretation of history in the broader and deeper holistic sense means that the first and foremost requirement of humanity is to develop culture and cultures in the comprehensive sense. While economics and economies will always play a powerful role in the world, the cultural interpretation of history confirms that the development of culture and cultures in the all-encompassing sense is, and possibly will always be, *the* most important task facing humanity. It should be what preoccupies both ordinary people and political and educational leaders in the years and decades ahead.

While asserting the importance of the cultural interpretation of history is important for many reasons, one of the most essential reasons is that it sheds light on culture's great theoretical and practical tradition. Making maximum use of this tradition is the fourth and final foundation that must be maneuvered into place if a cultural age is to be created in the future.

Clearly a priceless tradition of theoretical ideas, concepts, insights, and thoughts, as well as practical experiences, actions, and concrete accomplishments, has been created by humanity in the past that has enormous relevance and value to the present and the future.

This is especially important with respect to the theoretical component. This component possesses the potential to transform the world — and transform it for the better — in numerous ways. In every domain of public and private life, from the individual level to the international level, scholars have had a great deal to say that is relevant and valuable with respect to how people should live their lives and how the world can be improved. The time has come to make maximum use of this vast storehouse of thoughts, ideas, concepts, and insights.

This is also true for the practical side of this tradition. What this side reveals, and reveals convincingly, is that outstanding contributions have been made to improving the human condition and world situation in every period of history, part of the world, and domain of public and private life. This is evident in agriculture and industry, the arts and sciences, business and politics, recreation and technology, architecture and health care, and everything else. This confirms, once again, the importance of the holistic nature of culture and comprehensive character of cultures, and with it, the necessity of pressing culture and cultures into the forefront of the world system in the years and decades ahead.

Something equally essential is also necessary. People and countries throughout history have reached above and beyond themselves in order to realize ever higher levels of accomplishment. This desire to achieve the best humanity has to offer — what I like to call "cultural striving" — represents one of the most valuable aspects of human culture. While wisdom may be required to make sensible decisions about future courses in planetary civilization, and creativity may be required to create the new forms, structures, institutions, and innovations that are necessary, it is the human quest to reach for the highest ideals that is the most essential of all. As Herman Hesse said in his novel *Magister Ludi* (*The Glass Bead Game*):

> World history is a race with time, a scramble for profits, for power, for treasures. What counts is who has the strength, luck, or vulgarity not to miss the opportunity. The achievements of thought, of culture, of art are just the opposite. They are always an escape from the serfdom of time, man crawling out of the muck of his instincts and out of his sluggishness and climbing to a higher place, to timelessness, liberation from time, divinity.

Nothing typifies this better than the cultural heritage of humankind. As the pinnacle of humanity's most cherished accomplishments down through the ages, this indispensable legacy stands above the rise and fall of different cultures and civilizations. As the final foundation that needs to be put into place for a cultural age to become a reality, it is the shining star that possesses the potential to light the way forward in the new century and new millennium.

Once I had come to grips with the foundations for a cultural age in the second part of *Revolution or Renaissance: Making the Transition from an Economic Age to a Cultural Age*, I turned my attention to how such an age would function in fact. For just as the functioning of the economic age was based on an economic worldview and model of development, so the functioning of a cultural age would be based on a cultural worldview and model of development.

In a nutshell, this meant developing culture and all the diverse cultures of the world in breadth and depth, achieving balance and harmony between the component parts of culture and cultures in general and the material and non-material components of culture and cultures in particular, and situating culture and cultures effectively in the natural, historical, and global environment.

Just how different a cultural age would be from the economic age was revealed by the most dominant concerns of these two ages. As identified in the first part of *Revolution or Renaissance*, the dominant concerns of the economic age are specialization; products; production; consumption; capital accumulation; profits, the profit motive, and profit maximization; competition; centralization; materialism; the marketplace; globalization; and monetization. Obviously, these concerns would continue to exist in a cultural age. However, they would be subsumed by, and subordinated to, the concerns that would be most relevant to a cultural age. As identified in the second part of the book, these concerns would be holism; people; distribution; sharing; compassion; altruism; cooperation; excellence; beauty, creativity; democratization and decentralization; cooperation; conservation; spirituality; and the search for the sublime.

If, as the Russians say, "All is known by comparison," then it only makes sense to compare the concerns of the economic age with the concerns of a cultural age in order to expose the basic differences between the two. Once this was accomplished, I identified some of the principal priorities for a cultural age: new meanings and measures of wealth; a new corporate ideology; a new political system; a cultural approach to citizenship; a breakthrough in education; livable and sustainable cities; and a united world. Each of these priorities was required for a very specific reason – a reason that had to do with the effective functioning of a cultural age and the well-being of people and the natural environment in all parts of the world.

New meanings and measures of wealth were required because existing meanings and measures of wealth, based largely on economics, were not defining or measuring wealth accurately, and were producing incredible demands on the natural environment and world's scarce resources. Clearly a broader set of *cultural indicators* was required that included many metrics besides the more familiar *economic indicators,* ones that had to do with improving the state of the natural environment and the quality and character of people's lives.

In much the same way, each of the other aforementioned priorities was based on some specific change that was necessary to achieve a fundamental improvement in the human condition and world situation. For instance, a new corporate ideology was advocated that was predicated on corporations making reasonable rather than excessive profits and abandoning their penchant for profit maximization; a new political system was proposed that would make culture, cultures, cultural development, and ministries of culture — rather than economics, economies, economic growth, and ministries of trade, industry, and commerce — the centrepiece of political and governmental affairs; and a cultural approach to citizenship was required that would include people's *responsibilities* as well as their *rights*, and hopefully lead to the creation and adoption of a *Universal Declaration of Human Right and Responsibilities*.

Correspondingly, a breakthrough in education was required that would involve approaching education from a cultural rather than economic perspective; livable and sustainable cities were required that would situate culture, cultures, and the culturescape process at the centre of municipal planning, policy, and decision-making; and a united world was necessary that was based on making the development of culture and cultures in general — and a global federation of world cultures in particular — the principal preoccupation of international development and multilateral relations. Doing so was required to break down the walls and barriers that exist between the different peoples, countries, and cultures of the world, as well as to build many more bridges and connections between them.

While these priorities were of fundamental importance to the world of the future and needed to be implemented without delay, they paled by comparison with the two most essential priorities of a cultural age. The first was achieving a new environmental reality; and the second was fulfilling human needs.

These two priorities topped the list in my view because they held the key to creating reasonable standards of living and a decent quality of life for all people and all countries of the world. They also held the key to reducing the huge impact human beings were having on the natural environment and globe's scarce resources. Nothing was more important than this, and it could only be achieved by crossing the threshold to a cultural age.

Achieving a new environmental reality was predicated on three interlocking requirements: cleaning up the natural environment after the fact; taking the necessary precautions and actions to ensure that the natural environment was not abused or polluted before the fact; and visualizing and interacting with the natural environment in an entirely different way.

Due to the advocacy of countless environmental organizations and activists, a significant amount of headway was being made in cleaning up the natural environment after the fact when I was writing *Revolution or Renaissance*, even if a great deal was left to be desired. While such measures did not provide a permanent solution to the environmental problem, at least they were moving in the right direction and helped to alleviate specific aspects of this problem.

Nevertheless, these efforts paled by comparison with the need to take necessary precautions and actions before the fact. A battery of initiatives were required here — initiatives that were both preventative and precautionary in nature.

On the preventative side, the most urgent initiatives were reducing the use of fossil fuels; developing new technologies and alternative forms of energy such as wind, geothermal, solar, hydrogen, and tidal power; instituting and enforcing rigorous standards with respect to carbon emissions; preventing the use of toxic substances like chlorofluorocarbons and pesticides; purifying water and air; and protecting endangered species. Since these measures were not likely to occur on their own, a powerful and proactive role was required on the part of governments and other public institutions if real progress was to be achieved.

On the precautionary side, the most pressing initiatives were increasing the longevity of products so that they don't wear out as easily and last longer; designing products more efficiently, so that they take up less room and don't require as many resources to begin with; recycling and repairing commodities at every opportunity rather than throwing them out; and shifting from products and activities that are high in material inputs and outputs to products and activities that are low in material inputs and outputs.

However, the most essential requirement of all was visualizing and interacting with the natural environment in an entirely different way. While the ideas, insights, and actions of environmental activists and organizations were imperative in this respect, I felt that artists, artistic organizations, and spiritual leaders had a very important role to play here. This was because their contributions were the key to getting to know the natural environment as a spiritual entity, and in a far more intimate, sensitive, compassionate, and responsible way.

In every culture in the world, artists and spiritual leaders have played — and continue to play — a key role in exposing people to the character and capabilities of the natural environment and increasing their appreciation and reverence for it. There is no doubt that these individuals, and the institutions and organizations they represent, do a great deal to make people aware of how important it is to revere and respect the natural environment, renew it at every opportunity, and be sensitive to the fragile state of local, regional, national, and international ecosystems and habitats.

If achieving a new environmental reality was one of the most pressing and essential priorities of a cultural age, fulfilling human needs was the other. As long as a substantial percentage of the world's population was living on less than a few dollars a day and experiencing a great deal of difficulty making ends meet, it was not possible to claim that the welfare and well-being of all people was being attended to properly.

When human needs are viewed from a cultural rather than economic perspective — that is to say, from a holistic rather than partial perspective — it is clear that they extend far beyond the economic and material requirements of life to include many social, aesthetic, recreational, scientific, spiritual, and other requirements as well. This means that human needs should not be seen as a hierarchy with the economic and material needs constituting the base. On the contrary, they should be seen as a holistic constellation, with economic and non-economic, material and non-material, and quantitative and qualitative needs constantly interacting with one another and impinging on one another. This is imperative in order to ensure that people have access to the full spectrum of resources they require to live full, healthy, and dignified lives. This includes food, clothing, shelter, fresh water, and clean air, as well as many educational, social, health, recreational, artistic, and spiritual possibilities. This need was summed up most admirably by a group of scholars and statesmen assembled by the Kapur Surya Foundation in India in 1995:

> Development must assure the satisfaction of the minimum basic needs for food, habitat, health, education, and employment, and the quest for inner peace and self-realization. This can only be

> achieved if we can cultivate need-based, as against desire-based lifestyles, which are not superficial or self-indulgent, and are non-destructive of the environment and other cultures. These must be frugal in means and rich in ends, and not beyond the reach of increasing numbers of citizens. While being equitable, development must not sacrifice initiative and excellence, but be ecologically responsible, economically viable, cumulative, life-enhancing, culture-specific, and culturally sensitive.

I was convinced that humanity possessed enough productive capacity and creative potential to satisfy the basic requirements of *all* people and *all* countries in the world if it was properly directed. The problem was that the lion's share of wealth was confined to a small and elite percentage of the world's population, and not being shared equitably. What was required here, and required more than ever, was the public, private, and professional will – as well as the redistributive means, mechanisms, and channels – to share income, wealth, goods, services, and opportunities more broadly. This was particularly important when the environmental crisis, climate change, and global warming were beginning to signal that people and countries in all parts of the world could experience far more difficult health, medical, and survival problems in the future due to the increased frequency of floods, hurricanes, forest fires, coastal disasters, and disruptions in the flow of the basic necessities of life. And what was evident then is far more evident today.

These problems will only be addressed effectively if people's most fundamental requirements in all areas of life are addressed, and addressed first and foremost. When vast quantities of food, clothing, and other commodities are destroyed every day to keep prices artificially high, and when productive systems are operating at far less than full capacity, it is not possible to claim that humanity lacks the means, wherewithal, and ingenuity that are needed to come to grips with this most endemic human problem of all. While more will be said about this later, suffice it to say at this point that it is not necessary to double or triple world output in order to achieve this. At its root, this is a distribution problem and not a production problem.

What was beginning to take shape as I worked on this section of *Revolution or Renaissance* was a portrait of a future cultural age that was very different than the existing economic age. In a cultural age, every person in the world – young and old, women and men, girls and boys, Africans, Asians, Latin Americans, and Caribbeans as well as North Americans and

Europeans — would have enough of the basic requirements of life to live satisfying, creative, and fulfilling lives. At long last, the vast majority of people in the world would be able to move away from concern for basic survival and towards possibilities that would substantially enrich and embolden their lives.

What would be true for people's daily lives would also be true for their long-term prospects. Rather than having to constantly worry about survival and the survival of their families, they would be able to think great thoughts, dream exciting dreams, and focus their energies and efforts on doing worthwhile things. Creativity and imagination, rather than conformity and imitation, would be the norm. For as Albert Einstein observed, "A society's competitive advantage will come not from how well its schools teach the multiplication and periodic tables, but from how well they stimulate imagination and creativity."

This is what life and living could be like for all people in a cultural age if governments, corporations, educational institutions, and international agencies made a collective, sustained, and systematic effort to achieve this goal. While there would not be substantive changes in the way people at the top live their lives — except that they would likely have less income than they do now because income would be shared more equally — the ways of life of the less fortunate people of the world would be dramatically altered, and for the better.

In order to realize this improved state of affairs, it will be necessary to achieve a better balance between the physical, material, and quantitative side of development and life on the one hand, and the emotional, spiritual, aesthetic, and qualitative side on the other. This balance is what is most lacking in the world today, and a cultural age would set it right. For just as the most important challenge in the development of individuals is to combine the mind, body, heart, soul, and spirit to form an integrated, harmonious whole, so the challenge in global development and human affairs is to fuse all the diverse determinants of development together to form an inclusive, balanced entity. Humanity has suffered too long from major imbalances among the various determinants of development and life, and particularly because some determinants dominate and overshadow others. The time has come to change things, and a cultural age would be the ideal vehicle to achieve this.

It is impossible to think about entry into a cultural age without giving consideration to whether this age should be based on a single *world culture* shared by all citizens and all countries, or on many *world cultures*, each with its own identity, independence, and ability to function effectively in a global world.

Clearly both possibilities have their advantages and disadvantages. Proponents of a single world culture shared by all citizens and countries are quick to point out that this possibility possesses the potential to open up unlimited opportunities for cooperation, collaboration, and exchange among the diverse peoples and countries of the world, because they would all share the same or a similar worldview and value system. It would also minimize cultural differences and go a long way towards reducing fear and suspicion, thereby improving the potential for peace, stability, security, and harmony in the world. Those opposed to a single world culture are quick to counter these arguments. They contend that homogenization of the world through the creation of a single world culture is something that should be avoided at all costs, since it would stifle creativity and vitality and eliminate diversity and originality.

This is by no means the end of the argument. Far from it. Those favouring the development of a single world culture are quick to contend that there has been a relentless trend throughout history towards the creation of larger and larger cultural units. Humanity in this sense has moved progressively from the creation of small tribes and tiny towns to large cities, regions, countries, and now to a globalized world system. Pushed to its logical conclusion, it is clear that this trend ends with the creation of a single world culture shared by all citizens and all countries.

Proponents of this view also contend that this is where the entire world seems headed at present. As evidence of this, they point to the establishment of giant trade zones like the European Union and the North American Free Trade Agreement, the creation of multinational corporations and international institutions like the United Nations, World Bank, and World Trade Organization, the use of English as a kind of universal lingua franca, and the steady movement towards economic and cultural globalization. As additional confirmation of this, they point to international improvements in transportation and communications, the global popularity of American (or American-style) films, television programs, popular music, and consumer goods, the creation of the Internet and many different social media applications, the concentration of media ownership in fewer hands, and the emergence of what Marshall McLuhan called the "global village."

This trend is not only inevitable, say proponents of this point of view, but also desirable. They base their claim on the belief that it would open up myriad opportunities for cooperation among all the world's peoples and countries. Once differences in such matters as religion, politics, education, and culture are stamped out, the world (so they claim) will become safer and more secure. At the root of this contention is the conviction that all human beings have the same needs, concerns, and aspirations in the end, so it is high time we focused on the similarities and did away with the differences.

Opponents of a single world culture are quick to counter these arguments. They contend that a single world culture is anything but inevitable, or desirable, and that numerous factors stand in the way of ever actually achieving it. Their arguments are based on an equal number of compelling premises.

In the first place, they contend that virtually all movements towards the creation of larger cultural units have been accompanied by dialectic developments that have at the same time produced smaller cultural units. In the modern world, this is most evident in the affirmation of tribes and tribal affiliations, as well as the creation of many different local organizations, citizens' coalitions, social groups, and civil society associations. These have acted as counterweights to globalization.

Moreover, they contend that most people in the world derive their identity and sense of belonging from smaller and more human-sized cultural units like the family, the ethnic group to which they belong, the neighbourhood in which they are living, and the town, city, or region where they are located. Such units are more tangible and concrete than most of the international movements and transnational developments taking place throughout the world today. The world (proponents of this view add) is already made up of so many small, distinct units that it is unlikely that they will disappear. They are too deeply entrenched in the human condition and global situation. While many people in the world may watch the same films and listen to the same music, they still live in very specific cultural contexts and engage in local activities that have little or no resemblance to the activities that would prevail in a single world culture.

Opponents of a single world culture also claim that the establishment of such a "world monoculture" would be a curse, not a blessing. They emphasize the dangers of conformity, uniformity, centralization, and homogenization, and warn that control of the world would end up in the hands of a small group of powerful corporations, governments, countries, and wealthy elites. In their view, such an outcome should be avoided at all costs. Not only would it stamp out creativity and diversity — the very things that provide real spice and zest in life — but lethargy, apathy, and indifference would become the established norm. Some even go as far as to contend that "cultures of resistance" should be created to fight the forces of standardization and centralization. A particularly strong advocate of this view is Denis Goulet:

> All cultures and cultural values are assaulted by powerful forces of standardization. These forces homogenize, dilute, and relegate cultures to purely ornamental, vestigial or marginal positions in society. The first standardizing force is technology, especially media technology. . . . The second standardizing force is the modern state. . . . The third standardizing force is the spread of managerial organization. . . . The result of these standardizing influences is mass cultural destruction, dilution, and assimilation. The very pervasiveness of these damaging forces, however, gives rise to growing manifestations of cultural affirmation and resistance.

There is a great deal of validity to these arguments. Already the homogenizing forces of contemporary technology have permeated the world to the point where they threaten local (and already marginalized) cultures and traditional identities. This is a very disturbing development in the world in view of the fact that these changes are threatening to stultify innovation, imagination, and creativity, the very qualities needed to ensure human survival and well-being.

Presumably there will always be some people who want to see the creation of a single world culture and others who prefer a diversity of world cultures. Of course, much depends on what is meant by the term "world cultures." Without doubt, *all* cultures in the world are rapidly becoming world cultures in the sense that they are integral parts of the global village. As such, they are actively involved in the transformation that is going on in contemporary communications and less and less able to ignore what is taking place in other parts of the world, regardless of how insignificant those events may seem to be.

This is a new development in human history. Even past cultures that played an extremely powerful role in the world — such as the Chinese, Greek, and Roman cultures of ancient times, or the British, Dutch, Spanish, and Portuguese cultures of early modern times — were really national cultures with a great deal of international reach, not world cultures as such. There were large parts of the world that were totally unknown to them and untouched by their influence.

Not so today. What are emerging throughout the world today are the first signs of *world* cultures. When they are developed and fully operational, these cultures will be very different from the local, regional, and national cultures of earlier times and even today. Not only will they be fully integrated into the world, but also they will be totally dependent on the world. American culture is likely the first world culture of this type, but a number of other cultures also appear to be headed in this direction, most notably in Europe and parts of Asia.

If all cultures in the world will eventually become world cultures, they will have to develop their international capabilities to a much larger extent, while simultaneously maintaining their distinctiveness and identity. This challenge, undoubtedly one of the greatest challenges facing most cultures and countries in the world today, has enormous implications for the future. Though it is not unlike the challenges that confronted many local, regional, and national cultures in earlier periods of history, it will be infinitely more complex and difficult to manage. People in all parts of the world will have to exercise a great deal of control over their public and private affairs if they want to be successful in coping with a vast array of international developments that will confront any world culture in the future.

This is particularly important with respect to maintaining historical roots and traditions, ensuring that ownership and control of strategic industries and resources are in domestic rather than foreign hands, expanding internal as well as external cultural content, pursuing indigenous rather than imposed or imported development, and learning to function effectively in the world in a sustainable, systematic, and sophisticated manner. This will require cultures that are finely tuned to global developments, but that remain independent cultures in their own right and that don't allow other cultures to dominate or rule them.

With these thoughts in mind, we are now able to return to the question of whether it is possible to reconcile the two seemingly irreconcilable possibilities of a single world culture or many world cultures. Surely it is, and the answer lies in the creation of *a global federation of world cultures*. This would make it possible for all countries and cultures in the world to reap the advantages of a single world culture, while simultaneously reaping the benefits of many diverse world cultures.

In a global federation of world cultures, concepts like development, progress, and world system would have very different meanings than they do today. Development and progress would mean feeling comfortable with the specific directions that people, countries, and cultures are pursuing, rather than acquiescing to the worldviews, norms, values, and beliefs of others. The world system would be one in which it was possible for many different ways of life to prevail and thrive — each with its own distinctive identity, values, and legitimacy — while simultaneously coming to grips with problems that are global in nature and universal in scope. In such a world, all people, countries, and cultures would possess the freedom, flexibility, and adaptability that are necessary to pursue their own specific paths to development, while at the same time being able to participate actively in the collective responsibilities and common work of humankind. In one form or another, all this activity would involve engaging in causes that are devoted to improving living standards, the quality of life, and the natural environment for all members of the human family.

In order to achieve these goals, it will be necessary to draw on countless creative capabilities in the arts, sciences, education, economics, politics, technology, social affairs, and other areas of life. This need is yet another reason why it is so essential to enter into a cultural age and realize a renaissance rather than a revolution in global development and human affairs. Doing so would make it possible to improve the human condition in peaceful rather than violent ways, largely by propelling humanity out of an age preoccupied primarily with money, power, materialism, and the marketplace, and into an age concerned with human welfare and environmental well-being. It is difficult to see how standards of living and the quality of life will be improved and a new environment reality will be achieved if this does not occur.

As I was putting the final touches on the second half of *Revolution or Renaissance* and the manuscript as a whole, I received a letter from my friend Gao Xian, who was responsible for having *Culture: Beacon of the Future* translated into Chinese and published by the Social Sciences Academic Press in China. Gao asked me if I was working on any other manuscripts that might be of interest to Chinese readers and the Press.

I wrote back to say that I was just completing a manuscript that was concerned with the age of economics and the age of culture that might be of real interest to them. He asked me to send him a copy of the manuscript, which I did. Shortly after this, I received a second letter from Gao indicating that authorities at the Press had read the manuscript and decided to translate it into Chinese and publish it in China, much like

Culture: Beacon of the Future. I was very excited about this. I remember thinking how farsighted it was on the part of the Social Sciences Academic Press to have a program committed to translating works by foreign authors into Chinese and making them available to Chinese readers. I was not aware of any other country that had such a program.

Having the manuscript translated into Chinese and published in book form in China proved to be a strange experience because I had yet to find a publisher for the English version. This proved to be much more difficult than expected, since publisher after publisher turned the manuscript down because it did not fit with their "current lists" or "long-term publishing plans." Fortunately, however, I was able to find a publisher for the English version. This occurred in 2007, when the University of Ottawa Press decided to publish this version of the book in its governance section. In retrospect, I think that having two books translated into Chinese and published in China was the decisive factor in convincing authorities at the University of Ottawa Press to publish the manuscript in English. However, I have no way of verifying this.

By the end of 2008, *Revolution or Renaissance: Making the Transition from an Economic Age to a Cultural Age* was published and circulating in English as well as Chinese. I had worked on the manuscript for more than four years on a full-time basis and felt it was very relevant to the world situation. While I suspected that there would be many people who would disagree with the central premise of the book — namely that humanity should pass out of the prevailing economic age and into a future cultural age — I felt I was definitely on the right track. I believed that it would be a mistake to perpetuate the economic age for much longer in the future. The costs, consequences, and dangers of this were just too great, especially as world population increased and the carrying capacity of the earth was approached.

Without entering a cultural age and realizing a renaissance in global development and human affairs, I felt it would not be possible to improve living standards and the quality of life for all people and all countries in the world without straining the globe's scarce resources, fragile ecosystems, and natural environment to the breaking point. Having made this case and made it to the best of my ability, it was up to others to decide if this case had merit.

CHAPTER ELEVEN

Flourishing of a Cultural Age

As the twenty-first century and new millennium began to unfold, I was more convinced than ever that a cultural age was imperative. Not only was it required to come to grips with many existing world problems, but also to deal with the new problems that had loomed above the global horizon.

These problems, old and new, included the environmental crisis and with it climate change and global warming, huge disparities in income and wealth, and an increasing number of conflicts between specific ethnic groups, countries, religions, and civilizations, especially in the Middle East but also in other parts of the world. Other problems included the growing scarcity of natural resources, escalating prices for basic staples and fundamental foodstuffs, unacceptable levels of poverty, unemployment, and hunger, and mounting skepticism over the existing state of the world and prospects for the future. These problems, and others, were closely linked to culture in a whole series of deep, dynamic, and fundamental ways.

This meant that it was not only necessary to enter a cultural age, but also for a cultural age to flourish. This was especially important with respect to the need for new approaches to the world's most pressing and persistent problems, as well as for the creation of much more hope, optimism, and enthusiasm in the world. Without the ability to come to grips with such problems – an ability I felt culture possessed in abundance – the full potential of culture would not be realized and a cultural age would not flourish.

As I was thinking about how a cultural age might flourish most effectively and fully, my mind was transported back to the way the economic age flourished. This was largely because an elaborate theoretical and practical *system* had been created that was based on the centrality of economics, economies, and economic growth in the overall scheme of things. Like the economic age, I believed a cultural age must also be based on a theoretical and practical *system*. Much of this system's success would depend on creating a very different relationship between human beings and the natural environment, as well as on placing a much higher priority on people rather than products and profits.

While thoughts and ideas on this matter were important, they were not enough. What was needed was a *new* world system — a *cultural* system based on different foundations, principles, policies, and practices. This meant going farther, and digging deeper, into culture and its many diverse assets, capabilities, and secrets than had been achieved in the past. It also meant extending culture well beyond the existing boundaries that have been established for it by the vast majority of people, institutions, and countries in the world.

Creating such a system constitutes the next great leap in human history, thereby making it possible to achieve many things that are simply not possible to achieve in the present economic age. While many of the economic age's achievements will be sustained in a cultural age because of their importance to people's lives, it is mandatory to broaden and deepen knowledge and understanding of culture, as well as to make maximum use of the incredible theoretical and practical legacy that successive generations of cultural scholars and practitioners have created for us.

I am not exaggerating the size, scope, importance, or potential of this legacy. It is all there in black and white, as I discovered in the Bladen Library years earlier and tried to make manifest in such books as *Culture: Beacon of the Future* and *Revolution or Renaissance: Making the Transition from an Economic Age to a Cultural Age*.

Most essential in this respect is the need to treat culture as an end in itself rather than a means to other ends. As long as culture is held captive in the web of other disciplines and activities, its full potential to come to grips with the world's most demanding and debilitating problems and create the conditions for a better world will not be realized. For a cultural age to become a reality, flourish, and soar to great heights, culture must step out of the shadows and into the sunlight. The world desperately needs a new organizing principle and culture is the ideal vehicle to provide it.

This is because culture manifests itself in the world in many different ways. Each of these ways has a crucial role to play in the flourishing of a cultural age and the development of a new world system. Most prominent among these ways are culture as the arts; the humanities; the legacy from the past; shared values, traditions, beliefs, and behaviour; a complex whole; a total way of life; the relationship between human beings with the natural environment; and as the organizational forms and structures of different species. These main "manifestations of culture" have been mentioned on several occasions throughout the book. However, now is the time to examine them in detail because they hold the key to the flourishing of a cultural age.

These manifestations are what makes culture so indispensable to the world of the future. When culture is understood and dealt with in these terms, it possesses the potential to explain an enormous amount about all the complexity and diversity that exists in the world. This is of crucial importance. The world has become incredibly complex and diverse over the last century or so, and this trend is likely to continue and compound in the future. Without being able to deal with the implications and consequences of this, humanity will be at a severe disadvantage in the future. Clearly culture is the "missing link" that is required to confront and come to grips with these requirements.

Culture is able to serve as this link because it possesses the capacity to move horizontally as well as vertically — in breadth as well as in depth — across the vast spectrum of activities that exist in the world, from the human to the non-human, the simple to the complex, the individual to the collective, the local to the global, the public to the private, and the mundane to the profound. While the eminent economist and environmentalist, Barbara Ward, asked "Where is the thread that will lead us through the maze?" it is now clear that culture is this thread. It is capable of linking together and explaining virtually everything that exists in the world in depth and breath because it manifests itself in the world in so many different ways.

As the arts, culture does this first and foremost by bringing an enormous amount of happiness and fulfillment into people's lives. Not only does culture reach to the very depths of the human condition in this sense, but also it connects with people in profound, moving, and very intense ways. It also helps people to express their feelings, emotions, and frustrations, develop their sensorial and aesthetic capabilities, cultivate their creativity, imagination, and capacity for innovation and entrepreneurship, pursue the quest for excellence, perfection, and the search for the sublime, master other disciplines and activities, and reduce the demands they are making on the world's scarce resources.

This is equally true for culture's capacity to foster awareness, appreciation, and reverence for nature. There is no doubt that this is one of the arts' greatest assets and fundamental strengths. Virtually everything that exists in the realm of nature is revealed through the abilities, sensibilities, and creative capabilities of artists and artistic works.

Culture also broadens and deepens our understanding of cultures, countries, and civilizations as dynamic and organic wholes when it manifests itself through the arts. As indicated earlier, this is because artists create many of the signs, symbols, myths, legends, metaphors, stories, paintings, plays, musical compositions, and the like that "stand for the whole" and give us a more complete understanding of the whole. This is especially true of dramatic works. Such works deal with the full spectrum of people's emotions, customs, beliefs, educational experiences, and religious practices, among many other things, and consequently address culture in its totality.

It follows from this that it is impossible to know or understand any culture, country, or civilization in any real depth without exposure to, and familiarity with, the works of its artists. Take American culture as an example of this. Since American culture as a whole can't be known in its totality because of its infinite variety and complexity, it can only be known through parts of the whole that stand for the whole and give us a sense of what American culture is really like as a whole. This is achieved through the works of writers such as Ernest Hemingway, Mark Twain, Emily Dickinson, and Maya Angelou, dancers and choreographers such as Martha Graham, Ginger Rogers, and Fred Astaire, artists such as Andrew Wyeth and Jackson Pollock, composers and musicians such as Aaron Copland, George Gershwin, Irving Berlin, and Richard Rodgers, and photographers and documentary film-makers such as Ansel Adams and Ken Burns. Indeed, Ken Burns seems to have a particular knack for picking parts of the whole that are symbolic of the whole and communicate a great deal of information about the whole. Most notable in this regard are his documentaries on baseball, jazz, America's national parks, the Civic War, and the three Roosevelts, Theodore, Franklin Delano, and Eleanor.

Russian culture also provides an excellent example of this same principle. Think of how much our knowledge and understanding of the historical development and contemporary character of Russian culture is enlarged and enhanced by exposure to, and familiarity with, such artistic masterpieces as Tolstoy's *War and Peace* and *Anna Karenina*, Dostoevsky's *Crime and Punishment* and *The Brothers Karamazov*, Chekhov's

Uncle Vanya, *The Seagull*, and *The Cherry Orchard*, Pushkin's *Boris Godunov* and *Eugene Onegin*, Pasternak's *Doctor Zhivago*, Tchaikovsky's *Symphony Pathetique,* and many others. Both the light side and dark side of Russian culture are exposed through these and many other artistic works, all of which help to provide us with a more composite and compelling picture of one of the most complex and captivating cultures in the world.

The same holds true for Spanish culture. Exposure to and familiarity with Miguel de Cervantes' *Don Quixote de la Mancha*, Rodrigo's *Concierto de Aranguez* and *Concierto de Andaluz*, Granados' *Goyescas* and *Danzas españolas*, Albéniz's *Iberia*, de Falla's *Noches en los jardinas de España* and *El amor brujo*, and the paintings of El Greco, Velázquez, Goya, and many other masters is essential if we want to heighten our understanding of the historical development and contemporary nature of Spanish culture. These works evoke strong images of the Spanish countryside, the diverse regions of Spain, hot days, cool nights, splendid architecture in places like Seville, Cordoba, Segovia, Toledo, Madrid, and Barcelona, intoxicating gardens in Granada, flamenco music and dances in the caves of Andalusia, and majestic monuments throughout the entire country. While there is much more to Spanish culture than this, there is no doubt that exposure to and familiarity with these and many other works does a great deal to enhance our understanding and appreciation of Spanish culture in all its splendour, magnificence, and grandeur.

Nor is this all. The arts also uplift us and cause us to aspire to the sublime. It is not only classical music such as Beethoven's *Ninth Symphony* and especially his *Ode to Joy* — as well as Mahler's *Resurrection Symphony* and countless other musical works — that scale Herculean heights and inspire us to reach above and beyond ourselves. Popular music does this, too. Do such pieces as John Lennon's *Imagine*, Louis Armstrong's *What a Wonderful World*, and many others not uplift and inspire us in profound and moving ways, exhorting us to visualize a world full of peace, harmony, beauty, hope, and happiness, where it is possible to "live as one" and experience "the brotherhood of man"?

It is easy to see how essential culture in the form of the arts will be to the world of the future and to the flourishing of a cultural age. However, what artists have done for humanity in the past will have to be magnified many times over in the future. In virtually every domain of public and private life, from the individual to the international level, artists and arts organizations possess the ability to improve and enrich life. In fact, it would not be far off the mark to say that in a cultural age, every individual should become — and is capable of becoming — an artist in her or his own right. While a great deal of fulfillment can be derived from enjoying the arts as an audience member, even more can be derived as a practitioner. People are never too young or too old to become actively involved in painting pictures, taking photographs, creating music, singing songs, making movies, telling stories, and so forth, as well as to experience the infinite joy, satisfaction, and fulfillment that comes from such activities.

Just as culture manifesting itself as the arts has a great deal to do with the flourishing of a cultural age, so does culture in the form of the humanities. Indeed, when culture manifests itself in the humanistic sense, it has a great deal to do with ethics, morality, the finer things in life, and the highest standards of human conduct. These qualities are connected to culture in countless ways, from the quest to realize peace, order, equality, and justice to the need for sharing, caring, compassion, and cooperation. Commitment to ideals such as these is also of vital importance to the flourishing of a cultural age.

As mentioned earlier, I often think of Albert Schweitzer, Mahatma Gandhi, Mother Teresa, Nelson Mandela, and Dr. Martin Luther King Jr. when I think of these matters, largely because they led inspiring and humanistic lives. While these people are well-known and revered throughout the world, there are countless other people in the world who are struggling to put into practice culture's highest, wisest, and most humanistic values and ideals. They are doing so by dedicating themselves and their lives to worthy causes and concerns, such as battling crime, corruption, waste, oppression, pollution, violence against women, children, and seniors, inequitable distributions of wealth, and myriads of other injustices and inequalities that are evident throughout the world.

Building on the courage and determination of such people, it is not difficult to see how the humanities in general — and ethical values, ideals, and actions in particular — can lead to a great deal more equality and justice in the world. This is a categorical imperative in the future if humanity is to be successful in enabling all people and all countries to enjoy reasonable standards of living. To achieve this end, there will have to be far more giving in the world — giving that comes from culture and its ability to call forth things that have much more to do with the heart, the soul, and the spirit than materialism and the pocketbook.

Then there is the legacy from the past. When culture manifests itself in this way, it shines the spotlight on how humanity has evolved over the centuries, and with it, on the cultural heritages of all the diverse peoples, cultures, and countries in the world. This universal heritage of hope includes the cultural accomplishments of all the diverse peoples of the world; all the greatest cities and historical sites in the world; all the world's greatest achievements in the arts, sciences, religion, education, economics, medicine, philosophy, and so forth; all the most powerful ideas, theories, and writings; and especially all the myriad cultures and civilizations that have been created throughout the world, each with its own unique character and particular strengths. Little wonder Jacob Burckhardt called this precious gift "the silent promise" that possesses the potential to transform the entire past into a "spiritual possession."

One institution that has taken convictions like this to heart is surely UNESCO. This remarkable organization has been steadily and systematically translating such lofty ideals into concrete realities for more than half a century. It places an exceedingly high priority on preserving and protecting humanity's indispensable cultural legacy and making it accessible to everyone. We are the beneficiaries of this rich cornucopia of cultural achievements and environmental wonders. Fortunately, developments in contemporary technology, the social media, and modern communications are making it possible for people in all parts of the world to enjoy this magnificent legacy. I am elated whenever I think that virtually everyone in the world today possesses the means, or has access to them, to tap into these treasures regardless of where they are situated in the world.

This indispensable legacy from the past also provides a number of other possibilities that are of utmost importance to the world of the future. One of these is the ability to create strong bonds and links between the past, the present, and the future, and therefore to enhance people's sense of identity, belonging, solidarity, and ability to move backwards and forwards in time. Another is the ability to speak directly to people about what is most dear to them, and hence about their historical values, ideals, and origins in space and time. Still another is the ability to root education and learning in culture and make it possible for people to draw on insights and ideas from all the diverse cultures of the world to improve their own situation and enrich their own lives. And yet another — and one that is of utmost importance to the world of the future if peace and harmony are to be achieved — is the ability to expose people to their mistakes in the past, and consequently why and how it is essential to correct these mistakes in the future.

We must be ever mindful of the cultural baggage we inherit from the past. We will never create a better world and a cultural age will never flourish until we have come to grips with the negative aspects of this baggage as confirmed earlier. This is why leaders like Gandhi, Mandela, Archbishop Tutu, the Dalai Lama, and others have been so committed to engendering respect and appreciation for all the diverse peoples, countries, and cultures of the world. It is also why truth and reconciliation commissions, or their equivalent, have been established to come to grips with the causes and consequences of the many conflicts and hostilities that exist in the world.

Closely related to the legacy from the past are shared values, traditions, beliefs, and behaviour. This manifestation of culture is also of fundamental importance to the full flourishing of a cultural age.

The "shared" aspect of culture in this sense is exceedingly important. It is impossible to be a member of any human collectivity, be it a group, club, organization, community, or country, without sharing many things in common. It is this fact that makes it possible to bind people, institutions, countries, and cultures together when other forces exist to propel them apart.

Without doubt, we need a great deal more sharing in the world if we are to be successful in overcoming the huge social, economic, and educational injustices and disparities that exist throughout the world. Income, wealth, and resources will have to be shared much more equally if we want to eradicate poverty, hunger, and unemployment, which are the causes of a great deal of hostility and misery in the world. While some of the impetus for this change will have to come from corporations, governments, and international organizations, the bulk of it will have to come from citizens, community groups, and culture if it is to come at all. For the impetus to share, like the impetus to bond and to belong, emanates much more from the heart and the soul than from the head or the pocketbook.

There is another dimension to this particular manifestation of culture that should not escape our attention. It has to do with the way individuals, institutions, and groups organize themselves, conduct their affairs, and position themselves in the world. Increasingly, it is being realized that groups and institutions have "cultures" just as communities, regions, and countries do, and what is more, manifest these cultures as they go about the process of meeting the individual and collective needs and concerns of their members.

Whether it is clubs, communities, associations, governments, corporations, or service organizations, all human entities and collectivities – and the specific organizations and groups that comprise them – manifest cultures that say *this is who we are* and *this is the way things are done around here*. This is what makes it possible to talk about the cultures of different groups of people and different institutions, such as police culture, bank culture, hospital culture, corporate culture, educational culture, governmental culture, and so forth. Each of these cultures, and the specific institutions and groups that function within them, is designed to act as a cultural entity – a dynamic and organic whole – that exhibits very specific ways of organizing, functioning, and positioning itself in the world. Terms such as these are popular and commonplace today because they confirm the fact that all organizations, institutions, and groups display very specific ways of operating as they go about the process of meeting the individual and collective needs of their members, employees, customers, and so forth.

What makes this so important to the world of the future is the fact that many organizations, groups, and institutions will have to change "who we are" and "the way things are done around here" if the world is to become a better, safer, more secure place. It is often said in this respect that there is an "environmental problem." However, it is not really an environmental problem but, rather, a "human problem." We are the ones who are polluting and destroying the natural environment. This makes the "sociological manifestation of culture," as it is often called, one of the most important manifestations of culture of all, since it is concerned with *transformation* and *change* and all of the various methods, actions, and especially behaviours that are required to initiate and bring about this transformation and change.

The same holds true for culture when it manifests itself as a complex whole or total way of life. Could there be anything more essential or fundamental to the flourishing of a cultural age than this? Viewed from this perspective, culture includes every conceivable activity that people are engaged in – tangible and intangible, material and non-material, visible and invisible. It also includes the ordering process that is used to combine all these activities together to form a whole or overall way of life.

Like the other manifestations of culture, this far more all-encompassing expression of culture possesses many capabilities that are of utmost importance to the world of the future and the flourishing of a cultural age. In fact, these capabilities may be the most quintessential of all. Most of them have to do with a capacity that the other manifestations of culture do not possess, namely the ability to see things in holistic terms. Sight should never be lost of this capacity, nor should it be underestimated. It is one of humanity's greatest gifts and most fundamental assets.

In the first place, it makes it possible to see the world and the vast majority of things that exist in the world as they really are, not as we are conditioned to see them as a result of specialization and our penchant for dividing the whole up into parts in order to study those parts in detail. While specialization is very helpful in shedding light on the various parts of things, and studying those parts in detail, it is not helpful in understanding that the world, the world system, and most things in the world are wholes made up of an intricate interlacing of countless parts, not smorgasbords of disconnected or unrelated pieces.

Nowhere is this more important than with respect to people. Though our bodies and our lives are made up of many diverse parts, the fact remains that they are wholes in the all-inclusive sense, not collections of unrelated elements. Failure to recognize this fact and deal with the implications of it can have serious consequences for people struggling to live happy, healthy, and productive lives, but who are unable to do so because they cannot combine all the different parts of their bodies and their lives together to form harmonious and integrated wholes. *It is culture, possibly more than any other activity in society or in the world, that enables people to do this, thereby making it possible for them to become "whole people" in the most compelling and comprehensive sense.* We will never become whole people and live effectively in a cultural age until we recognize that this is first and foremost a cultural requirement.

The same holds true for the world and the world system. They are also wholes made up of many diverse and interconnected parts.

It is impossible to view culture in the holistic sense without recognizing that culture provides the *context* or *container* within which virtually everything in the world created by human beings is situated. If we have lost one thing in the modern world, surely it is our ability to see things *in context* rather than *in isolation*. We have become so caught up with the "contents" of things that we have lost sight of the overall "context" in which they are situated.

There are many examples of this. Failure to understand that culture provides the context within which corporate activities take place has yielded a situation where many corporate activities take place without proper control and oversight. This can lead to fraudulent accounting practices, financial irregularities, the payment of exorbitant fees and salaries to corporate executives, and the inability to regulate business activities and corporate practices in the public interest. Likewise, failure to understand that culture provides the context within which economic and technological activities take place has yielded a situation where preoccupation with certain types of these activities is having a deleterious rather than favourable effect on the global situation, especially when undue demands are made on the resources of nature and people's lives. Moreover, failure to recognize that culture provides the context within which education takes place means that cultural education is neglected everywhere in the world, despite the fact that culture has a great deal to do with how people and countries develop and interact, and consequently with international development and world affairs. Clearly there is a price that has to be paid when we get so wrapped up with the parts of things that sight is lost of the whole.

This ability to see things in context is not the only benefit to be derived from the holistic manifestation of culture. This manifestation is also the key to seeing things that are of vital importance to the world of the future. This is imperative if we are to come to grips with the environmental crisis and treat the natural environment and other species with the dignity and respect they deserve. Here, as well, we have lost sight of the forest for the trees, leading to environmental excesses and imbalances that are impossible to justify.

Culture in this all-inclusive sense also possesses the ability to shed light on the complex interconnections and interrelationships that exist between and among different human activities. Here, we must be successful in "connecting the dots" and coming to grips with the complex connections that exist – *or do not exist* – between such matters as economics and ethics, science and religion, education and health, politics and society, technology and spirituality, and many others. It is culture that enables us to connect the dots and bridge these gaps.

Clearly we are also paying a severe price for dealing with many things independently rather than *inter*dependently. We engage in activities that are high in material inputs, outputs, and resource utilization, while refusing to admit that these activities are intimately connected to environmental problems. We idolize technological developments while failing to realize that many of these developments are having a deleterious effect on religious practices and spiritual beliefs. We condone huge expenditures on health care while decreasing or eliminating the time spent on physical education and recreational activity in our schools. While culture may not possess the ability to deal with all of these problems, there is no doubt that it provides the best possible "container" within which to view them, as well as the ability to shed light on how to approach and overcome these problems in the future.

It is particularly important for governments to recognize this fact. Unfortunately, governments have become so accustomed to taking a partial or specialized approach to problem-solving — largely by creating and perpetuating separate "silos" within which all the various aspects of society are situated — that the left hand often does not know what the right hand is doing. What is needed now, and needed more than ever, is a holistic approach to governmental decision-making and problem-solving. It is culture, more than any other discipline, that makes this possible. It also provides the best possible framework for governmental planning, policy, and decision-making. It does so by providing the most effective device for achieving balance and harmony between the various parts of society and public planning, policy, decision-making, and development as a whole.

There is one final capability culture possesses when it manifests itself in holistic terms that has a great deal of relevance to the flowering of a cultural age. It is the ability of culture to bring things together rather than propel them apart. This ability is required on many fronts. It is required to unite people, communities, countries, cultures, and civilizations, as well as to establish strong bonds and connections among them. It is also required to create symbiotic relationships and synergistic connections between all the diverse disciplines and activities in society, as well as to unify knowledge and understanding of what is fundamental and most essential. It is likewise required to eliminate the fragmentation that exists in our lives — fragmentation that makes it difficult to blend all the various activities in which we are engaged together to form a harmonious entity.

While all the different manifestations of culture considered thus far are important and have a great deal to do with the flourishing of a cultural age, two much broader manifestations of culture have emerged in recent years that are also crucial. Both are concerned with the intimate connection that exists between human beings, nature, the natural environment, and other species.

The first is the ecological manifestation of culture. It is predicated on the conviction that culture is concerned with the complex relationship between people and the natural environment. Whereas all the manifestations of culture considered prior to this confine culture to human beings and the products of human creation, the ecological manifestation does not, but, rather, focuses on the intimate relationship between human beings and nature. This necessitates another quantum leap in our understanding of culture — a leap not unlike the one required to see culture in holistic rather than partial terms.

The ecological manifestation of culture has the advantage of focusing attention on the biggest challenge confronting humanity of all. For the evidence is clear and conclusive. Unless urgent attention is given to the intimate connection between human beings and the natural environment, cultures and countries in all parts of the world run the risk of over-extending themselves, collapsing, and disappearing entirely from the global scene because they are unsustainable.

Like the ecological manifestation of culture, the biological manifestation of culture opens the doors to a very expansive view of culture — without doubt the most expansive of all. It is predicated on the conviction that culture is concerned with the organizational forms and structures of all the diverse species of the world, both human and non-human.

With this view comes the belief that every species possesses culture. Culture is not confined to human beings in this sense, but rather exists throughout the entire realm of nature. It is possible, therefore, to talk about the culture of plants and animals in much the same way that we talk about the culture of human beings, even if those cultures are less sophisticated and complex. Terms in our vocabulary such as *agriculture* and *horticulture* indicate that culture manifests itself in virtually everything that exists in the world in the natural and human realms.

Not everyone will agree with the biological manifestation of culture or feel comfortable about this idea. Indeed, there may be many who will insist that culture is — *and always should be* — confined to human beings, because human culture and cultures are what separates the human species from other species and makes human beings unique.

People who share this conviction believe that human beings have the capacity to rationalize, reason, reflect, and engage in various forms of consciousness that other species lack, or do not possess to the same degree. Nevertheless, the belief that culture is not limited to human beings is rapidly gaining ground. More and more people around the world are becoming aware of the numerous similarities that exist between human beings and other species. Indeed, recent research is revealing that the differences between human beings and other species, once deemed to be very great, are not as great as previously thought.

All that is required to confirm this is to watch other species as they go about the process of meeting *their* individual and collective needs and working out *their* association with the world. Do they not do it in much the same way that human beings do, even if it is less sophisticated and complex? Like human beings, other species see and interpret the world, even if they see and interpret it in their way and not our way. Moreover, they organize themselves into communities and groups, conduct their affairs with a great deal of conviction, courage, and determination, elevate and embellish life by engaging in various forms of play and recreation, and position themselves in the world in much the same way that humans do, such as by fighting to maintain their turf when necessary. Anyone who has tuned in to the profusion of television programs that have been made about other species in recent years will instantly recognize and accept this fact. But it can also be confirmed by watching a flock of geese as they stare at us, observing a colony of ants as they prepare for the hunt, studying cats to see how much they enjoy playing with each other and basking in the sun, and observing a pack of wolves as they carve out a prominent place for themselves in the wilderness.

And there is more. Many species bond, mate, and create wholes and total ways of life in much the same way that human beings do. Consider bees, as we did earlier. Like human beings, bees create cultures that are composed of many different elements or parts, all of which are woven together in specific arrangements to form wholes and overall ways of life. These wholes and overall ways of life act to ensure the survival of bees and attend to their various biological requirements. They also guarantee a continuous supply of products. These products, such as honey, wax, the beehive, and the honeycomb, are much in demand in the human domain and have a functional, medicinal, and aesthetic value and significance. The beehive and the honeycomb, for example, are intricately designed cultural creations, comparable in their function and complexity to many of the cultural creations of human beings. And what is true for bees is also true for many other animal and plant species and their creations. Virtually every animal and plant species in the world has its own forms of culture and cultural creation, including its modes of organization, behaviour, procreation, consumption and production activity, and positioning in the natural environment. In fact, modern advances in botany and horticulture are revealing that plants, like people and animals, have feelings, emotions, and experience pain, and what is more, respond very much the way people and animals do when confronted with such unpleasantries.

There is a great deal to be learned from the cultures of other species that is relevant to the development of human cultures. Consider what can be learned about caring, sharing, bonding, and cooperation. While it is not true for all animal species, many animal species share more fully than human beings, and do so far more willingly and frequently. Elephants, for example, care for each other very deeply, and are each other's keepers, even if (like all species) they fight over mating, food, and other issues. Elephants also pay close attention to what is going on with their companions, something which explains why elephants are so revered, especially in many Asian cultures. Elephants also have incredible memories (possibly better than those of many people), and show great sympathy and affection for one another, especially when they are in difficulty. They gather around each other when they are sick, whenever there is work to be done, and when there is a need to rescue their companions from danger or distress. They also look after their young attentively and affectionately. And what is true for elephants is true for many other animal species, even if not to the same degree.

It follows from this that one of the best ways to understand the culture and ways of life of human beings may well be to study the cultures and ways of life of other species more intensively. Careful study of the reasons why other species (and their cultures) thrive and survive – or fail to do so – may be helpful in dealing with comparable human problems. Many animal species have evolved modes of organization, conservation, and behaviour that reveal an awareness of how large populations can be regulated, managed, and governed when resources are scarce and space is limited.

Nor are these the only advantages to be derived from studying the cultures and ways of life of other species. Another is to improve the relationship between human beings and other species. While many people get immense pleasure from their involvement with plants and animals (especially their pets), there is no doubt that our relations with other species will have to undergo profound change if we are to treat other species with the dignity, respect, and empathy they deserve.

When all the aforementioned manifestations of culture from the artistic to the biological are considered in totality, it is clear why they have a great deal to do with the flourishing of a cultural age. For each manifestation possesses many specific qualities, capabilities, and characteristics that are of utmost importance to the full flowering of such an age.

Like all ages, the cultural age will have to be built on all the ages that preceded it, and, most emphatically, the economic age. This is because it is not possible to wipe the slate clean and start over. However, it is imperative to go beyond previous ages if we are to be successful in coming to grips with the most difficult and demanding problems that exist throughout the world today. As indicated earlier, the key to this lies in making culture, cultures, and cultural development in the holistic sense the centrepiece of the world system and principal preoccupation of municipal, regional, national, and international development.

What we are talking about here bears a striking resemblance in certain ways to what Thomas Berry called the "*Great Work*," although in our case it is much more immediate and practical than ultimate and cosmological. Of course, great work has been achieved in every age. It results from the fact that human beings have been compelled to come to grips with many difficult problems that have loomed up in their paths over the course of history, sometimes by making large and epic, and other times by making smaller but imperative, changes in the prevailing ways of doing things. In each and every case, however, this has been necessary in order to cross over the threshold to a different kind of age.

This was true for the very first human age, when people had to protect themselves against the elements and the ravages of nature and wild animals. It was also true for the agricultural age, when a transformation took place in the production of food supplies that facilitated large increases in population and made it possible for some people to move "off the land" and live in the world's first urban communities. It was equally true for the Industrial Revolution and the economic age. In this case, the great work involved improving living standards and the quality of life for billions of people and countless countries throughout the world.

Now, the challenge is to do the great work that is required to bring a cultural age into existence and enable it to flourish. In order to do this, it is necessary to shift from economics to culture, so that a better balance will be achieved among all the diverse factors of development and a more harmonious relationship will be established between human beings and the natural environment. It is a tremendous challenge, but one which, if realized, will make it possible for all the diverse people and countries of the world to experience a great deal of happiness, fulfillment, and well-being in life without straining the globe's fragile ecosystems and limited resources to the breaking point.

CHAPTER TWELVE
Living a Cultural Life

I had been writing about culture and a cultural age for so long by this time that people were starting to ask me what it would be like to "live a cultural life." Would it be possible to provide them with some thoughts and ideas on this subject that would be helpful in planning and living their own lives?

As I was wrestling with this problem, my mind was cast back to the time I came across a phrase by Wolfgang von Goethe, the great German scholar and playwright, in a book called *The Meaning of Culture* by John Cowper Powys. As quoted earlier, the phrase was: "*Live in the whole, in the good, in the beautiful.*" This phrase hit me like a ton of bricks the moment I read it. It seemed to sum up in a few simple words what I thought living a cultural life was all about. I recall thinking at the time that I would likely have to write about this evocative phrase at some point in my life. Now, almost thirty years later, I have decided to do this, largely because I think it says so much about living a cultural life and all the happiness and rewards that can be experienced from this.

I have decided to tackle this task by breaking Goethe's captivating phase down into its three principal components — live in the whole; in the good; in the beautiful — and writing about each of these components separately. It is my hope that this approach will prove helpful to others who might also be wrestling with similar problems in their own lives and find my experiences in this area helpful.

For some curious reason that I have never been able to understand, I have always thought that living a cultural life is tied up with becoming a *whole person* in some way. I don't know where this idea came from, but it has always been there. Perhaps it is because I think a whole person is someone who is able to blend all the different parts of their lives together to form an integrated and harmonious whole. The problem is that life does not come to us this way. It comes to us in parts, not as a whole. As a result, we grow up knowing little about *the whole* and how it is possible to blend all the various parts of our lives together to form a whole.

When I went to elementary and secondary school, I learned quickly that the focus of attention was on the parts, not the whole. Whether it was physics, geography, chemistry, algebra, geometry, or any other subject I was studying, everything was divided up into parts in order to study those parts in detail. There was never a subject that dealt with how all the parts can be combined to form a whole, regardless of whether this was in the personal sense or any other sense.

This problem was compounded when I went to university. I was told that I would have to specialize in a single subject if I wanted to succeed in life. So I chose economics. It seemed to be the sensible thing to do, and the thing my parents and teachers wanted me to do.

The farther I went in university, the more I was encouraged to specialize. It was no longer sufficient to specialize in a single subject. It was also necessary to specialize in a specific branch of that subject in order to get to know it as well as possible. This was the key to getting a good job, earning a decent living, and realizing one's basic goals and objectives in life. So I chose the history of economic thought, because I was fascinated with the historical development of economics as a discipline and how economics had become the most powerful force in the world.

It wasn't until I was in my early thirties that I realized what was going on here. I was moving farther and farther away from the whole and becoming a whole person rather than closer and closer to this. Not only was I encouraged to specialize in a specific part of the whole — albeit an extremely important part — but also I was encouraged to specialize in the development of one of my faculties only, namely my intellect. While I wanted to understand the whole in a more profound and fundamental way, and to position myself as a "whole within the whole," so to speak, I was encouraged to close off to the whole and develop one of my faculties only.

I decided then and there that I would pursue a different course of action. I would endeavour to learn as much as I could about the whole in the most elementary sense, as well as to become a whole person, regardless of how difficult this was and what personal and professional obstacles stood in the way.

I got a terrific start in the right direction when I read a book by Mathew Arnold called *Culture and Anarchy*. In this book, Arnold talked about the need to attend to the harmonious development of all the powers that comprise human nature as noted earlier. Here, at last, was something I could hold on to and press into the forefront of my consciousness. Not only did Arnold recognize the need to develop all our faculties and not just one — our bodies, minds, hearts, souls, spirits, emotions, and feelings, as well as our intellects — but he also recognized the need to achieve balance and harmony between and among these faculties.

Since Arnold was a cultural scholar much like Goethe, I began to wonder if culture contained some clues with respect to what is necessary to become a whole person and to understand the whole in a broader, deeper, and more fundamental sense. I was encouraged to do so even more when I discovered that Arnold had something else to say that had a direct bearing on this subject. It was the need to see culture in proactive, altruistic, and external — and not just reactive, internal, and egocentric — terms.

In Arnold's view, it was not sufficient to observe and learn from the world without giving something back in return. It was equally necessary to ensure that the best knowledge, wisdom, and understanding prevailed, in the sense that they were made available to future generations and people living in all parts of the world and at all levels of society. In one of the most telling passages in Arnold's book, he states:

> The great men [and women] of culture are those who have had a passion for diffusing, for making prevail, for carrying from one end of society to the other, the best knowledge, the best ideas of their time; who have laboured to divest knowledge of all that was harsh, uncouth, difficult, abstract, professional, exclusive; to humanize it, to make it efficient outside the clique of the cultivated and learned, yet still remaining the *best* knowledge and thought of the time, and a true source, therefore, of sweetness and light.

For Arnold, "sweetness and light" were "the arts and education." These activities have a crucial role to play in realizing the harmonious development of all aspects of the human personality, as well as diffusing the best knowledge, ideas, and wisdom throughout the world. This is because they go far beyond oneself and one's own life, and embrace other people and their lives as well. In so doing, they make it possible for people to concern themselves with "the other" and not just "the self." This is essential if people want to become whole people, live in the whole, and live a cultural life.

If Arnold's thoughts on this matter got me moving in the right direction, Thomas Carlyle's great *Law of Culture* quoted earlier strengthened my resolve that I was on the right track. His advice to become everything we are capable of becoming and show ourselves in our own shape, substance, and stature hardened my commitment to becoming a whole person and "a person in my own right." It also gave me the confidence I needed to pursue the idea of culture with much more vim, vigour, and vitality than I had up to that point in my life. I knew that I was on to something powerful and profound here with respect to "living in the whole" and living a cultural life when I read Arnold's and Carlyle's thoughts in this area.

I received an even stronger boost in this direction when I came across the writings of Sir Edward Burnett Tylor. As indicated earlier, Tylor defined culture in his book *The Origins of Culture* as "that complex whole that includes knowledge, belief, art, morals, law, custom, and any other capabilities and habits acquired by man as a member of society."

Here was definitely something I could build on with respect to broadening and deepening my knowledge and understanding of culture and the whole. What Tylor's definition did was break with the long tradition of defining culture in terms of the parts – a tradition that can be traced back to the classical and medieval ages and the intimate connection between culture, the arts, and humanities – and started defining culture in terms of the whole.

Tylor's definition of culture as "*the complex whole*" had a profound effect on me the instant I read it. I was desperately searching for a way of looking at the world that was consistent with reality, and Tylor's definition of culture provided it. For despite our penchant for dividing things up into parts in order to analyze those parts, the fact remains that the world and most things in the world are wholes made up of many parts, not smorgasbords of disconnected and unrelated pieces. This is true not only for culture, but also for people, institutions, communities, cities, countries, cultures, the world, the world system, and virtually everything else. Each of these entities, and countless others, are complex wholes made up of many parts. While I appreciated the need to break these wholes up into parts, as well as the numerous benefits that can and are derived from this process, I was deeply concerned about the fact that humanity had lost sight of the whole in the individual, institutional, community, national, international, environmental, and historical sense. I felt that culture in general – and Tylor's holistic understanding of it in particular – was the key that was required to overcome this problem and set things right.

Armed with this holistic way of seeing, I began to realize the incredible potential culture possesses for broadening and deepening knowledge, understanding, and awareness of the whole in the most profound and quintessential sense. While culture is not the only discipline or activity that is capable of doing this, since this is also possible through disciplines and activities like philosophy, religion, and others, it made me far more aware of the whole within myself, as well as in the world. This was particularly true for my family, friends, neighbourhood, community, country, and culture. Each of these wholes was constantly evolving and mutating as changes took place in their diverse parts and the way these parts are woven together to form a whole. While it is not necessary to know all of the parts that make up such wholes, it is necessary to be conscious of them and how they are combined to form wholes.

To "live in the whole" in this sense is to allow the whole to penetrate into the interiors of our being and our consciousness, regardless of what type of whole it might be. As a result, whenever I step out the front door now, I am instantly aware of the whole that exists all around me. When I walk in the neighbourhood — which is so often that kids in the neighbourhood call me "the walking man" because I am always out walking when they see me — I am aware of it as a whole. Not only do I soak it up as a whole, but also I cherish it as a whole. This gives me an incredible sense of exhilaration because I am connecting with my neighbourhood in all its complexity, diversity, and vastness. Exactly the same is true for my community — Markham — and my country and culture — Canada and Canadian culture. Each of these complex entities is a whole made up of many parts. I want to learn as much as I can about them, as well as about how all their various parts are combined together to create a whole.

To live in the whole in this sense is to embrace the whole at every opportunity and in every possible way. In the process of doing this, it is possible to understand what Goethe meant when he said "live in the whole." To do so is to be conscious of the whole — and wholes — all the time and in all places.

Unfortunately, this is not the way we are taught to see and understand the world. Rather than opening up to the whole and embracing it at every opportunity, we close off to the whole, and "wholes within the whole," and tend to ignore them. This is because we have been trained — as I was trained — to identify with the parts and not the whole, especially parts that have some particular significance or value for us. Nevertheless, to live in the whole — *really* live in it — is to make a concerted effort to expand our knowledge, understanding, and awareness of the whole — and the wholes within it — whenever and wherever we encounter them.

There is an incredible sense of awe, unity, and oneness that comes from this, regardless of whether it is in the narrow, individual sense or in the broad, collective and environmental sense. For every whole possesses a unity that comes from the way all its parts are woven together. With this comes the realization that all things are linked, and everything is connected to everything else. This realization is of crucial importance as a result of the disconnected and fragmented nature of reality and the division of most things in the world into parts. This sense of unity and oneness could go a long way towards counteracting the fragmentation and disconnection so apparent in the world today.

As I began to live in the whole within myself as well as in the world, I began to understand why Goethe thought this was so essential. For in the process of living in the whole, I began to realize that I was not only identifying with the whole whenever and wherever possible, but also I wanted "the best for the whole" regardless of what kind of whole this happened to be.

I found this intriguing because Goethe also declared that *"who wills the highest must will the whole."* I interpreted this to mean that it is not only necessary to live in the whole, but also to "will the whole" if we want to realize the highest state of goodness within ourselves as well as in the world. This requires "getting out of our own skin" and wanting the best for everyone and everything. To do so is not only to live in the whole, but also to live in the good, the second component in Goethe's captivating phrase.

My parents gave me an excellent introduction to this when I was very young by taking me to church on a regular basis and enrolling me in a choir at Grace Church-on-the-Hill. It was part and parcel of the commitment they made to ensuring that I had an upbringing in religion as well as in the arts.

In retrospect, I realize how much this has affected my entire life and made it possible for me to want to live in the good and not just in the whole, despite the fact that I still have a great deal to realize in this area. While I am not a religious person today in the formal sense, I have a keen interest in all the different religions of the world and what they have to say about life and living in the ethical sense. Like living in the whole and wanting the best for the whole, I feel the religious training I had in my youth has made me a better person in many ways.

This is particularly true with respect to realizing a harmonious balance between the material and non-material dimensions of life. When too much emphasis is placed on the material dimension, gratification of our material desires and development of the egotistic aspect of our personalities tend to get out of hand. This is why all the different religions of the world advocate abstinence from *excessive* consumption and preoccupation with the material dimension of life, as well as the need to put more emphasis on the non-material dimension of life and on cultivating the altruistic, aesthetic, and spiritual sides of our personalities and our lives. As Pablo Picasso said, "the meaning of life is to find your gift; the purpose of life is to give it away."

We don't need to be a member of a specific religion, institution, or group to achieve this. While being rooted in a specific religion, religious institution, and group has its advantages, all we have to do is open our minds, hearts, and souls to all the diverse religions of the world and what they are able to provide in life.

As important as religion is, it is by no means the only way to live in the good as Goethe proposed. This can be achieved in many other ways, especially through making donations of one kind or another or doing volunteer work. This may include giving money to a worthwhile cause, helping at a local school, hospital, or seniors' home, assisting an arts organization, or organizing a social event or community celebration. All these things, and many others, enable people to devote a significant amount of their time to helping others and people in need.

Over the course of my life, I have tried to maintain a judicious balance between my career responsibilities and my voluntary activities. When I was in my thirties and forties, for example, I had several "foster children" in different parts of the world at one time or another and sat on the board of Foster Parents Plan of Canada for several years. Since I was engaged in the arts later in life, I did voluntary work for a number of arts organizations and served as a board member and president of one of these organizations for many years.

As the years have gone by, I have tried to learn how to contribute to the welfare and well-being of other people and in other ways. Strange as it may sound, I have discovered that one of the best ways to do this is to "be myself" and "true to myself" as much as possible. I have endeavoured to do this by enabling the things that are most essential in my life — commitment to the arts, culture, and the cultural cause; holism; becoming a whole person; promoting and perpetuating the cultural heritage of humankind; living in the whole, the good, and the beautiful; and manifesting goodness, kindness, and compassion in life — to radiate outwards and affect other people. While this doesn't involve helping other people with a specific problem or need, except when they ask me to do this, it does involve giving to people in other ways, especially when it is combined with making a real effort to be friendly, happy, and set a good example for others.

Lately, I have been trying to do other things that are related to living in the good. When I read somewhere that Gandhi said "Be the change you want in the world," it struck a responsive chord in me. For it meant instituting the changes I wanted to see in the world in my own life, first and foremost. Since I believe less pollution is imperative in the world, for example, I have been trying to make changes in my life that are consistent with this, especially in terms of engaging in activities that make fewer demands on the resources of nature. Since I also believe that there is a need for more understanding and compassion in the world, I am trying to be more understanding and compassionate with other people, and make this a fundamental part of my personality, behaviour, and life.

If living in the whole and the good are essential, so is living in the beautiful. This third element in Goethe's captivating phrase is important because there are many things in the world that are incredibly beautiful and are meant to be enjoyed and savoured because they bring so much happiness and fulfillment in life. In so doing, they make the world a better place — a place filled with more joy and contentment than misery and discontent. This is probably what Dostoyevsky had in mind when he said in one of his novels that "beauty will save the world."

Beauty manifests itself in the world in many ways. For some, it manifests itself in an exquisite sunrise, sunset, gesture, deed, picture, or musical work. For others, it manifests itself in a splendid park, garden, poem, story, or bonding with their favourite pet. And for still others, it manifests itself in a unique play, discovery, insight, or idea. It all depends on how people see and experience beauty — thereby confirming the old adage that beauty is in the eyes of the beholder — as well as what lingers on in the mind and memory after these experiences have taken place.

While beauty manifests itself in different ways for different people, it manifests itself for me much more in the arts and nature than in anything else. This is probably because the arts and nature lift me to incredible heights — heights that often border on the sublime and occasionally the divine. This is especially true of the arts. I had a musical experience one night, for example, that had a profound effect on my life. Here is how it came about.

For many years, I have been in the habit of setting my radio to a particular station before falling asleep. The station plays soft and soothing music — a rare commodity these days — to help people end their day on a pleasant and peaceful note.

One night, I set my radio to the usual station and fell fast asleep. I don't know how long I was sleeping, but I slowly became aware that I was hearing one of the most exquisite pieces of music I have ever heard in my life. As I lay there in a semi-conscious state — stupor might be a better word — I remember thinking I had died and gone to heaven. *The music was just that beautiful!* Then I heard an announcer say, "You have been listening to 'Grant Us Peace' by Felix Mendelssohn. It was sung by the Corydon Singers." As soon as I heard the announcer's voice, I knew that I had not actually died and gone to heaven.

This piece of music has a wonderful melody, as many of Mendelssohn's pieces do. This melody is sung first by one section of the choir, then another section joins in, and finally the melody is sung by the entire choir. I have often thought this piece of music should be adopted as humanity's "universal anthem." Not only is it exceedingly beautiful, but also it would serve a very useful purpose at this time. With all the violence, terrorism, conflict, and confrontation in the world, its plea to "grant us peace" is valuable and timely.

This is not the only piece of music I find exceedingly beautiful. While every person has his or her favourites and personal preferences, I can't resist mentioning some of the pieces that rank at the top of my list. Included here are Handel's *Ombre ma fú, Lascia ch'io pianga*, *Minuet* from *Berenice,* and *Zadok the Priest*; Strauss's *Four Last Songs*; Bizet's duet *Au Fond du Temple Saint* from *The Pearlfishers*; Liszt's transcription of Schumann's *Widmung*; Schubert's *Impromptu* Number III, Opus 90; Caesar Frank's *Panis Angelicas*; Glazinov's *Autumn Adagio* from his ballet *The Seasons;* and Thomas Tallis's *Spem in Allium*. Also included on my list are Mahler's *Resurrection Symphony*; Mascagni's *Intermezzo* from *Cavaleria Rusticana*; Rachmaninoff's *Second Piano Concerto*; Brahms' and Beethoven's violin concertos; Chopin's *Etude Opus 25, No. 13* (Aeolian Harp); the second movement of Albinoni's *Concerto Opus 9, No. 2 in D Minor*; the last movement from Saint-Saëns' *Organ Concerto,* Arthur Sullivan's *The Lost Chord*, Puccini's *Vissi d'arte* from *Tosca*; Giordani's *Cara Mio Ben*, Fauré's *Cantique de Jean Racine*, and Johann Sebastian Bach's *Prelude No. 1 in C Major*.

I hope I don't leave the impression it is only classical music that ranks at the top of my list, because this is not the case. As noted earlier, I also find many songs in musicals extremely beautiful, especially songs by Richard Rodgers and Oscar Hammerstein II. This is also true for certain pieces of film music, such as Ennio Morricone's *Gabriel's Oboe* from *The Mission* and *Dinner* from his *Lady Caliph Suite*, as well as many popular songs.

What makes the aforementioned pieces so beautiful is that they transport me into an ethereal state and place whenever I hear them. So does Beethoven's *Ninth Symphony*. It evokes such strong feelings and emotions that I have the impression that Beethoven was "walking with the gods" when he wrote it, and I am "walking with the gods" when I hear it. It is undoubtedly one of the most beautiful pieces of music ever written, and *the* most beautiful piece in the minds of many.

Of course, music is not the only art form that brings a great deal of beauty into my life. The visual arts do this too, especially artistic masterpieces that have some association with nature. This is especially true for many of the paintings of Vincent van Gogh, Claude Monet, Canada's Group of Seven and Emily Carr, and Chinese brush painters. Interestingly, music also figures prominently in this area. Think, for example, of Smetana's *Moldau*, Beethoven's *Moonlight Sonata*, Dvorak's *Ode to the Moon,* Debussy's *Le Mer* and *L'après-midi d'un faune,* and Alan Hovaness's *Mysterious Mountain* (*Second Symphony*) — all of which are extremely beautiful and remind us of the incredible beauty of nature. As Marc Chagall said, "Art is the unceasing effort to compete with the beauty of flowers — and never succeeding."

What is true for music and paintings is equally true for other art forms. Literature is filled with many beautiful works — works that run the gamut from short stories and poems to novels and epics. This is also true for theatre, film, dance, opera, the crafts, architecture, and so forth, as plays by Shakespeare and Molière, films like *Doctor Zhivago* and *Gandhi*, dances like those from *The Rite of Spring* and *Swan Lake*, operas like *La Bohème* and *La Trivata*, architecture like the Taj Mahal and the great Gothic cathedrals of France and Great Britain, constantly remind us.

And what is true for the arts is also true for nature. Nature is also filled with countless beautiful things. I discovered this many years ago when I was having some health problems. I went to doctors first to seek solutions to these problems, much as many people do. When this didn't work, I turned to my family and friends, and read numerous books and articles on the specific health problems I was experiencing. While this helped a little, it didn't provide the lasting solution I was looking for. Finally, in a fit of desperation, I turned to nature. I began taking long walks in the countryside near our home. There seemed to be nothing quite like "getting out in nature" and enjoying everything nature has to offer that helped me with these problems. Slowly but surely my health returned to normal, thereby confirming the old adage that "nature is one of the world's best healers." Somehow, enjoying all the beautiful trees, flowers, streams, meadows, lakes, rivers, sunsets, and sunrises provided the lasting solution I was looking for.

All of these experiences, and many others, have made it possible for me to live in the beautiful and not just in the whole and in the good. They have also made me aware of how important it is to be surrounded with beautiful things and make beauty a fundamental part of our lives if we want to live happy, healthy, and contented lives. For beauty, and beautiful things, play a key role in making us feel enthusiastic and excited about life, rather than despondent and depressed.

As time wore on, I began to realize why Goethe's wise phrase — live in the whole, in the good, in the beautiful — had become the driving force and principal preoccupation of my life. There was little that I had come across that compared with it. It became the centrepiece of my life, it was as simple as that.

Nevertheless, Goethe's phrase was not the only one that has had a profound effect on my life. This is also true of Joseph Campbell's advice to "*follow your bliss*." Much like Goethe's phrase, it is short, simple, and to the point. I first heard this phrase when I was watching a television program on Campbell (another well-known cultural scholar) and his ideas about myths, myth-making, culture, and cultures. It was during an interview with Bill Moyers, where Campbell was talking about the need for people to follow their bliss if they want to do what they were intended to do in life. What made Campbell's phrase so valuable was the fact that I was going through a period of intense struggle within myself at the time I heard it to determine who I was as a person and what I was intended to do with my life. This is also a concern of many religions, since it is associated with the idea of a "calling," and therefore with the belief that every person is put in the world for a specific purpose. The challenge in life is to discover what that purpose is and then realize it to the best of our ability. This belief is prominent in many Christian religions and sects, particularly Calvinism, although I suspect it is prominent in many other religions and religious sects as well.

In order to come to grips with this challenge, it was necessary for me to descend deep into myself. This was required to draw from myself what I felt was most imperative to actualize in my life. As a result, I was constantly asking myself such questions as: What is the ultimate purpose of my life? What capabilities and qualities do I possess that were meant to be realized in some way? And perhaps most importantly, who am I at the core of my being and in my fundamental essence? As this introspective process evolved, I began to understand that I was intended to participate in the quest to broaden and deepen knowledge and understanding of culture and cultures and the central role they are capable of playing in the world, as well as to make the case that humanity should pass out of the present economic age and into a future cultural age.

In Campbell's view, following our bliss is the key to living a full, fulfilling, meaningful, and purposeful life. Once we discover what our bliss really is, according to Campbell, we need only pursue it on a sustained and systematic basis to live in a permanent state of bliss. We "walk with the gods" and "soar with the eagles," so to speak, because we have made the effort to determine what we were intended to do with our lives and then worked diligently and relentlessly to achieve this end. It may be something large or small, simple or profound, admired by many or admired by a few, but it is the thing that is right for us. While this process can be painful and extremely difficult at times, it also brings a great deal of happiness and countless rewards when it is achieved.

With insights as valuable and timely as the ones provided by Goethe and Campbell uppermost in my mind, I began to realize that my life was becoming "*all of a piece*" in a way it never was before. I began to refer to this as "*living a cultural life*" because everything seemed to fit together nicely to form a harmonious and integrated whole.

In recent years, these benefits has been enhanced by participating in a number of specific activities. Here, as well, most of these activities have to do with the arts and nature in some way, something that is not surprising in view of the fact that the arts and nature have played a phenomenal role in my life ever since I was seven or eight.

Many of the artistic activities began shortly after the twenty-first century began and I had a bit more free time on my hands. Included here were Chinese brush-painting classes at the Pacific Mall in Markham for a number of years, singing in a seniors' choir at the Markham Community Centre for several years, assisting the Chinese Opera Group of Toronto with its financial and administrative problems, and, more recently, practicing the piano for an hour or so each day. Although I have not been able to do some of these activities especially well, I have tried to do them to the best of my ability and to become actively engaged in them. I have learned over the years that there is a big difference between being involved in artistic activities as a spectator or audience member compared to being involved in these activities as a participant. While these are different experiences that produce different results for different people, there is a tremendous amount of satisfaction that comes from being able to sit down at the piano and play a piece of music, pick up a brush and paint a picture, or sing in a choir or musical group.

While I really enjoyed the Chinese brush-painting classes and singing in the seniors' choir, practicing the piano has brought me the greatest happiness and fulfillment in recent years. This is because it provides a marvellous opportunity to express my feelings and emotions. There are so many beautiful pieces of music that can be played on the piano that it is never possible to run out of options. Not only is this true for pieces that have been written expressly for the piano, but also it is true for pieces that have been transcribed for the piano.

I must confess that I am deriving immense pleasure from playing some of the simpler pieces of Bach, Brahms, Beethoven, Chopin, and other composers. I have also discovered that Schumann wrote many beautiful pieces of piano music — such as *About Strange Lands and People*, *The Poet Speaks*, *Dreaming* (*Träumerei*), *Little Study*, and songs like *The Nut Tree* — that are relatively easy to learn even if they are hard to play well, and that some of Handel's most beautiful pieces, such as the *Minuet* from *Berenice*, *Lascia ch'io pianga*, *Ombra mai fú*, and others are available in piano versions.

These are not the only benefits I have derived from becoming actively involved in a variety of artistic activities late in life. I seem to be much more energetic, relaxed, lively, and creative when I am engaged in these activities. Not only do they provide the outlets and vehicles I need to express my feelings and emotions — I have never been very good at this — but also they are making it possible for me to respond to life's challenges and opportunities in more imaginative, resourceful, and creative ways.

Over the last few years, these activities have been complemented by making a systematic search for beauty and beautiful things a fundamental part of my life. Collecting information on exquisite pieces of music, paintings, plays, poems, literature, architecture, gardens, historical sites, and the like is enhancing my life in myriad ways, as well as making it possible for me to live a richer, fuller, and more meaningful life than would have been the case otherwise. I also feel that I am keeping a part of the natural and cultural heritage of humankind alive when I am engaged in activities of this type.

What participation in artistic activities and collecting information on beautiful things is doing to enhance my life in aesthetic and sensorial ways, participation in physical activities like tai chi and qi gong is doing to enhance my life in physical, mental, and metaphysical ways.

It all started seven or eight years ago when I had the good fortune to come across a group of people doing *Yuanji Dances* at the Markville Mall, close to where we live. These are dances based on a number of tai chi and qi gong movements that are related to nature and set to the most exquisite music imaginable. They go on for an hour each morning five days a week, and are followed by massaging all parts of the body and a number of fan dances. They have literally changed my life, since they have proved to be not just physical in nature but mental and metaphysical as well. As a result, I am feeling better than I have felt in years, with much more energy, vitality, and creativity.

I have complemented these activities by walking for an hour or so each day. Most of this walking occurs in our neighbourhood, as indicated earlier. However, some of it takes place at the Milne Conservation Area close to our home, as well as around Toogood Pond in Unionville, not far away. I never do this, however, without thinking of Henry David Thoreau — a great walker in his own right, as his famous article on walking reveals — and what it must have been like for him to turn his back on urban life in order to experience the fullness, richness, freshness, and diversity of the countryside.

Over the last few years, I have also been taking long walks in the forests of York Region, a few kilometres north and east of us. What a wonderful find these forests have been! I love walking in them any time of the year — spring, summer, fall, and winter — but particularly in the spring and fall when they are at their most magnificent. In the spring, the leaves are myriad shades of yellow and green that give the forests a delicate appearance and silky quality. However, it is in the fall that they are at their best. With a vast array of hardwoods, softwoods, and evergreens — maples, elms, birches, hemlocks, and so forth — the profusion of reds, yellows, oranges, browns, and greens at this time of year is breath-taking and a sight for sore eyes. The aromas are equally enticing, including the pungent smell of pine cones and the intoxicating scent of decomposing leaves.

What never ceases to amaze me is how few people use this remarkable resource, especially when there is nothing quite like a good walk in the forest to renew, revitalize, and invigorate us. The forest soothes us in times of trouble and rejuvenates us in times of anguish.

I have also begun to understand how valuable it is to be in tune with nature and bond with nature as much as possible through these and other activities. This has led me to examine nature's rhythms, cycles, patterns, themes, and elements very carefully. Not only is nature full of all sorts of ingredients that have been immortalized for their medicinal qualities and soothing and healing properties, but also it dances to the tune of its own drummer and has a life and character all its own.

As my understanding of all this has evolved, I have found myself applying what I have learned from nature to my own life. I have discovered that my life is much more fluid, flexible, and relaxed when I am in tune with nature and create rhythms, patterns, and cycles in my own life that correspond to those of nature. Not only have I discovered that for everything there is a season, but also I have come to realize *why* there is a season for everything. This is especially true for Canada. Since I live in a country where all seasons are dominated by one season — winter — I have begun to understand why it is so sensible to conduct certain activities in the spring, others in the summer or fall, and still others in the winter. It is simply a matter of getting in tune with nature and paying close attention to its various moods, melodies, and mysteries. So much is revealed when we study nature, examine its elements, understand how it cleans, cleanses, renews, and heals itself, as well as how it sings, dances, and has voices and music all its own.

All these activities, and many others, are part and parcel of what I have required to live a cultural life. While learning to live such a life has not been without its challenges and difficulties, it has also produced countless benefits and opportunities.

Looking back, I can see that living a cultural life has broadened, deepened, and enriched my life in countless ways, just as getting to know the many secrets of culture has. It has brought me an enormous amount of happiness in life, made me more aware of other people and their needs, increased my sensitivity, patience, and compassion for others, especially those who are experiencing major difficulties in life, suffering from certain types of illnesses, or are less fortunate than myself, and helped me to become comfortable in my own skin and more at ease with others. It has also expanded my respect and tolerance for people from different cultures, as well as for worldviews, values, customs, traditions, beliefs, and ways of life that are different than my own. I have also become far more conscious of how much I have learned from other cultures, not only in terms of coming to grips with my own problems and possibilities but also in terms of enriching my entire life. This has made my life expansive rather than contractive, as well as filled with life-long learning and a great deal more curiosity in life.

And this is not all. I have also come to realize that culture is not only the key to understanding the world and what is required to change and improve it, it is also the key to experiencing much more spirituality in life. This is true not only for "specific moments of spirituality," but, more importantly, for achieving a "permanent state of spirituality."

This is as it should be. For culture possesses everything that is required to produce a great deal of fulfillment in life, as well as to make the world a better, safer, and more secure place for all the diverse people and countries of the world. This is why is it essential to unlock all of culture's secrets and ensure that culture plays a central rather than marginal role in the world. The future of humanity and the world depend on it.

Acknowledgements and References

My journey over the years to unlock the secrets of culture and make the case for a cultural age would not have been possible without a great deal of help, encouragement, and support from many people. I am particularly grateful in this respect to my parents, Harold and Belle, my wife Nancy, my daughters Charlene and Susan, my son-in-law Alan, and many of my closest friends and colleagues, most notably Walter Pitman, Biserka Cvjetičanin, Gao Xian, Sheila Jans, Jack Fobes, Guy Métraux, André Fortier, Eleonora Barbieri Masini, Erika Erdmann, Joyce Zemans, Prem Kirpal, Joy MacFadyen, John Hobday, Bill McWhinney, Herman Greene, James Gillies, Mavor Moore, Thierry Dufay, Magda Cordell McHale, Isabella S.C. Scanderbeg, Galyna Shevchencko, Manickam Nadarajah, Polly Tong, Diane Dodd, Réal Bédard, John Gordon, and Peter Sever. These people have "hung tough" with me over the years and given me the strength, endurance, and companionship I have needed to make the case that culture, cultures, and cultural development have a central rather than marginal role to play in the world.

I am especially indebted to David Stover who has been a close friend for many years and has edited and published this book in addition to others I have written. While recognizing these contributions, I nevertheless assume responsibility for everything contained in this text.

Information on the books and documents referred to in this book, as well as other publications I have written on culture, Canadian culture, and the world system, is available on my LinkedIn Profile and the Publications section of the World Culture Project website (www3.sympatico.ca/dpaulschafer). Because this book is meant to be more informal than some of my previous works, I have not included academic apparatus such as footnotes. However, information on the sources of the quotations included in the book can be found on the Rock's Mills Press web page for *The Secrets of Culture*. You are also welcome to contact me by email at dpaulschafer@sympatico.ca.

D. Paul Schafer
2015

www.ingramcontent.com/pod-product-compliance
Lightning Source LLC
Chambersburg PA
CBHW060825170526
45158CB00001B/91

* 9 7 8 0 9 8 8 1 2 9 3 5 1 *